Architectural Guide
Aarhus

... building is an elementary activity of man,
intimately linked with evolution and the
development of human life ...
CIAM, La Sarraz Declaration, 1928

Architectural Guide
Aarhus

Author: Heiko Weissbach
Concept: Heiko Weissbach/Ulf Meyer

With contributions from Johan Bender, Nils-Ole Lund, Mogens Brandt Poulsen, Gøsta Knudsen, Stephen Willacy

DOM
publishers

Contents

How to Use this Guide
All buildings are numbered and sorted geographically.

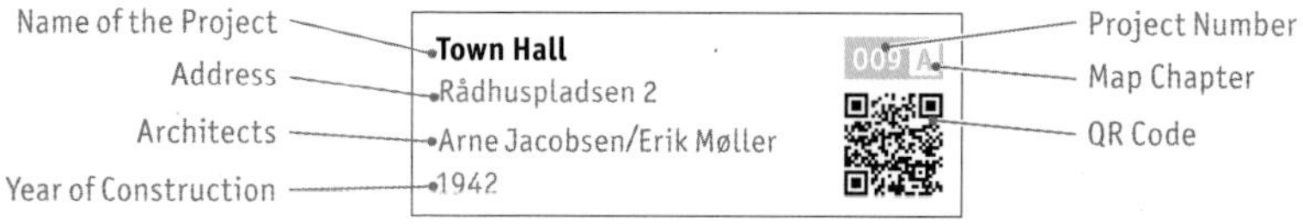

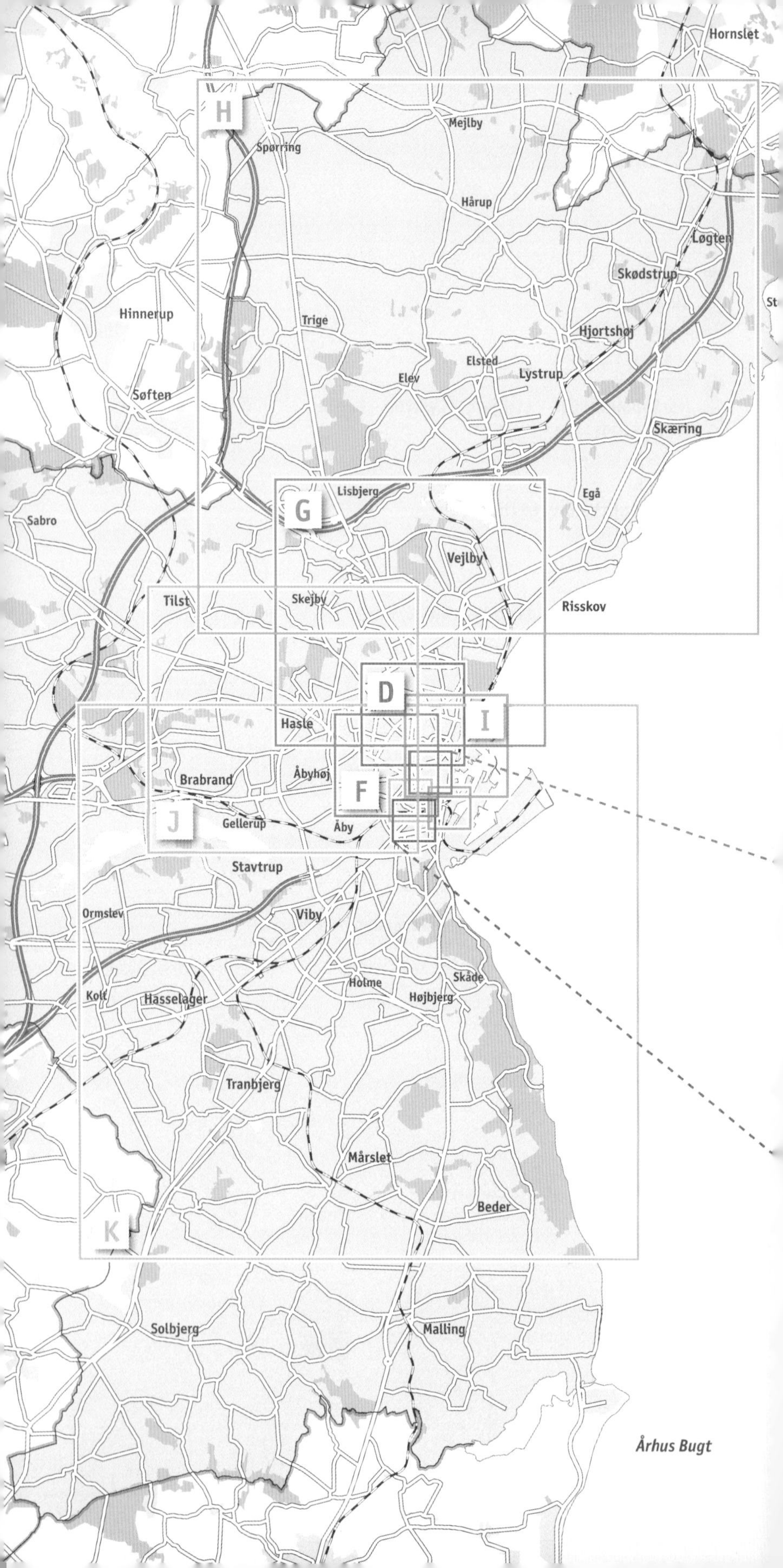
Hornslet
H
Mejlby
Spørring
Hårup
Løgten
Skødstrup
Hinnerup
Trige
Hjortshøj
Elsted
Lystrup
Elev
Søften
Skæring
Lisbjerg
G
Egå
Sabro
Vejlby
Tilst
Skejby
Risskov
D
I
Hasle
Brabrand
Åbyhøj
F
J
Gellerup
Åby
Stavtrup
Ormslev
Viby
Holme
Skåde
Kolt
Hasselager
Højbjerg
Tranbjerg
Mårslet
Beder
K
Solbjerg
Malling
Århus Bugt

https://goo.gl/VeHDUa

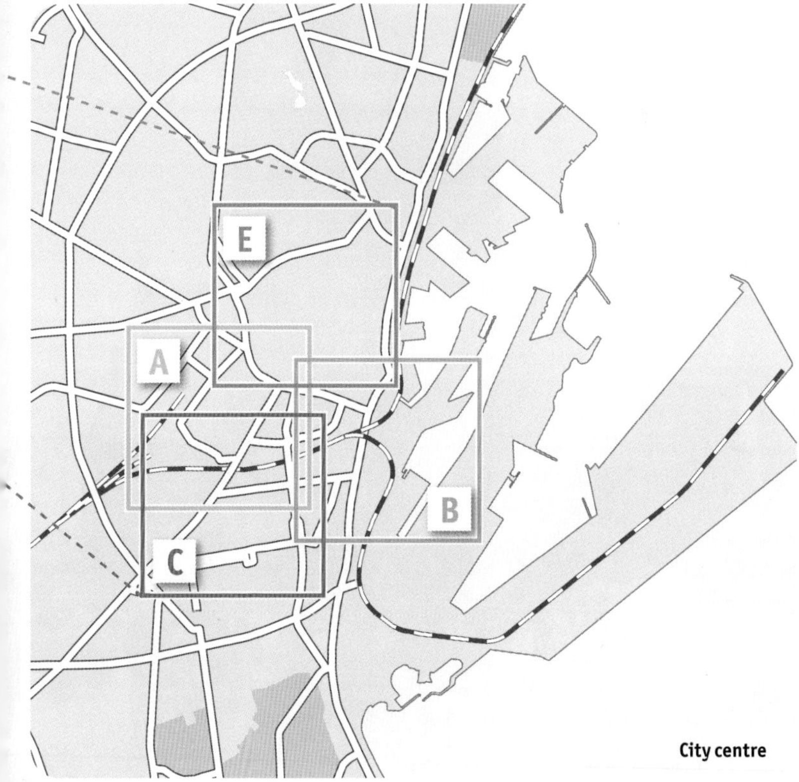

City centre

Per Rasmussen

Aarhus or Århus?

Heiko Weissbach

On 1 January 2001, the city changed the spelling of its name: in lieu of the traditional Scandinavian letter which the Danes affectionately call *bolle-å* (a with a doughnut), as had been the case hitherto, Aarhus was to be written with double-a with immediate effect, taking into account international keyboards. However, the three Scandinavian vowels æ, ø and å continue to appear at the end of the alphabet and may still be used in proper names.

The earliest known spelling of the city of Arus has been known from 1231 and arguably stems from the terms *å* (river) and *ōs* (mouth) which was subsequently refashioned *hus* ("house"). Aarhus thus means "house" or "houses at the mouth of the river" – an obvious name for the waterfront city.

Aarhus has borne the pet name City of Smiles (*Smilets By*) since 1938 in order to promote itself (and its positive atmosphere). When arriving in the 1990s by ship from Zealand, people would hear a catchy tune from the band PS12 with the title *Hjem til Aarhus* (Back at Home in Aarhus) blaring out from the ferry terminal designed first and foremost for this purpose – a fine, white cube on Europaplads. Perhaps because of this Aarhus has long been ridiculed, especially by Copenhageners. Metropolitans are only too happy to arrive in the province for a weekend in good spirits, attending a concert by renowned musicians during the jazz festival, or an international performance during the festival week, or merely a family celebration, since many residents of the capital originally hail from Jutland. But to live permanently in Aarhus? Any such suggestion brings out the prejudice against all things provincial.

Perhaps because of this the city unveiled its new title, the *World's Smallest City*, in order to draw attention to the many qualities of the "capital of Jutland" –which had long ceased to be a secret –and rid it of its provincial status. In the meantime, Aarhus has achieved a degree of popularity owing to the high standard of living which draws many here – including Copenhageners. The architect Søren Leth described it thus in a conversation: "In the morning, when I bring my children to kindergarten or to school by bicycle, I meet friends and colleagues, staff and customers en route. People are acquainted with each other and exchange greetings, taking the time to order a cup of coffee together – from

← Daily life unfolding on the large square in front of the Cathedral

Den Gamle By/VisitAarhus

Open-air museum Den Gamle By (The Old Town)

Den Gamle By, Open-air Museum
Viborgvej 2
Since 1914

001 F

one of the numerous baristas, take note – before entering the office and dedicating themselves to their daily work."

Those who have the privilege of living and working in the city centre refer to a quality of living that is hardly attainable in other larger cities, be it Copenhagen, Berlin or London. The short distances to be covered by bicycle, the proximity to forests and water and the sense of familiar closeness attributable to close-knit circles of acquaintances and ranges of activities provide many Aarhusians with an unusually high standard of living in comparison with other Europeans. However, it seems that many Aarhusians have yet to discover that their hometown has indeed become a "genuine" metropolis.

In the City of Culture year of 2017, Aarhus is primarily a city for education and knowledge. With nine educational institutions – among which is the second-largest university in the country (see Essay 2) – and 150 different study courses,

Lively café atmosphere along the reopened riverbed

Henrik Bentsen/VisitAarhus

Evening scene within the Latin Quarter

Aarhus has the country's largest concentration of students, namely 50,000, in proportion to the size of the population. At just under thirty-eight years old, the average age of the population is correspondingly low. The population of 330,000 (1 January 2016) is growing by 1 to 2 per cent each year. Up to 365,000 inhabitants are expected for the year 2025. Well over one million people, of whom many make a daily commute here, reside in the catchment area – e.g. within the radius of one hour's drive – since it is not only educational establishments but also large companies which have their headquarters here, i.e. Arla Foods (the seventh largest dairy company in the world), Vestas Wind Systems (the largest European wind power plant supplier) and Dansk Supermarked (the largest Danish food distributor).

Of course, the increasing number of inhabitants and jobs is accompanied by a growth in traffic volume and demand for housing (see Essay 4). In this context it is useful that Aarhus has its own School of Architecture, as well as the highest density of architects throughout the country, and is itself committed to the urban development and architectural planning necessary (see Essay 3). Vast tracts of the port areas – which have increased to cover 260 ha and almost 10 km of quayside over the course of centuries – offer the greatest potential for urban development in close vicinity to the city centre, although these are no longer fit for purpose owing to the development of shipboard transportation. This provided an opportunity to allow the inner city to grow back out to the waterfront, making use of its accompanying properties (see Essay 5). The desire for a new, international airport expressed by enterprises and holidaymakers is also affiliated with the new assertiveness of the world's smallest big city. There is repeated and ongoing discussion on this topic. Most recently, however, the European Union had stated that that there are two comparatively nearby airports in Billund and Aalborg, thus removing the need for a further airport. Since mid-2016, the dream of fast air transport links has been counterbalanced by a seaplane which transports businessmen in a hurry between the city centres of Aarhus and Copenhagen in just under an hour at most.

As of spring 2017, Aarhus will obtain a new regional railway track in lieu of an airport. This is named the Letbane (light rail) and is a hybrid of tram and regional railway. The new lines connect the centre of Aarhus with the cities of Odder to the south and Grenaa to the northeast, specifically to relieve commuter traffic.

Aarhus Cathedral

A new ferry terminal that is worthy of the name will not materialise in the eastern harbour until 2020 at the earliest.

About this Book

This guide is not intended to give architectural aficionados alone the opportunity to discover a small urban treasure on the northern periphery of continental Europe which has arguably been hitherto overlooked. Nor is it merely a road map to 135 buildings and projects sorted geographically from over the past 100 years – it also contains in-depth texts by prominent guest authors which steer the reader through urban and architectural history from the end of the nineteenth century, continuing into the foreseeable future. The texts by the guest authors are in chronological order beginning with an article by the historian Johan Bender, who espoused a commitment to the work of the architect Hack Kampmann in the years preceding the publication of a major monograph in 2014. Here, he describes in a concise manner his life, work and impact on the architectural and urban development of the city. It was Johan Bender who drew attention to the fact that Aarhus is the only provincial city to be represented by two architectural masterpieces in the Danish Cultural Canon: the city hall and the university.
The article by Nils-Ole Lund, one of the first professors at the School of Architecture founded in 1965 and its subsequent Rector, is devoted to the genesis and significance of the university campus.
The third guest author, Mogens Brandt Poulsen, was also a longstanding lecturer and Rector at the School of Architecture. In order to mark its fiftieth anniversary he wrote a book entitled *Den Gode Skole – og arkitektmiljøet i Aarhus* (The Good School – and the Architectural Environment in Aarhus) in 2015 where he expands upon the origins, development and arguably unprecedented collaboration between the School of Architecture and the numerous planning bureaus of the city.
Gøsta Knudsen was not only a student, lecturer and Rector at the School of Architecture, but also a practising architect and master builder of the city between 2007 and 2012. He describes at great length the overarching urban development of recent decades.

Coincidentally, Gøsta Knudsen's son-in-law, Stephen Willacy, became his successor in the office of master builder of the city. In his article entitled *Utopia in Aarhus*, Stephen describes, among other things, the major challenge in terms of urban development of turning a ghettoised satellite city from the 1970s into an integral part of the city worth living in.
Besides the countless architectural treasures of the twentieth century and the sometimes spectacular new buildings of the twenty-first century, the old Aarhus is also worth discovering, for example in the open-air museum Den Gamle By (The Old Town) with sixty-five historic buildings which were brought over from all parts of the country, or in the Cathedral which was built as a Romanesque basilica in the twelfth century and converted into a gothic cathedral in the fifteenth. Diagonally opposite, in the basement of Nordea bank (see 058), you find the Viking museum featuring a model of the first city Aros. A mere stone's throw away is probably the oldest sacred stone building in Scandinavia: the crypt of the Church of Our Lady from the year 1060.
Therefore, culture has a long tradition at Aarhus and is not just newly being paraded under the title *European Capital of Culture*, but rather is something practised daily and is a way of life. Testimony to this is a stroll along the new waterfront or through the historic quarter which, drawing inspiration from Paris, is fondly and somewhat presumptuously referred to as the Latin Quarter. Perhaps this explains why Aarhusians and Danes in general are repeatedly named the happiest Europeans according to polls.

Aarhus Cathedral 002 E
Store Torv
Unknown
ca. 1197

Church of Our Lady and Cloister 003 E
Vestergade 21
Unknown, ca. 1100

Per Rasmussen

Crypt beneath the Church of Our Lady

Per Rasmussen

Above: Church of Our Lady, next double page: Aarhus – a waterfront city among forested areas

Jan Kejser

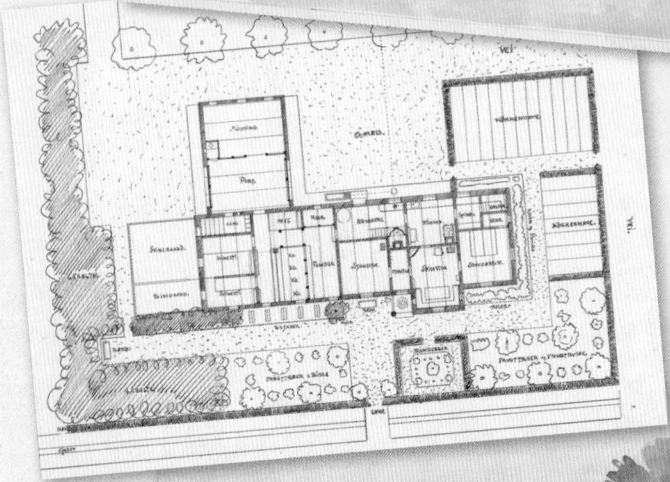

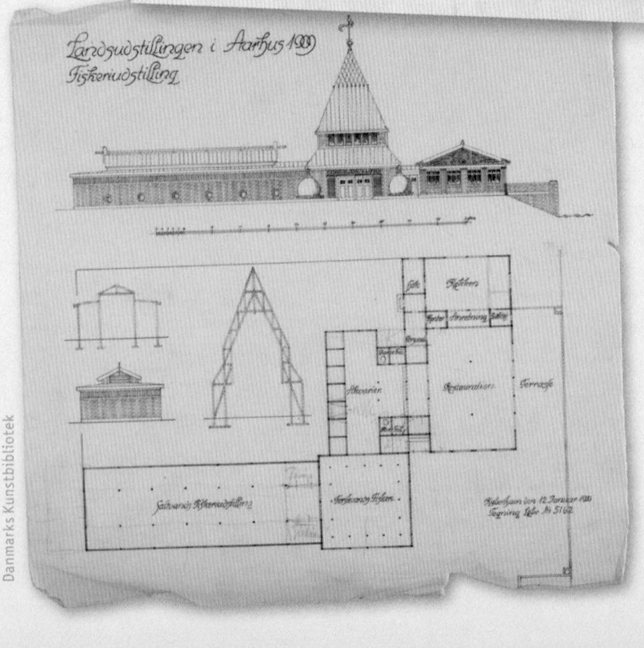
Landsudstillingen i Aarhus 1909
Fiskeriudstilling

Hack Kampmann
When Aarhus Entered the History of Architecture

Johan Bender

The National Exhibition of 1909: An Architecture-Inspirator

By the turn of the century (1900), the development of Aarhus was more pronounced than in any other Danish provincial city, and the city fostered an ambition to demonstrate such progress to the competing cities of Jutland and the rest of the world! Initially, a series of striking buildings spreading out from the port and the city centre formed the visible expression of this.

However, city patriotism reached out beyond the construction of spectacular buildings and brought forth the National Exhibition of 1909 – the hitherto largest investment by the municipality. The large World Expos in London, Paris and Chicago etc. provided sources of inspiration. In 1909, everything that Danish industry, artisanry and art were able to muster was exhibited and negotiated over six months. The National Exhibition played host to 667,000 people, among whom were 1,200 guests from the USA.

Although the expenditure almost crippled the city, it enabled it to gain experience with collaborative urban communities, something that would henceforth continue unabated throughout the century – especially in the construction sector with planning and cooperation between suppliers, tradesmen and architects. The significance of the National Exhibition for that which has come about in Aarhus ever since cannot be overstated.

Hack Kampmann (1856–1920)

Hack Kampmann was the architect who lent Aarhus the first semblance of a large metropolitan city. His breakthrough work on the regional archives in Viborg made him the royal building inspector (*Kongelig Bygningsinspektør*) for Northern Jutland in 1892. He settled down in Aarhus and stayed there for sixteen years. During this period, he built a series of beautiful buildings prior to his appointment as professor at the School of Architecture within the Academy of Fine Arts in Copenhagen. He had of course been earmarked to be the architect for the National Exhibition of 1909, but since he was in the process of settling down in Copenhagen he put in a recommendation for a fellow architect, Anton Rosen. Kampmann continued to exert a major influence on the plans for the National Exhibition and would run through detailed architectural problems with Rosen whilst continuing as Head of the Arts Committee.

He was also the inspiration behind the greater part of the National Exhibition entitled *Model Town* or *Station Town*. This was the response of the architectural profession to the deterioration in the culture of construction – a struggle against ugliness. Kampmann himself drew up the site plan for this Model Town and designed its twelve buildings, including The Danish House, or the small farm. Kampmann mastered the construction of castles and other stately houses, but also had very

← Watercolour and drawing of the Danish Pavilion by Hack Kampmann, watercolour of the Kampen Villa by Hack Kampmann, drawing of the Fishery Pavilion by Anton Rosen

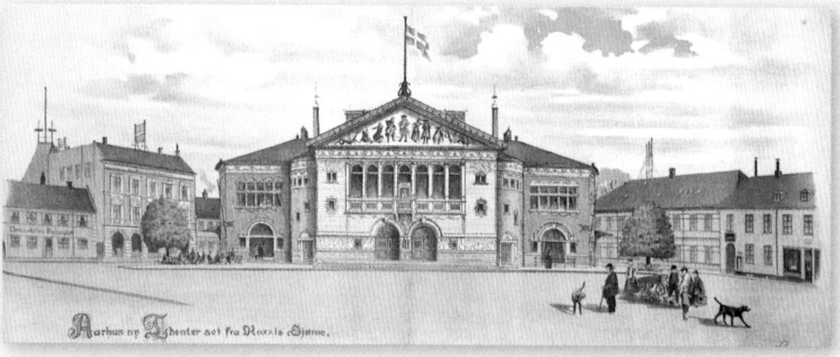

Aarhus Theatre, drawing on the cover of *Aarhus Stiftstidende*, 23 January 1898

much of an appetite for the house of the common man. As professor at the School of Architecture in Copenhagen, he also drew the distinction between the Danish Class (also referred to as the Servant Class) and the Temple Class.

Kampmann's first and most beautiful building in Aarhus was the Customs House (Toldkammeret) down at the port – heavy, majestic and medieval, drawing inspiration from the travels he undertook in France and Germany, to Lübeck for example. It is characteristic of him that he designed his buildings to act in concert with their immediate vicinity. The Cathedral with its three towers dominated the city centre, and the complex of the Customs House featuring three towers came to be seen as a more worldly, more modern twin to the temple of faith which had been a sacred emblem of the city for centuries.

Kampmann subsequently designed the red building of the Cathedral School, again drawing inspiration from the Cathedral in terms of the three towers – together the three buildings make up the Kampmann Trinity.

The heavily set red building of the Customs House is augmented by masonry ornamentation such as figures of seabirds on the roof, or in the form of reliefs. Two vigilant sleuth dogs in sandstone relief are visible on each side of the entrance. Further injections of flair give an opportunity for reflection and imbue the building with a humorous touch.

Aarhus Theatre

Inaugurated in 1909, Kampmann's most magnificent offering within the city is the theatre which features lavish ornamentation both inside and outside, entirely reflecting a city of culture. The style is classical with arches, columns and a triangular pediment featuring extensive use of Greek theatre mask. The architect abandoned the classical gods and goddesses in this frontispiece and, in lieu thereof, staged a local Holberg scene – a masquerade which has since turned Carl Nielsen's music into Denmark's national opera. The façade emanates melodiousness and joie de vivre, capturing that which unfolds inside. Kampmann's buildings were intended to render the interior function as visible as possible from the outside.

This classical style is combined with national romanticism and a smidgeon of art nouveau upon the vibrant main façade of the theatre. Eleven swans with golden crowns upon their heads float around an illuminated solar system within the auditorium. Kampmann availed himself of Hans Christian Andersen's epic poem *The Wild Swans* – wherein the latter are transformed into princes. The spectator is thus given a taste of adventure before the curtain goes up.

A Town Plan for Southern Aarhus

While Kampmann was engaged with his buildings at the heart of the city, the city council entrusted him with the composition of a town plan for southern Aarhus after the city had acquired the land expanse of Marselisborg Jorder. It was proposed to incorporate this vast expanse into the city zone. In 1898, in collaboration with the Copenhagen-based engineer Charles Ambt, he compiled an extensive development plan featuring the overriding principles of a modern city, the majority of which were followed during the topographic expansion. Thus the newly acquired rural culture was coupled organically with urban civilisation by means of wide avenues, boulevards, squares and parks.

With much foresight Kampmann and Ambt outlined a ring road in order to detour approaching traffic around the city. Fifty years later this prevented the city being partitioned by a four-lane motorway. Incidentally, the bypass road was studied and imitated when Copenhagen was set to be expanded with a ring system. Furthermore, the urban plan had already earmarked an excellent venue for the National Exhibition which would illustrate the potential of the city a few years later. Everyone can enjoy Hack Kampmann's splendid buildings – they are immediately visible – but the ingenious urban plan is obscure, embedded within the spinal cord of the city and not readily visible to the naked eye.

Marselisborg Castle

The new regions south of the city were an excellent setting for the castle which sought to strengthen the royal family's ties with Jutland following the loss of the royal palaces in Schleswig. Several cities in Jutland stood at the ready, but Aarhus claimed victory. At this point both the site and a gifted royal building inspector were available and the latter was commissioned with the construction of Marselisborg Castle.

Marselisborg Jorder was an extensive area, but Kampmann's sense of orientation identified the ideal location for the castle. Visible from the city and arrivals from the sea, the white castle facing the park and the bay is located amidst the green forest like an emblematic landmark – a greeting to newcomers or returnees.

The building is reminiscent of no other work of architecture by the all-round oriented architect, although he was well versed in all styles. Even if he had constructed his buildings in the style of national romanticism from local materials, such as red brick and granite, his architectural area of expertise lay in classicism. This is self-evident for a castle, here in both a somewhat baroque and neo-classical model. However, Kampmann did not give contrasts a wide berth. He mingled the classical style of Marselisborg with art nouveau outside and more particularly inside. Swallows, eagles and gulls fly across the ceilings; the plasterer of the master builder planted floral friezes wherever he felt it appropriate.

The architect marked the fact that this could be interpreted as a castle for Prince Christian (the subsequent King Christian X.) by a frieze beneath the roof overhang bearing the initials C and A – A for Princess Alexandrine of Mecklenburg, whom the Prince married – and also symbols of the contract of love between the young royal couple. Such emblems lend the stylish castle a touch of national romanticism.

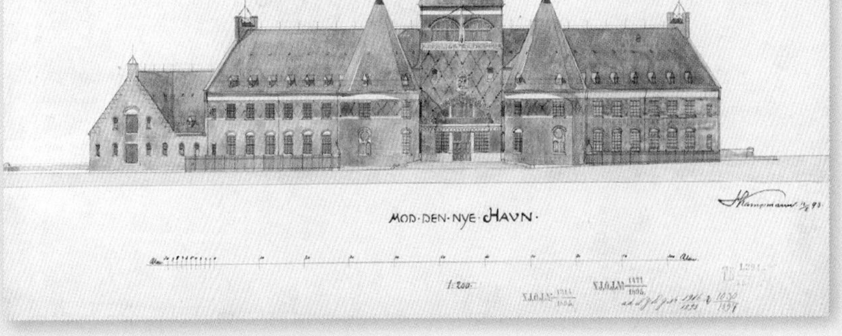

Customs House, watercolour by Hack Kampmann

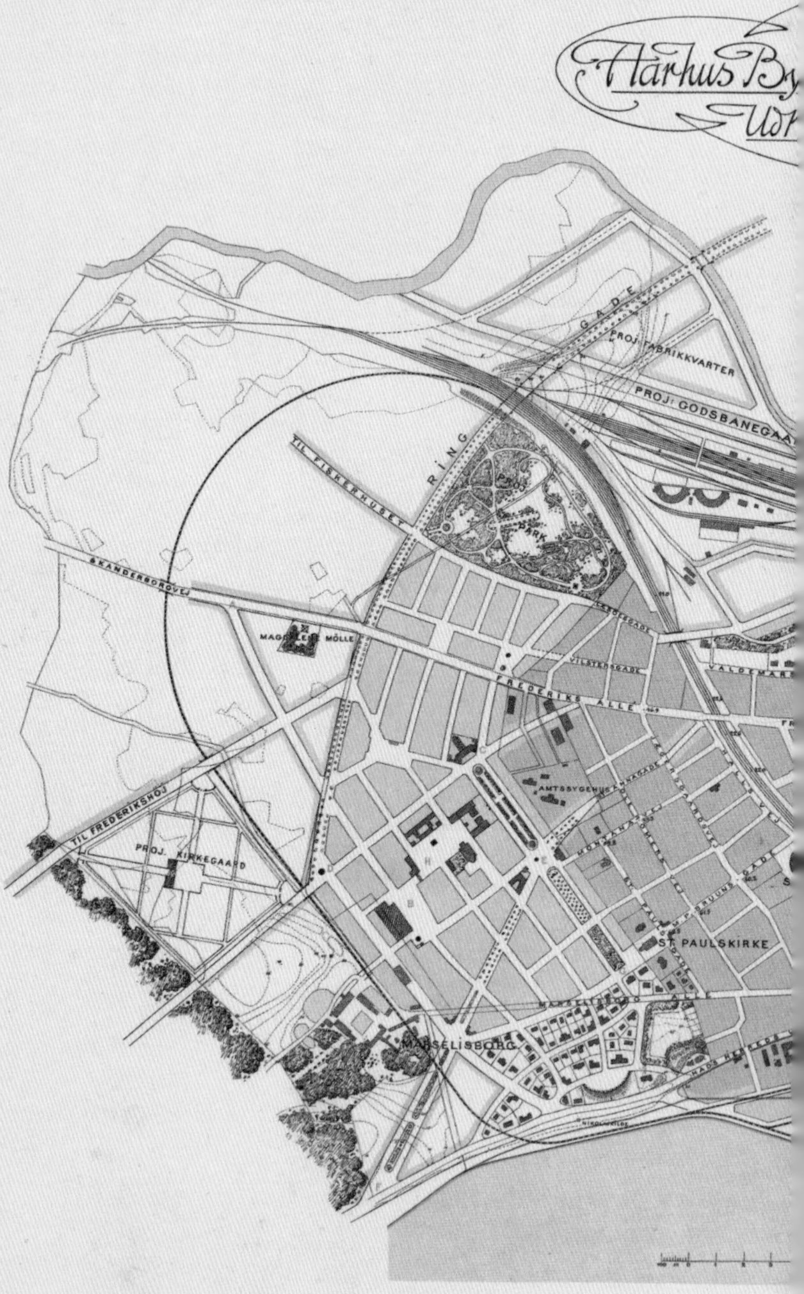

Urban layout plan for southern Aarhus, drawing by Hack Kampmann

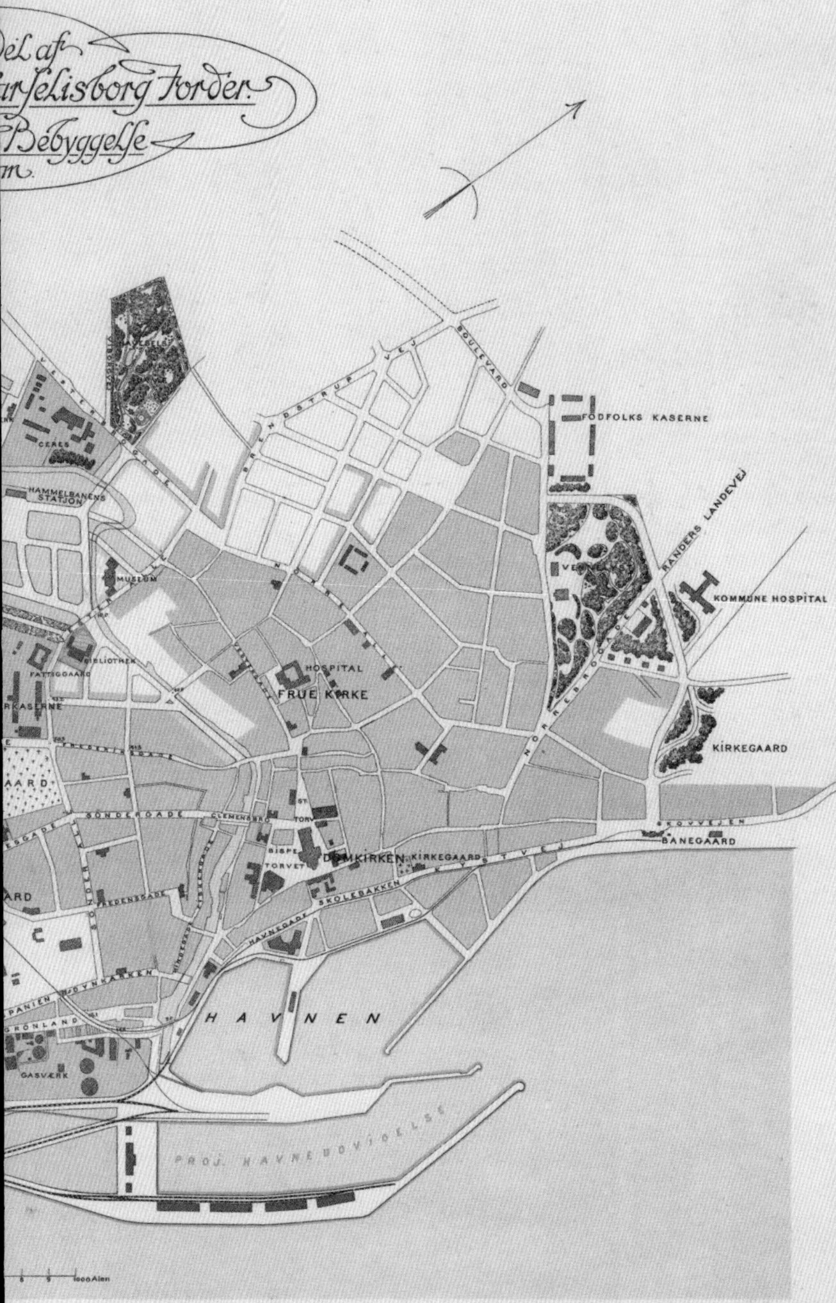

Danmarks Kunstbibliotek

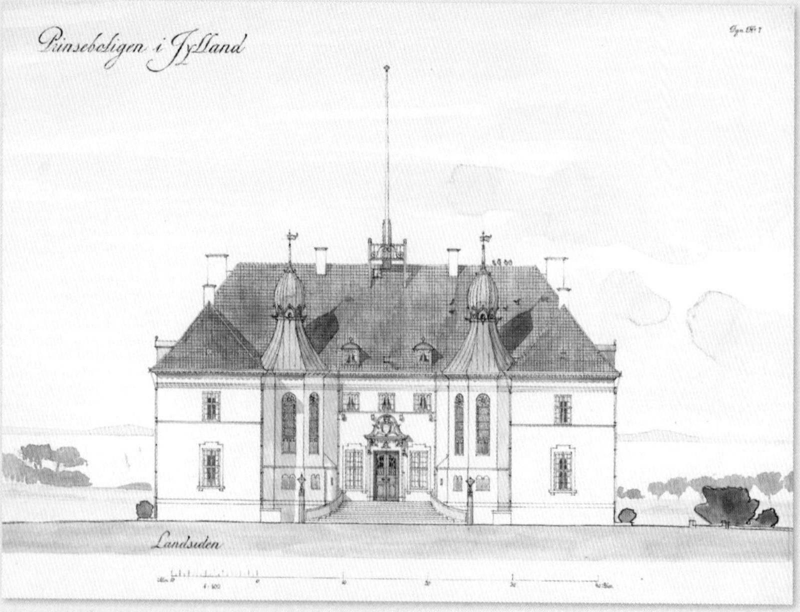

Marselisborg Castle, watercolour by Hack Kampmann

Two months before the royal couple were to occupy the castle in the summer of 1902, Hack Kampmann and his family moved into the newly built villa Kampen am Strandvejen. The national library was inaugurated shortly thereafter – also referred to as Hack Kampmann's jewellery box – which is regarded by many as his most interesting building in the city.

What Kind of Man was Hack Kampmann?

Hack Kampmann was born in the presbytery of Ebeltoft and was thus proud to call himself a *Molbo* (an inhabitant of the peninsula Mols). Jutland was his preferred region. When he was eight years old, his father was appointed Provost of Herning and the family moved to Vendsyssel. It was the fateful year of 1864, and the collective national shame made a lasting impression on him – something which is felt in his work. Trained as a mason, there developed within him a heartfelt relationship with building materials. He was aware of the brick plants and marble quarries in the Mediterranean region, even at the heart of Turkey from where he

Aarhus National Library, watercolour by Hack Kampmann

fetched marble for the burial monument of Christian IX. in Roskilde Cathedral. At technical school his pronounced drawing skills and especially his gift for lending ambience to technical strokes by using watercolours was noted. Consequently, he moved to Copenhagen and took further courses of study at the School of Architecture. The classical European orientation had governed here since the golden age circa. 1820, but after 1864 this was countered by a younger generation of architects drawing inspiration from Danish and Nordic building traditions. One pioneer was the architect Hans Jørgen Holm, to whom Kampmann affiliated himself, even becoming his son-in-law. He won both silver and gold medals and carved out a broad footing in the history of architecture through comprehensive study trips.

Kampmann was a very introverted person who became so obsessed by his "God-given" talents that he curbed his nature towards the outside world in order to fully capitalise on his work and his reputation. He wrote almost nothing and ignored requests to do so. He once said to a diligent journalist: "I am nothing interesting. There is nothing interesting to write about me." Perhaps it was a style of workmanship, but in a particularly introverted manner of Kampmannesque calibre. What is interesting about him was that he did not seek to awaken interest in himself. He designed his buildings and it is therefore these which must portray him. Hack Kampmann left Aarhus in 1908, but his architectural spectre continues to loom large over the face of the city. Countless architects and craftspeople are affiliated with him and his perfectionist influence. His Aarhus denotes a thriving period accompanied by the exemplary metamorphosis of the city. He initiated that which was set to evolve into a continuing architectural tradition, with several generations of master builders following him. In 1965, this culminated in the foundation of the first School of Architecture outside Copenhagen; Aarhus came to the fore as the home of leading architects. Aarhus is thus the only provincial city with works in keeping with the architectural canon – no less than two, equal to the number in the capital.

An acknowledged connaisseur of Kampmann, the subsequent royal building inspector Niels Vium, once said about his predecessor: "Hack Kampmann was a curious blend of country-bumpkin complete with Jutish stubbornness and a highly cultivated man of the world." A briefer, more accurate and more refined outline of Kampmann arguably does not exist.

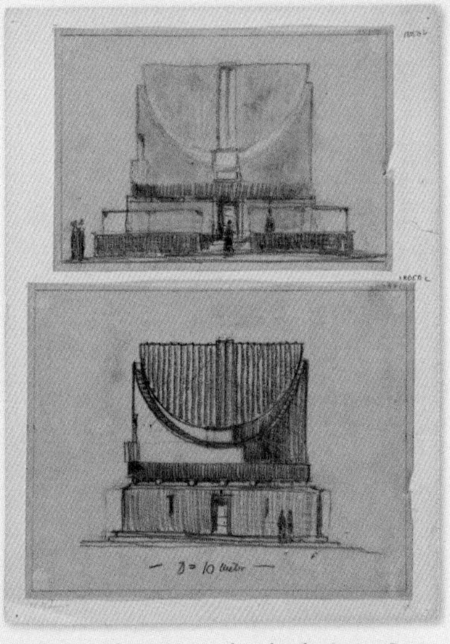

Danmarks Kunstbibliotek

Ole Rømer Observatory, drawing by Anton Rosen

Aarhus Theatre 004 E
Teatergaden
Hack Kampmann
1900/1953/1982

National Library 005 E
Vester Allé 12
Hack Kampmann
1902

Marselisborg Castle 006 K
Kongevejen 100
Hack Kampmann
1902

Customs House 007 I
Nordhavnsgade 1
Hack Kampmann
1897

Ole Rømer Observatory 008 K
Observatorievej 1
Anton Rosen
1911

Design for the theatre ceiling, drawing by Hack Kampmann

Danmarks Kunstbibliotek

From the Town Hall to Cultural Buildings and the Former Freight Depot

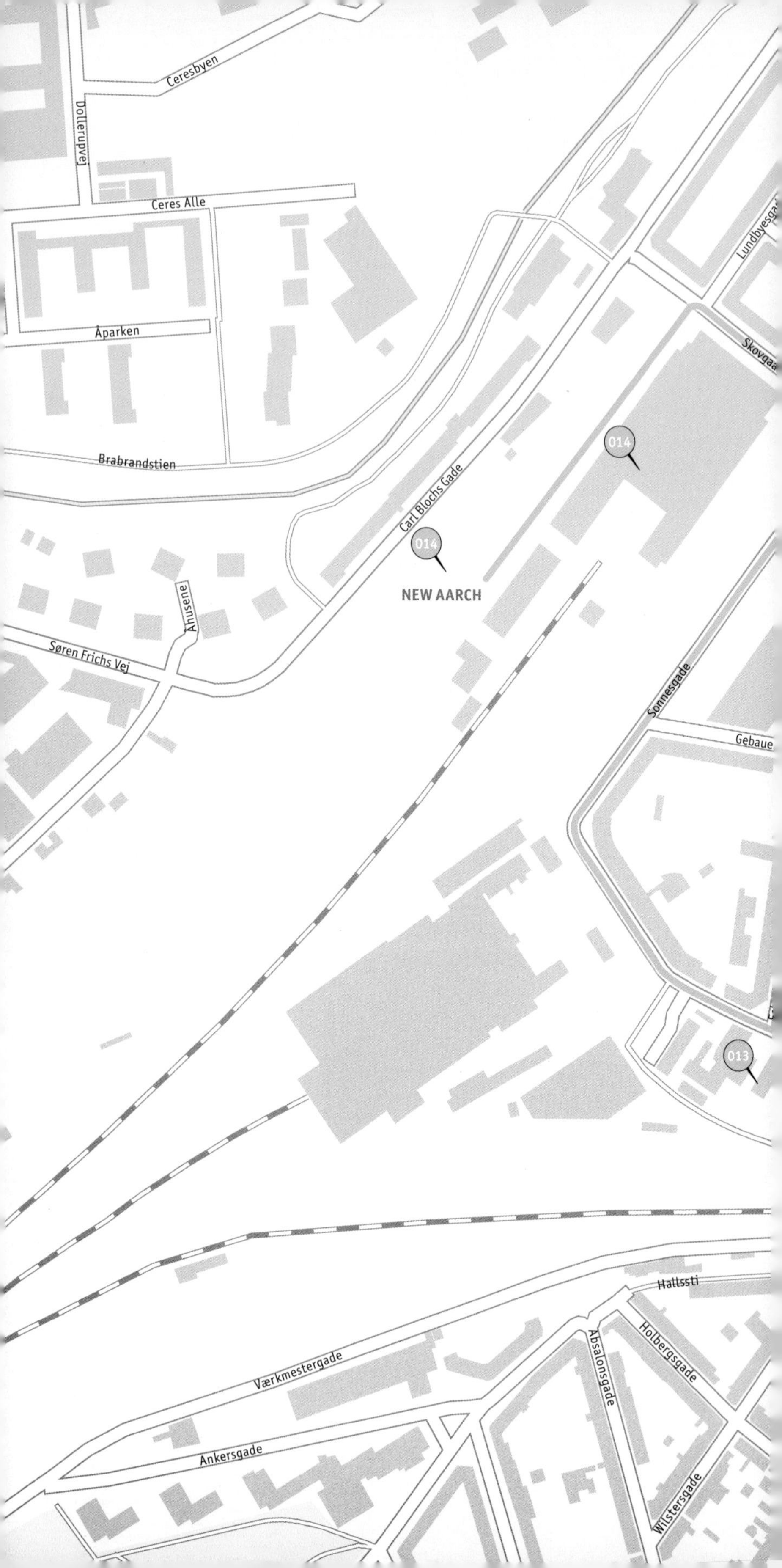
Ceresbyen
Dollerupvej
Ceres Alle
Åparken
Brabrandstien
Lundbyesgade
Skovgaa
014
Carl Blochs Gade
014
NEW AARCH
Åhusene
Søren Frichs Vej
Sonnesgade
Gebaue
013
Hallssti
Absalonsgade
Holbergsgade
Værkmestergade
Ankersgade
Wilstersgade

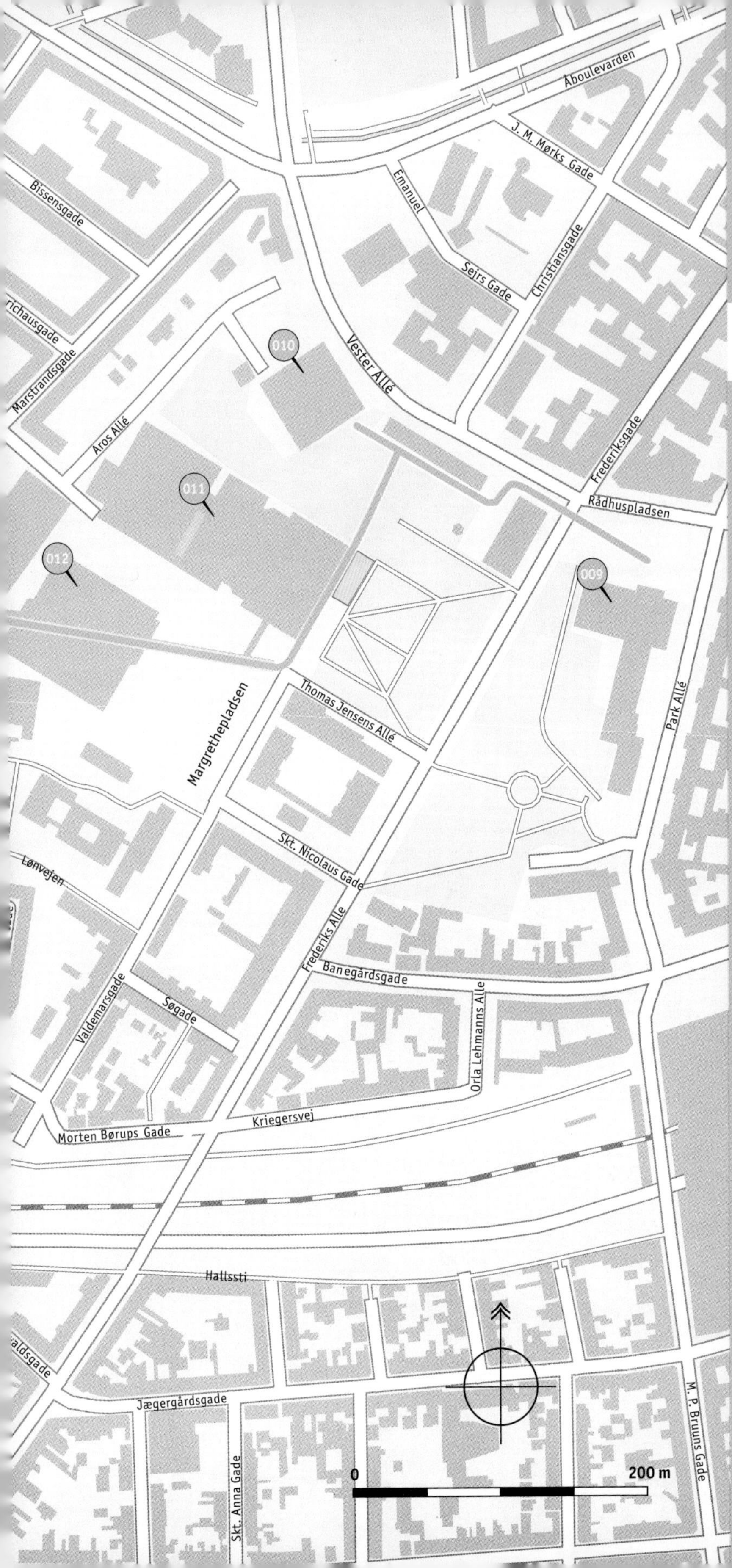
Åboulevarden
J. M. Mørks Gade
Emanuel
Sejrs Gade
Christiansgade
Bissensgade
Marstrandsgade
Aros Allé
010
Vester Allé
011
012
Frederiksgade
Rådhuspladsen
009
Thomas Jensens Allé
Park Allé
Margrethepladsen
Skt. Nicolaus Gade
Lønvejen
Frederiks Alle
Banegårdsgade
Orla Lehmanns Alle
Valdemarsgade
Søgade
Kriegersvej
Morten Børups Gade
Hallssti
Jægergårdsgade
Skt. Anna Gade
M. P. Bruuns Gade
0
200 m

Teknik & Miljø

003
049
052
048
060
009

009 A

Jan Kejser

Town Hall
Rådhuspladsen 2
Arne Jacobsen/Erik Møller
1942

009 A

The genesis of the fourth town hall in the history of the city of Aarhus is long, controversial and closely linked to the political development of Denmark since the abolition of absolutism in 1849 and the accompanying growth of democracy. These circumstances placed completely new demands on public administrative buildings. In light of the rapidly growing population (approximately 100,000) and lack of administrative space, the social democrat city council decided to commission the construction of a new town hall to reflect this new age heralding a growing democracy and prosperity. In the brief of the architectural competition held in 1937 one could read that the new building "is to be conceived as a distinctive administration building, as a place of work – without seeking to impose anything pompous and without any fake town hall style". The architects Arne Jacobsen and Erik Møller embraced this challenge and created a sombre, modern building which is today considered a masterpiece of Nordic functionalism. The building is located on a former cemetery. Part of the ancient tree population remains intact and has been transformed into a park which continues to serve as a popular grassy space in the city centre. The building has an asymmetric composition featuring three overlapping structures offset against each other. The main building containing the foyer, large hall and reception areas is located on Town Hall Square; the city council hall accounts for a cantilevered element above the main entrance. Elongated, panoptic office wings along Park Allé house

Wikimedia Commons

the main body of administration. Towards the station, the city hall culminates in a lower office building featuring a roof with a slight curvature to it. Everywhere daylight streams into the interiors from which there are views across the park and the city. Diffuse daylight penetrates from above into the atrium of the entrance hall and the panoptic wings, as well as the city council hall from the side through a west-facing window extending to the full height of the building. Each detail has been carefully crafted by the architects. Originally the mere twenty-six-year-old Hans J. Wegner was solely commissioned with the design for the furniture, yet the task was enlarged to cover the entire interior and many details. The jury had unanimously marked out the design as the best of the fifty-three entries to have been submitted, but public opinion found the building not monumental enough and that it did not embody its purpose and must have a tower. Following many weeks of a partially polemic debate, the city council put forward a compromise proposal to execute the competition design with three modified aspects – a prestigious main entrance, façades clad in natural stone (in lieu of the proposed plaster surfaces) and a tower. Although the architects saw no reason to build a tower, the emblem of ecclesiastical or royal power, they took up this architectural challenge. Commenting on the outcome, Arne Jacobsen subsequently said: "As a compromise we proposed that the tower be designed as a campanile which was to be located in the garden of the town hall – of course in the vicinity of the town hall – although this also met with resistance. The tower was to be elevated atop the town hall and this is how it comes to stand in this somewhat despairing fashion, its legs directly lumbering through the roof. It cannot be said that this is the most satisfactory architectural approach." It was to be the last town hall tower that was built in Denmark. Since 1994, the city hall has been a listed building and in 2006 it became part of the Danish Cultural Canon on the grounds that it is "...one of the most sensual buildings in the country, but also a magnum opus marking the transition to a regional interpretation of international modernism in Denmark."

Ole Hartmann Schmidt

Elevation of Sønder Allé

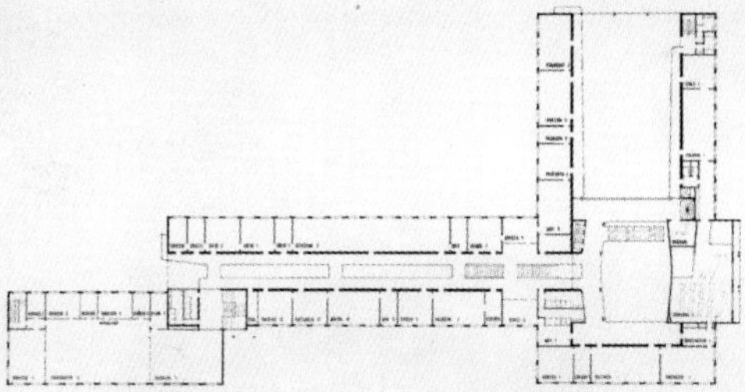

Floor plan of second floor

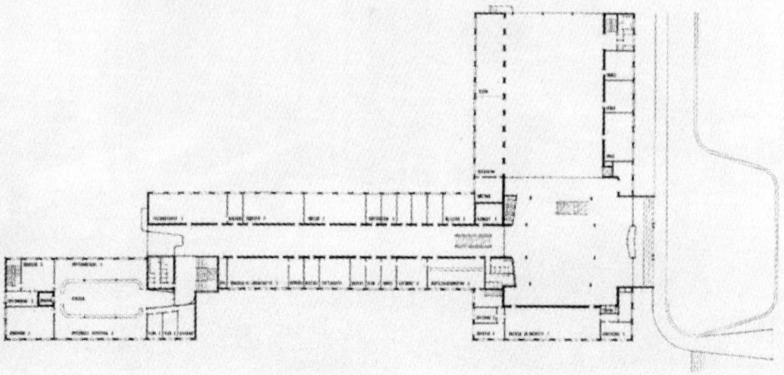

Ground floor plan

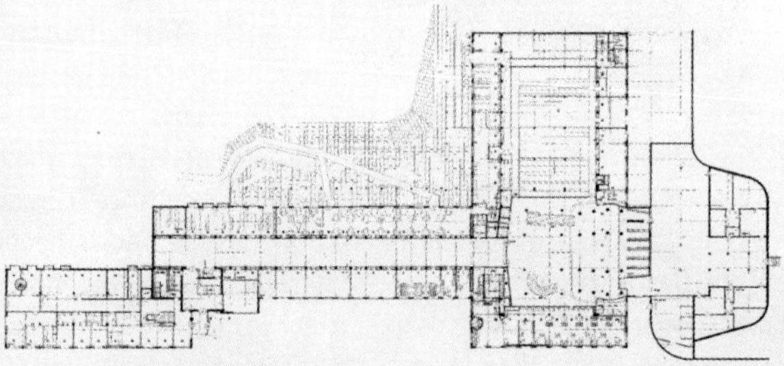

Basement floor plan

Adam Mørk / Schmidt/Hammer/Lassen

ARoS, Art Museum 010 A
Aros Allé 2
Schmidt/Hammer/Lassen, 2004,
Olafur Eliasson, 2011

As early as the 1980s, it was quite clear to the city of Aarhus that the former art museum in Vennelystparken, at the southern end of the University campus (see essay no.2), no longer met the demands of the modern art scene. A plot of land next to the Musikhuset (see 010) was made available with the notion of creating a cultural mile and in 1997 an international competition for the new building was held. The winning design was executed prior to 2004 and consists of a cube-like structure made of red brick which the so-called Museum Street slices through. This glazed public arcade allows people to visit the museum shop or the café on the ground floor without an admission ticket and is at the same time a unifying element in terms of urban design. The foyer extending to

Adam Mørk / Schmidt/Hammer/Lassen

Adam Mørk / Schmidt/Hammer/Lassen

the full height of the building divides the building into two functional domains: the exhibition wing featuring galleries and the service wing with workshops and storage rooms, offices and a library, and a restaurant too. A spiral projecting staircase comprising two lift shafts connects the various levels and lends the ascent a spatial experience. The greatest work of art and highlight of the collection awaits the visitor on the roof: *Your Rainbow Panorama* by the Danish-Icelandic artist Olafur Eliasson. This circuit has a glass façade in a range of colours, enabling the 150 m long arcade to evoke a stroll across a rainbow affording spectacular views over the city. With ca. 7,000 m^2 of exhibition space and more than 500,000 visitors, ARoS is among the largest art museums in Scandinavia and is already setting forth plans for the next attraction: a new oeuvre by the American artist James Turrell aims to propel the museum into the world elite of modern art museums under the name *The Next Level*.

ARoS Kunstmuseum / VisitAarhus

Musikhuset, Concert Hall 011 A

Thomas Jensens Allé 2
Kjær & Richter/
Sven Hansen, 1982,
C. F. Møller Architects, 2003/2007

Since it was inaugurated in 1982, the Musikhuset has been at the heart of musical life in Aarhus and is the largest facility for musical events in Northern Europe. It is home to the Aarhus Symphony Orchestra, Den Jyske Opera, Det Jyske Musikkonservatorium and the children's theatre group Filuren. Musikhuset draws ca. 700,000 visitors per year. The original building was the outcome of an architectural competition in 1977 from which the practice Kjær & Richter emerged triumphant. The building lies in a parkland landscape, the former barracks area, intersected by Frederiks Allé and bordered to the south by the park of the town hall. The building adjoins flat terrain and the slope leading down to the river valley and the former railroad property (see 028). In common with the open-air amphitheatre, the large hall with a seating capacity of 1,588 and the small hall with 319 seats have also been built into the embankment, while the service wing featuring performers' dressing rooms, administration, and, most importantly, the stage towers is located at the lower end of the slope. All closed off parts of the structure were built with yellow exposed brickwork, while the fully glazed foyer opens up invitingly

Kjær & Richter

Jan Kejser

on to the park. The total area of the 17 m high bright foyer with open balconies on several storeys underwent expansion in 2003 to include 2,000 m^2 of usable space by projecting the façade outwards. Today, the roof of the foyer is supported by forty columns. The foyer contains restaurants and cafés, information and ticket desks, a cloakroom, exhibition space and recreational areas dispersed over different levels. A large number of events are also held here. It is a place of many experiences and is used by the general public at all hours of the day. In order to mark the twenty-fifth anniversary, the Musikhuset was enlarged by three new halls as well as facilities and rehearsal rooms for Det Jyske Musikkonservatorium in 2007. This included a symphony hall with 1,184 seats, a rhythmic hall with 465 seats and standing room for 1,000 people and a chamber music hall which can hold up to 100 people. Today, Musikhuset has no less than six stages and nine halls covering a total area of 35,000 m^2. Scattered across the whole foyer one finds artworks by Robert Jacobsen, Jean Arp, Pierre Soulages and Ingvar Cronhammer, among others. In Sven Hansen's garden installation there are sculptures by Anker Hoffmann, Ejler Bille and Gudrun Steen-Andersen, among others. The original colour scheme of the main hall is attributable to the painter Emil Gregersen. The interior of the hall was decorated anew by the artist Mogens Gissel within the course of extensive renovation work in 2011.

Adam Mørk

Heiko Weissbach

Scandinavian Centre, Hotel and Conference Centre

012 A

Margrethepladsen 1
Friis & Moltke, 1995

The construction of the Scandinavian Centre was a huge endeavour. The prominent sloping site, which covers a difference in altitude of circa. 12 m and is located right next to the Musikhuset (see 011) and opposite the town hall (see 009), prompted the architects to deliver a monumental gesture, uncommon in Aarhus. Two slab-like high-rises are connected by, and made accessible with, a glass-roofed arcade. This constructed axis is aligned with the town hall tower which would have been visible if it were not for the coarse spatial lattice structure of the glazed roofs obscuring the view. At the opposite end the axis leads to the former freight station site (see 014), the building site preparation and urban development of which only started in 2010. Four-storey administrative buildings adjoin the railway premises. Owing to the yellow-grey natural stone cladding, the material properties of the building are aligned with both the yellow clinker brick of the neighbouring Musikhuset and the grey Porsgrunn marble of the town hall. The building complex contains a conference centre and a hotel, a private hospital, a fitness centre and a number of retail premises, as well as an underground car park. The arcade with bridges connecting both wings of the hotel is a spectacular space, although the shops on the lower storeys suffer particularly from a lack of customers since a destination is absent at the end of the axis. It is hoped that this may change with the development of the abandoned freight station site. Approximately 11,000 m² of commercial space has been converted into 133 new two- to four-room student apartments since the centre struggles to rent out space. The move-in period is scheduled for 2018.

Friis & Moltke

Frijs & Moltke

013 A

Rasmus Hjortshøj / SLETH

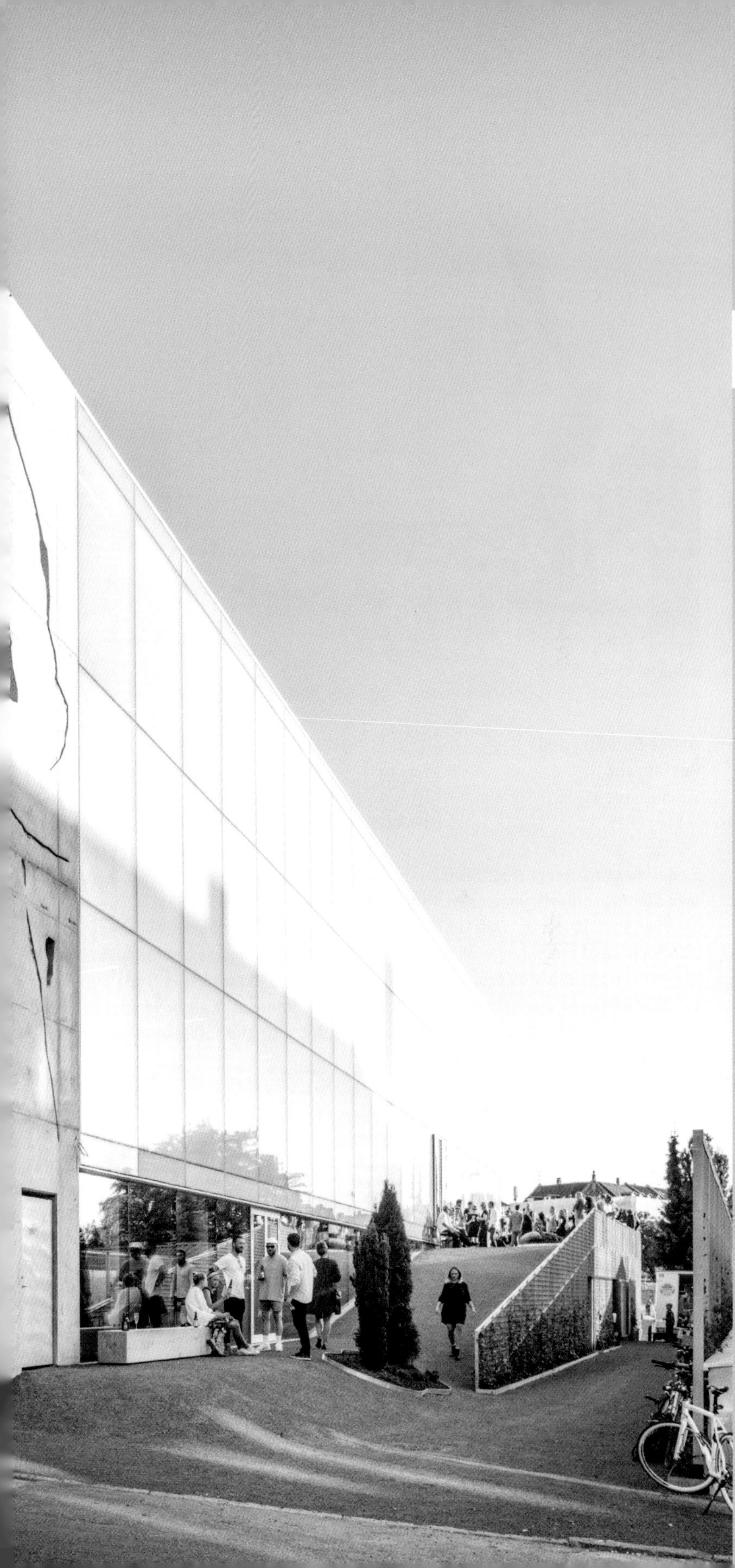

Rasmus Hjortshøj / SLETH

Office Building and Restaurant
Sonnesgade 11
SLETH, 2016

013 A

Sometimes architects must become their own clients in order to implement a design as they envisioned it. The SLETH practice took up the challenge of assuming the concurrent roles of property owner, project developer and architect in order to build their new domicile in Aarhus as a manifesto of their architectural philosophy. The architects themselves describe their building as a collage which, with six (!) different façades, reflects the manifold identities of the surrounding area and enters into dialogue with its multi-faceted, somewhat vague context. The building was thus established upon the foundation remains of a former industrial building and comprises three 50 m long office floors, not all of which have been rented out. The loft-like office premises

Rasmus Hjortshøj / SLETH

Rasmus Hjortshøj/SLETH

boast an open and flexible design. Parking spaces and a restaurant – which is also used as a canteen – have been furnished on the ground floor of the building. The building is accessed by means of an exterior stairway extending from street level to the roof and covering the entire east façade. Auxiliary functions are arranged in a linear fashion on this side and are punctuated on each floor by an entranceway at another point. The closed gable overlooking the street contains another stairwell which, cast in concrete and complete with cracks as a design feature, marks the entrance to the building, looking like an affixed stone. The restaurant has been "shoved" beneath the stone. The façade to the west is fully glazed and, in addition to optimum daylight, provides spectacular views across the railway line and the entire western region of Aarhus. As the sixth façade, the roof bears the entire building services and offers a 360-degree panoramic view over the city.

Rasmus Hjortshøj/SLETH

Adam Mørk / 3XN

Godsbanen,
Freight Depot and Site

014 A

Skovgaardsgade 3
Heinrich Wenck, 1923
3XN/E + N Arkitektur, 2012

Adam Mørk / 3XN

At the end of the nineteenth century, development in Aarhus was rampant and was thus seen as a major transportation hub in Denmark. At that time, although goods were being handled between the main railway station and the port, increased freight volumes forced a relocation. Following many years of discussion, Hack Kampmann and the Copenhagen-based city engineer Charles Ambt drew up a master plan for the site near Mølleengen. The freight depot, a palatial main building with two long, orthogonal cargo halls, was designed by the chief architect for the Danish State Railways (DSB), Heinrich Wenck, who is also the author of the main train station in Copenhagen. The activities of the freight depot were discontinued in 2000; eight years later the site and buildings were purchased by the Aarhus municipality in order to establish the city's new arts and cultural centre. During the restructuring of the site, traces of industrial architecture were to remain intact, as well as being augmented by and contrasted with new buildings and extension work. The historic buildings underwent careful renovation on behalf of the Exners Tegnestue (today's E + N Arkitektur) practice. Administration offices and workshops for the performing arts, pictorial art, cinematography and literature together with guest accommodation were furnished within the main building. One of the cargo halls has been preserved almost wholly intact in order to host exhibitions, trade fairs, shows and conventions. The other hall contains studios and workshops based on free artistic expression. Between the two longitudinal halls, the firm 3XN has placed approximately 9,000 m² of flexible halls and auditoriums, a restaurant and a music café beneath a new, large-scale folding roof which visitors can enter to enjoy the views across the site. The roof area is perforated by large, circular skylights which supply the space below with natural light. The new building is designed to mediate between the landscape and the existing buildings, establishing new interconnections between the elongated halls. Preserved rails have been incorporated into the design for a new inner courtyard between the new and existing buildings. The next new building on the site is supposed to be the new School of Architecture. Under the acronym NEWAARCH, architects from across the globe competed for the contract to design the new School buildings. Two hundred and thirty firms from forty-seven countries participated in the first open phase of the competition. Three designs were awarded a prize and competed in the second phase against three architects of global standing: BIG (Denmark), Lacaton & Vassal (France) and SANAA (Japan). Surprisingly, the young Danish bureau vargo nielsen palle won.

E + N Arkitektur

014 A

Adam Mørk / 3XN

Between the Main Railway Station and the Port

Fiskergade
Busgaden
Telefonsmøgen
Posthussmøgen
Ferdinand Sallings Stræde
Mindebrogade
Hans Hartvig Seedorffs Stræde
Søndergade
Østergade
Fredenstorv
Mindegade
Amaliegade
Ridder Stræde
Sønder Allé
Dynkarken
Rosenkrantzgade
Fredensgade
Toldbodgade
019
Ryesgade
018
017
Banegård-pladsen
Ny Banegårdsgade
Værkmestergade
016
Spanien
Frederiks Plads
015
022
Jægergårdsgade
Kalkværksvej
H. N. Clausens Gade
St. Blichers Gade
Brammersgade
Hekse-Trappen
Marselisborg Alle
Strandvejen
Skt. Pauls Gade

Hack Kampmanns Plads
Narvagade
Libaugade
Honnør-
kajen
Revalgade
Kovno
Gade
Mindet
Polensgade
Balticagade
Vilnagade
Danziggade
021
020
Havnevej
Filmbyen
Sydhavnsgade
Silovej
Celebesvej
Samoavej
0
200 m

017
002
015
016
Comwell

019
018
103
020
021
Sydhavnen
Teknik & Miljø

Ivar Mjell/3XN

Jægergården, Town Hall Annex 015 B

Værkmestergade 15
3XN
2001

As its name implies, Jægergården (hunter's court) was a clubhouse built in 1724 and originally belonging to the estate of Marselisborg. Later, it housed the administration of the Danish State Railways (DSB) prior to 1885, but was demolished in 1910 in order to provide the space required for new warehouse buildings (see 063). The municipality of Aarhus built their new administrative building on the same site which is named after the original development. Today's Jägerhof serves to enhance capacity at the town hall by a good 500 employees. Since the town hall (see 009) is the architectural icon of the city, the architects drew inspiration from its design principles and details. Steps and bridges made of white concrete elements featuring elegant metal balustrades interconnect the four office wings within the central atrium. The red brick façades are interspersed with serigraphic pale green glass elements featuring motifs by the designer Finn Skjødt. Inside, the southern wall of the atrium is adorned with a large-scale painting by Lise Malinowsky.

Ivar Mjell/3XN

Ole Hein / CUBO

Central Workshop
Værkmestergade 9
CUBO
2006

016 B

The halls of the former railway workshops behind the station have been listed since 2005. Their unique identity recounts the increase in railway architecture since the mid-nineteenth century. With the commissioning of the first railway line in Jutland – between Aarhus and Randers – three buildings featuring a forge, electrical and bogie workshops and the associated administration were built in 1862 and run by the firm Peto, Brassey & Petts.

Ole Hein / CUBO

Ole Hein / CUBO

In 1880 railway companies across the country underwent a merger and the Danish State Railways was founded (DSB). The complex proceeded to become the main workshop in Jutland and Funen which conducted repairs on hundreds of locomotives and thousands of rail carriages each year. Spare parts and tools were also manufactured on site. Up to 1,850 people were employed at the end of the 1940s. However, the use of diesel locomotives heralded the dwindling need for maintenance as of 1950. In 1990 merely 140 employees remained and the DSB decided on the closure of the workshops and the sale of the site and accompanying buildings. In tackling the rehabilitation, the architects set great store by the preservation of the industrial character of the buildings. Rails and other details evoking its former use remain intact both inside and outside. Today the former forge (Smedien) is occupied by a venue for staging events. In addition, several new buildings, such as the job centre and an extension of the town hall (see 015), have emerged in the neighbourhood.

Heiko Weissbach

City Tower,
Hotel and Office High-rise
Værkmestergade 2
Arkitema Architects, 2013

017 B

The coal-black City Tower is situated within an intricate urban development area between the main train station and the port. With a height of 94 m, it is a mere 2 m lower than the tower of the cathedral and is, at the same time, the fourth tallest building in Denmark comprising twenty-three storeys. One of the two slender slab-like high-rises contains 240 hotel rooms including a conference centre and restaurant, whereas the other contains rented office space. The investor established a private apartment for himself on the penthouse floor. Well aware of the fact that high-rises are difficult to incorporate into their surroundings, the architects have created a base construction which accommodates the differences in level on site and creates pleasant recreational areas at street level. The new landmark meets the requirements posed by the Danish low-energy class of 2015 through the integration of photovoltaic elements into the balustrades of the southern façades, among other things.

Mads Møller

Low-energy Office Building 018 B
Kalkværksvej 10
C. F. Møller Architects
2010

The municipal administration sought to create a landmark amidst the cityscape and a benchmark project for new energy-saving architecture with this new building tailored for its own planning department. These intentions are clearly visible from the design for the façade. The full height of the corner of the building facing southward is marked by roughly 200 m² of photovoltaic panels in the form of lamellae and an area of 170 m² for thermal solar energy collectors. Energy for the warming up of indoor air in winter and for cooling in the summer is collected here. The recessed windows feature solar protection panels in the form of solar cells. Only materials with low thermal conductivity have been used, such as vacuum-insulated glazing. The construction has double the thermal density of that required by the Danish Building Code, thus meeting the requirements of the low-energy class of 2015 as well as elements of the German passive house standard.

Julian Weyer

Julie Bertelsen/KADK

Spanien Public Baths

019 B

Spanien 1
Frederik Draiby, 1933
Arkitema Architects, 1995

The bureau of the city architect was first launched in 1919 and Frederik Marius Draiby was the first person who was to fill this post for twenty-five years. When the Spanien Public Baths – many streets of the port were named after countries and regions – opened, it was the fifth of its kind in Denmark and the first in Aarhus which, in addition to a large swimming pool, also contained baths, steam baths, sun beds, massage and pedicure rooms, a hairdressing salon and a confectionary. Draiby created a public space imbued with the ideals of health and hygiene, as well as new building materials (reinforced concrete). It was only in the 1980s that its popularity gradually waned since many urbanites now owned a fully furnished bathroom in their flats. In 1989 the public baths facility was declared a listed building and underwent renovation in the mid-1990s. The original polychromatic interior was re-installed , but regrettably the large swimming pool was scaled back in order to make space for whirlpool baths and paddling pools on the basis of the family and wellness concept. The red brick façade, the copper roofs with a green patina and the neon letters visible from afar have been overhauled and the baths technical installations restored to state-of-the-art condition.

Julie Bertelsen/KADK

Filmbyen, Administrative Building of the Movie City

020 B

Filmbyen 23
CUBO, 2004

The movie city of Aarhus (*filmbyen*) is a commercial centre within the former industrial area between the port and the main station. Roughly eighty firms from the film and media sector are based here. The coal-black administration building is located parallel with the former turbine hall which underwent conversion in 2003 to become film recording studios and a venue for hosting events. The horizontal and vertical elements of the reinforced concrete structure are clad in black anodised aluminium panels. The storey-height windows on all six storeys are dark tinted. The uppermost storey, double in height, grants access to a south terrace. The visible constructions and installations of the interior are modelled on the raw architecture of ports.

Villy FinkIsaksen

Five Sisters Silo Facility ↑ 021 B

Kornpier
Engineer: Jørgen Christensen,
Architect: Hjalmar Kjær
1927

Commonly known as The Five Sisters, the silo facility at the port is the first building made of reinforced concrete in the city. Measuring 33 m, it approaches the height of the cathedral and is visible from afar, especially upon arrival by boat. This prompted the local newspaper to write: "Many find this colossus in grey reinforced concrete ugly, yet it has its own poetry: it speaks of the port and labour and is part of the new Aarhus emerging along the southern port...." Since the 1870s, silos have been built for the storage of grain with farmers themselves increasingly organising the trade of lining materials. In 1898 they founded the agricultural cooperative Jysk Andelsfoderstofforretning (JAF, today's DGL), which commissioned the construction of this complex. A total of 1,200 foundation piles with a length of 14 m were required in order to build on the marshy terrain. The storage capacity is up to 14,000 m^3. The sequence of these silos afforded the advantage of allowing the restacking and aerating of grain. Another strength is its location on the quayside, enabling the vessels to load and unload directly. Hjalmar Kjær, who sought to incorporate the silos into the urban landscape, was responsible for the architectural design. Although, from a distance, the silos evoke Dutch gabled houses from the seventeenth century, the plain design of the relatively large building complex in reinforced concrete is groundbreaking for early modernism in Denmark. The Five Sisters facility has thus been listed as a national monument since 2005.

Helene Høyer Mikkelsen/CUBO

Danske Bank Headquarters
Spanien/Jægergaardsgade
Arkitema Architects
2018

022 B

The new administrative building is to serve as the new headquarters of Danske Bank in Aarhus. Roughly 650 employees of the bank are to be brought together on a site covering 11,000 m^2 and blended in with employees of other firms, such as the real estate chain HOME and the pension fund DANICA. The southern port is the nearest large-scale urban development area, and it is hoped that this new building too will stimulate development. The building resembles a stack of containers which are slightly offset in relation to each other. This displacement was capitalised on to create terraces where employees may reside. The bank's customer functions have been assigned to the ground floor. Well aware of the fact that the establishment of a bank within this – still raw – urban district may not be the first choice of residents, skateparks and sports fields have also been integrated into the compound. Work is already underway by the architects to create a similar building in Kolding.

Arkitema Architects

Arkitema Architects

Frederiksbjerg

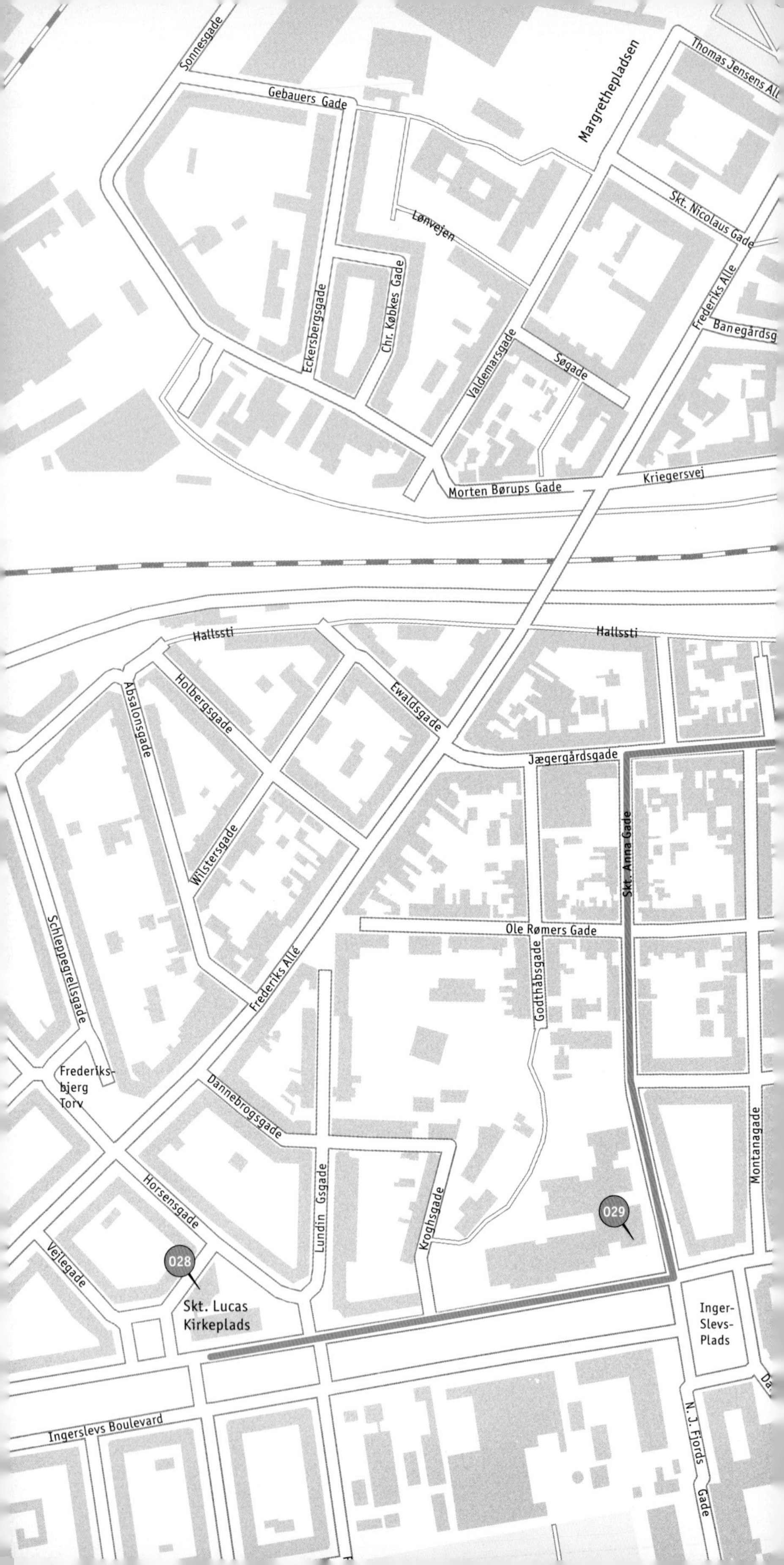
Sonnesgade
Gebauers Gade
Margrethepladsen
Skt. Nicolaus Gade
Lønvejen
Frederiks Alle
Eckersbergsgade
Chr. Købkes Gade
Valdemarsgade
Søgade
Morten Børups Gade
Kriegersvej
Hallssti
Hallssti
Absalonsgade
Holbergsgade
Ewaldsgade
Jægergårdsgade
Skt. Anna Gade
Wilstersgade
Ole Rømers Gade
Godthåbsgade
Schleppegrellsgade
Frederiks Allé
Frederiks-
bjerg
Torv
Dannebrogsgade
Montanagade
Horsensgade
Lundin Gsgade
Kroghsgade
029
028
Vejlegade
Skt. Lucas
Kirkeplads
Inger-
Slevs-
Plads
Ingerslevs Boulevard
N. J. Fjords Gade

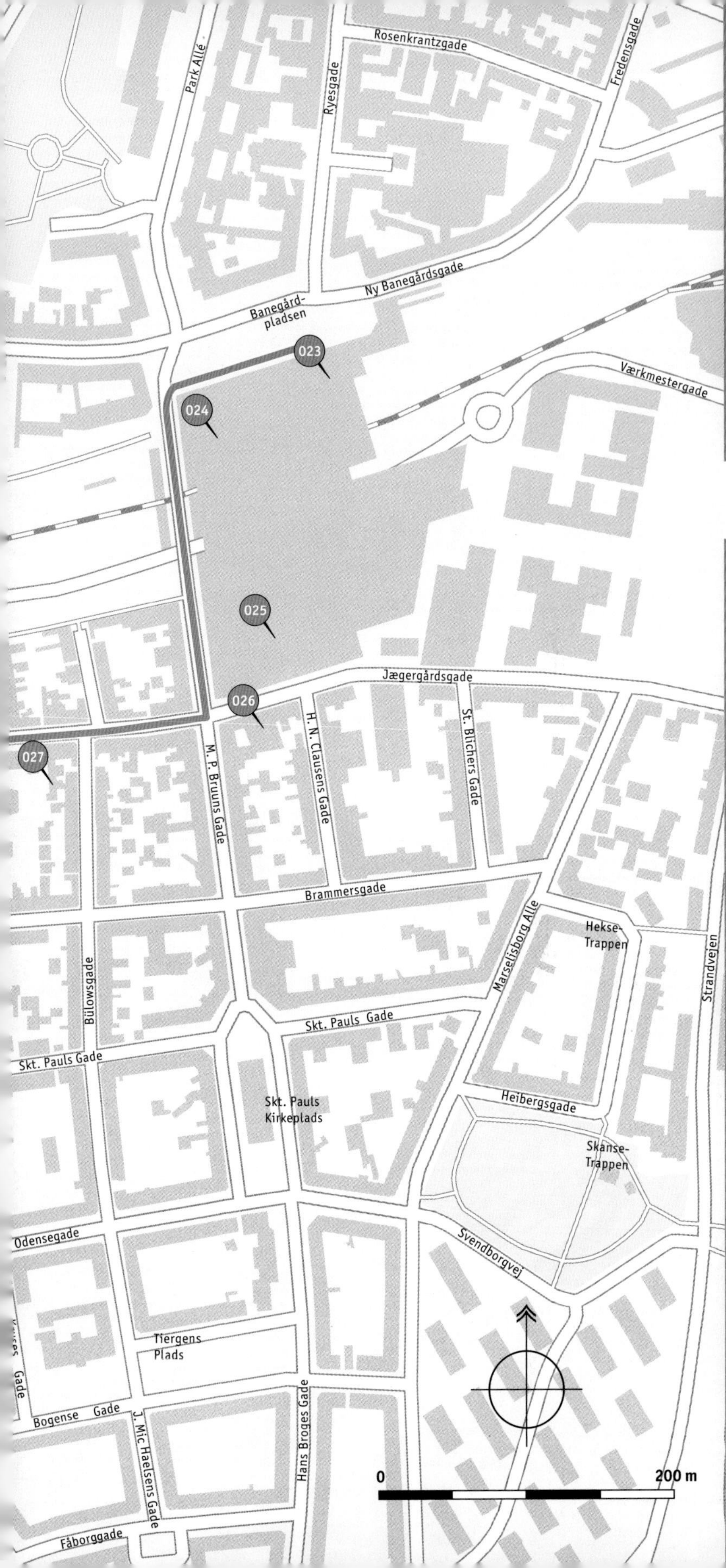
Rosenkrantzgade
Fredensgade
Park Allé
Ryesgade
Ny Banegårdsgade
Banegård-
pladsen
023
024
025
026
027
Værkmestergade
Jægergårdsgade
H. N. Clausens Gade
St. Blichers Gade
M. P. Bruuns Gade
Brammersgade
Marselisborg Alle
Hekse-
Trappen
Strandvejen
Bülowsgade
Skt. Pauls Gade
Skt. Pauls Gade
Skt. Pauls
Kirkeplads
Heibergsgade
Skanse-
Trappen
Svendborgvej
Odensegade
Tiergens
Plads
Bogense Gade
J. Mic Haelsens Gade
Hans Broges Gade
Fåborggade
0
200 m

C

021
017
009
023
025
024

029
028

Leif Wivelsted

Central Railway Station and Central Station Square 023 C

Banegaardspladsen 1
Knud Tanggard Seest/
Axel Høeg-Hansen, 1929

Today's railway station is already the third building on the same site. In 1862 the first station was built on an open space but was found to be too small as early as 1888 and was thus built over. In 1929, today's terminus was put into operation and appointed as the main railway station in conjunction with a major urban overhaul of the city centre in the 1920s. The station building was designed by the architect Knud T. Seest in the neo-classical style. In 1920, Axel Høeg-Hansen and the engineer Oluf Jørgensen won the urban planning competition for the precincts of the station and the new street Park Allé. Høeg-Hansen also designed the buildings around the Central Station Square which consort with the station in terms of height and materiality. Each building contains four storeys, is made of yellow exposed brickwork with details in sandstone and has tiled mansard roofs. The homogeneity of the Central Station Square is largely intact. It was only in 2005 that the open corner towards Bruuns Gade was bridged with the newspaper publishing house *Aarhus Stiftstidende* (see 024). The interior of the station was augmented by new ticket counters, waiting rooms and shops in the 1990s. There has been direct access to the shopping centre Bruuns Galleri (see 025) since 2003. The railway lines are situated roughly 5 m below the station building since the revamp of the Central Station Square in the 1920s. A new so-called light rail line between Odder and Grenaa will connect the station with the new dock area and the Skejby district. Commissioning is scheduled for 2017.

Visit Aarhus

Bruuns Arkade and Aarhus Stiftstidende 024 C

Banegårdspladsen 11/
Bruuns Bro
Exners Tegnestue, 2005

The new building of the station and its surroundings brought forth a new topography of the city centre at the end of the 1920s. The city and the urban district of Frederiksbjerg, south of the station, had to be bound to each other via a bridge spanning the railway tracks. The Bruuns Bro (bridge) was originally an infrastructural necessity, but its central location at an important traffic junction lent itself to a place of commerce. This initially gave rise to some barracks on the eastern side of the bridge which continued to develop over the decades and were ousted by a new building made of steel in 2003. Eight assembled, three-storey edifices clad in copper sheet with vaulted roofs acquired fully glazed shops facing the pavement which emerged in the aftermath of the neighbouring shopping centre, Bruuns Galleri (see 025). The full height of the structure is best discovered inside. Small intermediate landings have been inserted merely to house auxiliary functions, such as storage or personnel rooms, and are accessible via a white steel stair. Facing Central Station Square, the corner, a non-built up area since the 1920s, has been bridged with a five-storey office building featuring a yellow clinker façade. This houses the administration and customer centre of the major local newspaper, *Aarhus Stiftstidende*. The arched roof shape of the arcade has also been applied to the stacked storey and is intended – together with the sun protection lamellae made of copper – to forge a rapport between both buildings in terms of their design. In keeping with the traditional practice of the Exner architectural bureau is its thorough analysis of the neighbouring building stock and the extension in a modern interpretation. The yellow exposed masonry of the peripheral development on Central Station Square is shaped by special brick bonding, perforation dwindling in height or the diminished proportion of glass within the new building.

E+N Arkitektur

amo / 3XN

Bruuns Galleri, Shopping Centre 025 C

M. P. Bruuns Gade 25
Centrumtegnestuen (Schmidt/Hammer/Lassen + 3XN), 2003

Since the early 1990s, the municipal administration, the Danish State Railways (DSB) and private investors have focused on how to convert the partially abandoned site of the former railway workshops. It had been a lengthy and laborious path prior to the inauguration of the largest intra-urban shopping centre in Denmark. The concerns of citizens and individual councillors centered on the mass of the building with roughly 90,000 m² of floor space and on changes to transport and infrastructure. Furthermore, owners of small shops on M. P. Bruunsgade protested, nursing fears of being marginalised by major brands and supermarkets. The urban compromise involved the construction of a new bypass road on the track bed as well as the integration of housing. The high-rise is just under 70 m and has sixteen storeys, nine of which contain office space. It is crowned by two storeys containing apartment complexes. Below is located a multi-storey shopping centre with a cinema and car park. The centre is approached from three sides: via M. P. Bruunsgade and Værkmestergade and the neighbouring station. Both the cubature and the range of materials in grey hues – glass, steel and natural stone – stand in stark contrast to the small-scale neighbouring development in red brick with saddle roofs and no more than five storeys. The protests against the construction quietened down on the inauguration day in October 2003, when 100,000 Aarhusians began streaming into the newly opened stores. Fears regarding the potential disappearance of the heterogeneity of the shops on neighbouring streets have proved to be unfounded. In terms of urban development, the ensemble has been offset by further high-rises in the vicinity, so that Bruuns Galleri has today been incorporated into the cityscape.

Adam Mørk / Schmidt/Hammer/Lassen

Claus Hermansen

Kobberhuset

026 C

Jægergaardsgade 100
Claus Hermansen
2008

This residential and commercial building opposite Bruuns Galleri (see 025) bridges a longstanding gap on the street, which is animated by retail and catering outlets, in the popular Frederiksbjerg district. The building named Copper House derived its name from its façades clad in rectangular, perforated copper sheets which ensure protection from the sun and privacy. They may be slid sideways and folded. One flat containing approximately 90 m² of floor space is located on each of the four storeys above the two fully glazed shops on the ground floor.

Claus Hermansen

E+N Arkitektur

Nosy House

027 C

Jægergaardsgade 78
E + N Arkitektur
2008

This residential building with a mere four apartments squeezes itself in between two different buildings: on the left a pharmacy from the *Gründerzeit* period, the gable of which stands orthogonal to the street, and on the right a recessed, sober post-war building with a supermarket. The architects E + N take advantage of the existing misalignment of the façade contour towards the street to design a curved glass alcove above four storeys, affording residents an extensive view across the streetscape. Similar to the lamellae cladding of the former Historical Museum (see 101), here too, the glass façade is clad in larch wood lamellae. According to the architects, this is intended to imbue the building with "poetry and a human scale".

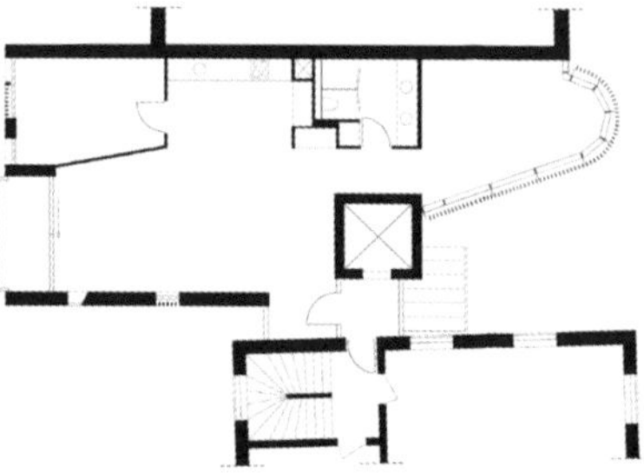

E+N Arkitektur

Leif Wivelsted

St. Luke's Church

028 C

Skt. Lukas Kirkeplads 1
Kaj Gottlob/
Anton Frederiksen, 1926
with Sognehus (Community Hall)
by Anders Bové Christensen/
Arkitektgruppen Regnbuen, 2000

The architects Kaj Gottlob and Anton Frederiksen had worked together at the practice of Hack Kampmann. There, they drew up competition entries with neo-classical motifs prior to their victory under their own name in the competition for St. Luke's Church with another neo-classical design. Regrettably, it took eight years before Kaj Gottlob was able to execute the church between 1921 and 1926, thus resulting in changes to the design which lent the finished building an austere, almost puritan, appearance. The church is located at the northern end of Stadion Allé, an axis which the urban development plan by Hack Kampmann and Charles Ambt had already set out. To the south, it leads to the stadium by Axel Høeg-Hansen (see 131). It was his idea to place the 35 m high church steeple at the point of alignment of the axis, thus spawning an urban contrast. The church façades consist of Faxe limestone and the interior is whitewashed. Since 1962, the ceilings have been adorned with paintings by J. G. Andersen. The subsequent extension building on the north side – the minimalist design of which is assimilated with the church and the urban district – houses a community hall, rooms for confirmations and administration. There is access to the crypt of the church between the church and the extension.

Heiko Weissbach

Hufton+Crow

School in Frederiksbjerg

029 C

Ingerslevs Boulevard/
Skt. Anna Gade
Henning Larsen/
Møller & Grønborg, 2016

The new school in the Frederiksbjerg district replaces what was once Skt. Anna Gade Skole and is the first new school in the city centre for a hundred years. The school is not merely a school, but also a resource for learning and playing, a community centre and a meeting place for the entire district. It is also accompanied by a kindergarten and an after-school care club, as well as multi-functional exterior spaces – which are accessible to the entire city outside school hours – for ball games and educational games. The very urban street façades are composed of reddish-brown exposed brickwork – which has partially been reused from the former school building – and irregular windows, intermeshing with the homogeneous development of the district which is attributable to a plan by Hack Kampmann and Charles Ambt dated 1898. The entrance is located at the offset and elevated corner, leading to an arrival plaza featuring podiums where one may reside and climbing walls. The school is arranged in four contours. Each contour has its own atrium around which technical rooms and pedagogical kitchens are oriented. The combination of limited floor space and a large number of pupils (650, 80 teachers) led to the result that outside facilities have also been designed on terraces to which each class has direct access. Younger children reside on the lower storeys and older children on the upper ones. The building thus approaches the smaller scale of the townhouses behind it. Pedagogical objectives are governed by the vision of a healthy school which involves the architects' concept of sustainability encompassing everything from daylight optimisation, a healthy interior climate, the recycling of building materials and consideration of quality and long lifespan. In addition, the school is a "living laboratory for studies on the interaction of daylight and artificial light and its significance for the learning process" – a development project chaperoned by the architects, several universities and the Danish State Building Research Institute (SBI).

Hufton+Crow

Møller & Grønborg

Hufton+Crow

029 C

Hufton+Crow

Julian Weyer

Aarhus University – History and Significance

Nils-Ole Lund

Aarhus University 030 D

Nordre Ringgade 1
Kay Fisker/C. F. Møller/
Povl Stegmann, since 1933

In 1919 the Ministry of Education in Denmark established a commission to grapple with the founding of a second university in Jutland. It called for a "modern university with student accommodation" and "in which students and professors live together and share a common everyday life", and lastly "where provision is made to ensure a sense of well-being within a scenic and beautiful university development."

In 1921 a foundation under the name of *Aarhus Universitets-Samvirket* was launched. The commission marked out the area of the campus four years subsequent to this: south of the proposed Ringgade and north of Vennelystparken, a morainic valley extending from Katrinebjerg north of the city to the bay of Aarhus.

In 1925 the foundation commissioned the architect Martin Borch with the task of examining the eligibility of the site as part of an initial development proposal. However, the hilly terrain gave rise to problems owing to its axial physical composition. One year later, the Academy of Fine Arts in Copenhagen held a so-called gold medal competition for the University in Jutland which the architect Frits Schlegel won. Contrary to Borch's approach, Schlegel respected the topography and his design affirmed the selection of the site. Its proximity to the community hospital on the other side of the street also played a role (see 036). In May 1931 the foundation and the city council invited Danish architects to take part in two competitions: one involving a development plan for several institutes, residential accommodation for male students and seven professorial dwellings, and the other involving plans for an Institute of Chemistry, Physics and Physiological Chemistry. The desire for buildings which "were cost-effective in terms of their construction and operation" had already been touched upon in the call for submissions.

The winning entry came from the architects Kay Fisker, Christian Frederik Møller and Povl Stegmann in collaboration with the landscape architect Carl Theodor Sørensen. One year previously the same team, minus Stegmann, won the competition for the community hospital. The mayor expressed that the architect ought to live in the city in light of such a major construction project. Accordingly, C. F. Møller decided to set up a practice in Aarhus and relocate to the city.

← **Material homogeneity in yellow brick**

C. F. Møller Architects

C. F. Møller at the office of Axel Høeg-Hansen, ca. 1920

The slogan for the winning design was *Jyde* (Jutlander) and the presentation consisted of thirty-eight panels which revealed five development plans and three different approaches towards the institute buildings, as well as analyses of foreign universities. The project drew up a range of alternatives, upon which the competition jury was able to comment, including four proposals which identified opportunities encompassing the entire valley. The valley had been left open in all proposals with the buildings placed on the uppermost point of the slope. The vegetation on the site – upon which allotment gardens had hitherto been located – was to be cleared and a hilly grassland featuring clusters of oak trees laid out. The architects proposed the construction of a small lake. The building earmarked to be built first – the objective of the second part of the competition – was placed on the high ground jutting out into the valley. It consisted of three clear-cut, interlocking structures made of exposed masonry with pitched copper roofs, horizontal strips of slender steel windows, and the horizontal façade composition was combined with simple buildings featuring gabled roofs.

Stegmann, Fisker and Møller had been raised within the spirit of neo-classicism, although the Bauhaus and modernism wielded influence on their architectural

C. F. Møller Architects

Model of the university campus featuring several unrealised buildings

C. F. Møller at the design studio – a.k.a. *skuret* ('the shed") – for the university with Gunnar Krohn, Peter Worm, C. K. Gjerrild, Jörgen Nordskov Kristensen, Baldur Moll and Aage Windeleff, ca. 1939

philosophy. Their design was marked by both Schlegel's project and the experiences of Kay Fisker and C. F. Møller during a study trip to Germany, where they paid a visit to Hannes Meyer's Bundesschule in Bernau, among other things. This school sets itself apart with its asymmetric complex featuring a long wing divided into individual blocks. These are offset parallel to each other in both the floor plan and the elevation, intermeshing with the terrain. Such a motif is also found in the plan for the University of Aarhus as well as the lake of the school in Bernau.

Fifty years later, C. F. Møller described the journey to Germany as follows: "It was the new forms that preoccupied us, the freedom to shape buildings in a sober and appropriate fashion. We barely paid heed to the general philosophy of functionalism. It played no role in our internal discussions. We worked under severe economic pressure and therefore it was often the economics which we discussed".

The first building complex, which was completed in 1933, was the Institute of Physics, Chemistry and Anatomy. Its architecture differed from that envisaged in the competition – not solely in that features had changed, but also because the buildings were to be as inexpensive as possible. The University Foundation was a private company; the economic crisis and

Institute of Physics, Chemistry and Anatomy, ca. 1933

The first halls of residence, ca. 1938

the lack of financial resources elicited a donations of materials, including brick (Hasle Clinker), oak parquet, spruce wood fixtures and doors. The gift of one million bricks and roof tiles from a brick factory led the architects to opt for yellow clinker brick. In order to ensure homogeneity of material in keeping with the Italian model, yellow roof tiles were also used which had never been produced in Denmark before. The choice of materials led to an increase in the roof pitch to 33 degrees, somewhat steeper than outlined in the competition design, but still slight enough that no useable rooms could be furnished in the attics; hence, no windows were required in the roof areas.

The three structures of the competition design proceeded to become four. This fourth slab-like edifice was set at an angle to the others, with a high gable facing the valley. The three slab-like edifices oriented in a north-southerly direction merely touch each other at the ends and were offset to each other in such a manner that allowed them to assimilate different building heights and depths. All workspaces have been amassed along a central circulation space – larger halls within the transverse slab, whereas auditoriums and the like with a large building depth and interior height are assigned their own wings. This principle of the parallel shift of the slabs and the north-south orientation have since been enshrined in the design for all subsequent buildings.

The simple design vocabulary featuring rigorous structures with an integrated gutter – to avoid disrupting the profile, albeit consistent with the Danish building tradition – is the outcome of the economic plight. The influence of modernism survived in the form of the white steel windows with slimline profiles and the robust building volumes.

C. F. Møller has said that Fisker felt he would give in too easily and alter the competition design too much. What was so peculiar was that this blend of neoclassicism, modernism and Danish tradition became so devoid of conflict that it merged to form one entity which endured throughout the evolution of the university. No one could have envisaged back then how large the university would eventually become.

King Christian X. was dissatisfied with the spartan architecture at the formal inauguration of the Institute of Physics,

Chemistry and Anatomy. He suggested C. F. Møller should study the typology of Danish manors. C. F. Møller was threatened with the withdrawal of the design contract and forced to defend his austere style. The year of 1934 saw the expansion of the site involving land bordering to the south and the conversion of the valley into grassland. Although the influence of the German New Objectivity movement upon the initial buildings had been mitigated, it remained discernible in the development plan.

Following the construction of the new institute and four professorial dwellings which had been built in 1934 on the north-eastern outskirts of the campus, a proposal was put forward to site future buildings west of the valley.

The architects executed three student residences with the same design in subsequent years. These combined the desire for regular repetition with the architecture of the Prellerhaus in the Bauhaus complex at Dessau: each room was embodied in the façade as an asymmetric composition with balconies featuring steel railings, tripartite windows and a balcony door. Nine dormitories were built in the same architectural style on both sides of the valley between 1935 and 1962.

The Institute of Biochemistry and Physiology was completed in 1937; this was accompanied four years later by the construction of the Natural History Museum which boasts three clear-cut structures and is therefore synonymous with the functional Danish tradition. The view towards the steps between the three wings underscores the virtues of this combining of structure and regard for materials.

Since Kay Fisker had been appointed Professor at the Academy of Fine Arts in Copenhagen in 1936 and was in receipt of major commissions there, the collaboration between Fisker and Møller had already come to an end at the time the main building was being planned. Work began in 1937 and the only assistant C. F. Møller had was the young Gunnar Krohn.

The main building was constructed in a period when a scaling down of materials reigned supreme and it was not a question of finishing as soon as possible.

C. F. Møller Architects

Typical gable with an asymmetrical balcony

Completion was even to be delayed in order to prevent German occupying forces inheriting buildings, as indeed they did in the case of the student residences. The design for the main building has been configured into 155 m long slabs along the newly laid out Ringgade which transverse buildings slice through at three locations. The gable sides facing Ringgade jut out, thus forming two courtyards – including the entrance courtyard facing Ringgade which is enclosed by masonry arches.

The central wing facing the park was used as a ceremonial hall. The differences in height on the side facing the park were offset by 10 m high retaining walls and terraces which culminate in masonry arches. The main building thus stood as

C. F. Møller Architects

Amphitheatre at the main building

Julian Weyer

Main building with the assembly hall and the amphitheatre

a monumental culmination of the valley. The piped source of the lake emanates from the walls on the valley floor and an amphitheatre on the slope along the Sørensen.
Grundtvig's Church near Copenhagen by Peder Vilhelm Jensen-Klint served as a source of inspiration for the auditorium. The hexagonal ceremonial hall not only has the same height (19 m) as the church hall, but also similar brick ornamentation. The pendant luminaires were designed by Poul Henningsen, whose acquaintance C.F. Møller made in the 1920s in Kay Fisker's practice.
The detailed design for the main building is richer and the artisanal standard – both inside and outside – higher than that of previous purist buildings. There were bricked columns above the supports and openings in walls, decorative masonry bonds on the gables and within the auditorium, undulating ceilings and floor patterns. C.F. Møller referred to these details as "romantic" and justified them on the basis of the war and as a response to harsh reality.
The main building at the end of the valley with the large window of the auditorium became one of the few Danish examples of

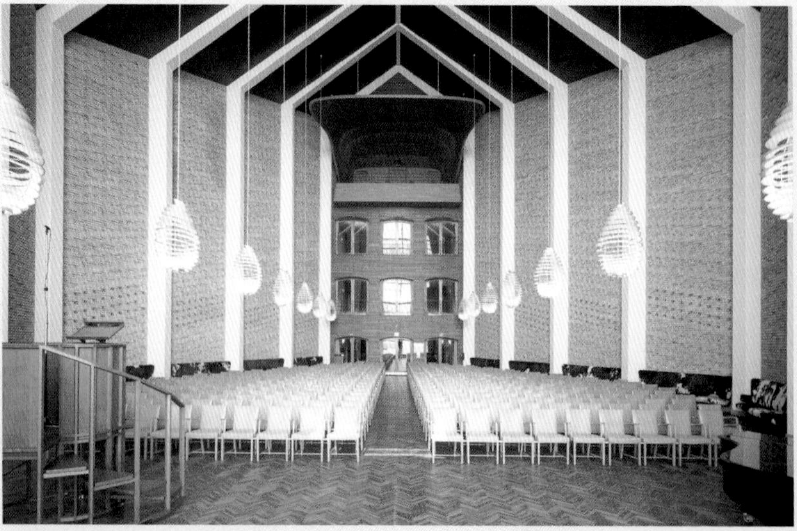
Torben Eskerod

Assembly hall

Torben Eskerod

Main building with the arcade, the sun dial and the amphitheatre

modern monumentality. Criticism levelled at the initial buildings turned into praise. In 1949 Axel G. Jørgensen wrote: "In the same manner as we believe that the entire university town, once complete, will be regarded as one of the most outstanding examples of architecture in Denmark, we can state by now that the university building is a magnum opus of Danish architecture from the 1940s."

On 31 October 1944, bombs dropped by English Mosquitos destroyed two student residences accommodating the headquarters of the Gestapo in Jutland. Many soldiers and police personnel were killed in the attack. Regrettably, several bombs fell on the main building which was on the cusp of completion. Shortly before the attack took place, C. F. Møller visited the construction site and got covered in debris and rubble when parts of the building collapsed. The only thing that protruded from the dust and debris was his hair. With a broken arm and crushed ribs, he was admitted to the hospital where the first thing he asked the nurse, once he had recovered from his initial shock, was: "Have we been lucky and the arches have fallen down?" However, the brick arches survived the bombing and

Poul Ib Henriksen

Benches outside the assembly hall

Poul Ib Henriksen

Stairs in the main building

Julian Weyer

Detail from the façade of a student residence

the university received a pinch of that which would subsequently be referred to as post-modernism.
In the 1960s, the long slab of the main building was augmented at the western end by the 43 m book tower of the state library and at the eastern end by premises for the humanities in the 1970s. A coherent shield against the traffic and noise on Ringgade thus emerged. Since the route between Ringgade and the park had been disrupted by the elongated main building, a winding underpass was built – a masterpiece of masonry.
C. F. Møller designed further buildings for the university for more than forty years.

Julian Weyer

Passage beneath Ringgade

Vigorous growth exerted pressure on the original proposals, such as the undeveloped valley and the open three-storey development. The expansion of the campus north of Ringgade, Vennelystpark and the barracks enabled the creation of space for many buildings, although a couple were higher than originally envisaged. Several construction phases could not be implemented in as free-standing a manner as desired in 1931; in some places the development became very compact. Over the years there were changes in construction methods and window formats; clinker walls proceeded to become the outer shell of a double-skin wall. C. F. Møller set out in a form of testament guidelines to be observed during conversions, expansions and repair work to ensure that his architectural oeuvre was not played havoc with. Permitted materials and acceptable signage are described therein. Flat roofs must not be built, nor should sculptures be installed in the park. Similarly, it was prohibited to plant both flowers or flowering shrubs and the oak population was to be thinned on a regular basis.

The University of Aarhus is an unrivalled oeuvre and also regarded as a place of recreation, evoking a park, for students and residents near the city centre. The first buildings with their beautiful proportions and elegant façades were met with sturdier successors. Yet, it is to the credit of C. F. Møller that he could follow through on the original proposals for over sixty years despite changes in technical and functional requirements.

The strength of the architecture lies in its coherence and the upkeep of the landscape. In the past, the impression of an unrestrained interplay between nature and buildings gained further traction than today as the oak trees have since grown large and partially obscure the view. Virginia creeper and ivy lend greenery to many buildings, concealing their robust forms. The Norwegian architectural historian Norberg-Schulz even once stated that it is not merely a matter of buildings, but rather of bushes that is usurping the art of gardening. C. F. Møller himself often expressed concern that greenery might dominate.

The ongoing development and customising of the landscape continued in collaboration with C. F. Møller up until the death of C. Th. Sørensen in 1979. Extensions were undertaken with consideration given to the guiding principle; vantage points come to full prominence owing to the maintaining and thinning out of the tree population. C. F. Møller passed away in 1990; the practice, which continues to bear his name, has since assumed responsibility for the further expansion of the university.

Resumé of a text from *Bygmester C. F. Møller* by Nils-Ole Lund, Aarhus Universitetsforlag, 1998. Published with kind permission of the author.

Lars Kruse/AU Kommunikation

View over the campus, the city and the harbour

From the School of Architecture and the University Campus to IT City

Malmøgade
Bodøvej
Mandalsvej
Hasle Ringvej
Stockholmsgade
Narviksgade
Farsundsvej
Kristiansundsvej
Haugesundsvej
Lillehammervej
Porsgrunnsvej
Møllevangs Alle
Tromsøgade
Laurvigsgade
Arendalsvej
041
Ålesundsvej
Frederikshaldsgade
Bildbjergvej
Vardøgade
Nordøgade
Brendstrupvej
Dybkjærvej
Thorshavnsgade
Myggenæsvej
Paludan-Müllers Vej
Vågøgade
Thingvalla Gade
Rytterknægten
Sandøgade
FÆRØSTIEN
Østerøgade
Heklagade
Reykjaviksgade
Islandsgade
Bly
Tværdalsvej
Kobbevej
Hammershusvej
Geysergade
Højlyngen
Slotslyngen
Katrinebjergvej
043
Finlandsgade
042
Ekkodalen
Helsingforsgade
Åbogade
Høgevej
Dybedalen
Uglevej
Paludan-Müllers Vej
Jens Baggesens Vej
Vestre Ringgade
Vilh. Bergsøes Vej
Bogfinkevej
Peter Fabers Vej
Gustav Wieds Vej
Falkevej
Nattergalevej
Otto Benzons Vej
Viggo Stuckenbergs Vej
Møllevangs Alle
Helge Rodes Vej
Blåmejsevej
Tornskadevej
Fuglesangs Allé
Paludan-Müllers Vej
Emil Aarestrups Vej
Spættevej
Fuglebakkevej
Jens Baggesens Vej
Solsortevej
Poul Martin Møllers Vej
Vestervang
Duevej
Vagtelvej
Ørnevej
Fasanvej
Drosselvej
Svalevej
Vestre Ringgade
Vestervang
Peter Holms Vej
Martin Vahls Vej
Johan Langes Vej
Eugen Warmings Vej
Møllevejen
0
500 m
Viborgvej
Mønsgade

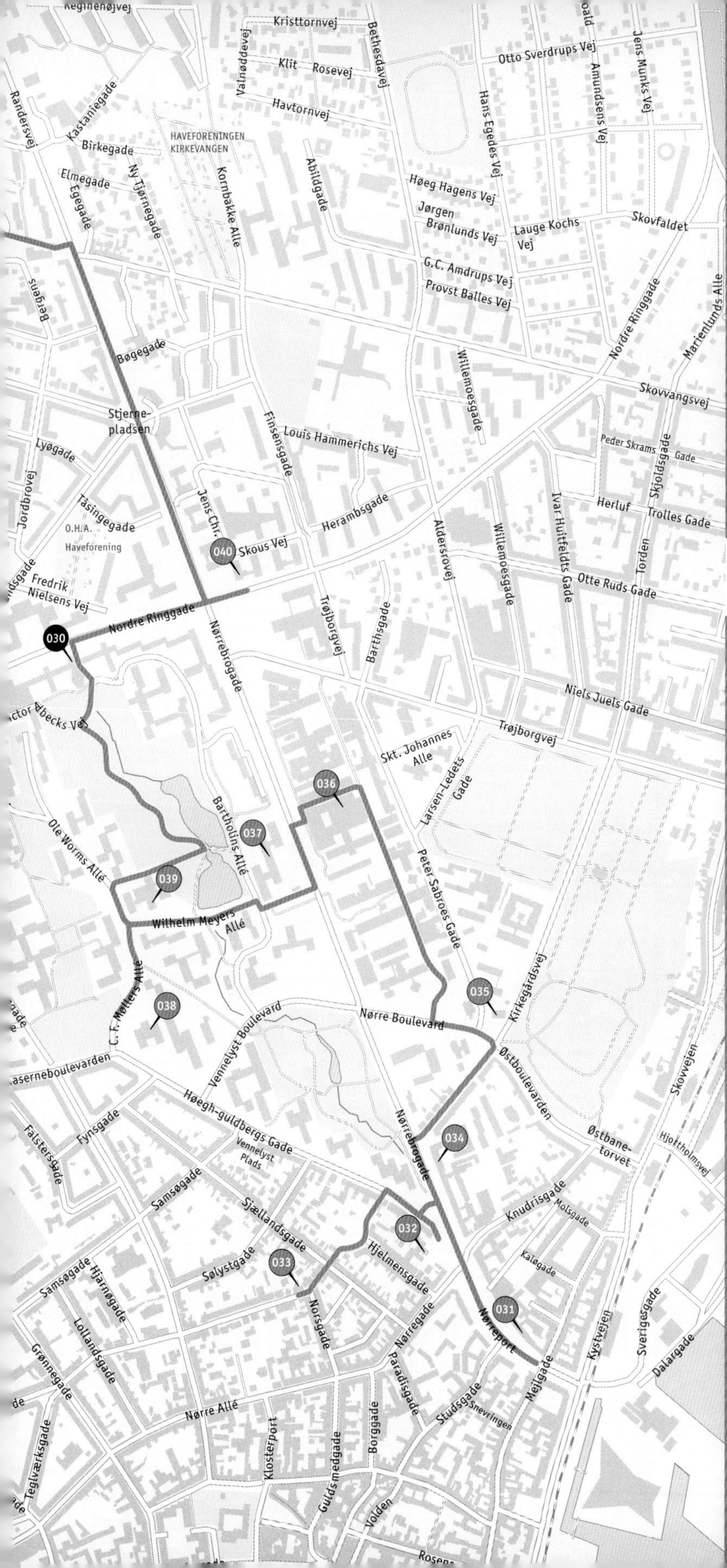
Kristtornvej
Valnøddevej
Klit
Rosevej
Bethesdavej
Otto Sverdrups Vej
Jens Munks Vej
Amundsens Vej
Havtornvej
Randersvej
Kastaniegade
Birkegade
HAVEFORENINGEN
KIRKEVANGEN
Hans Egedes Vej
Elmegade
Egegade
Ny Tjørnegade
Kornbakke Alle
Abildgade
Høeg Hagens Vej
Jørgen Brønlunds Vej
Lauge Kochs Vej
Skovfaldet
G.C. Amdrups Vej
Provst Balles Vej
Bergensgade
Nordre Ringgade
Marienlunds Alle
Willemoesgade
Bøgegade
Skovvangsvej
Stjerne-pladsen
Finsensgade
Louis Hammerichs Vej
Peder Skrams Gade
Skjoldsgade
Lyøgade
Jordbrovej
Tåsingegade
Herambsgade
Ivar Huitfeldts Gade
Herluf Trolles Gade
O.H.A. Haveforening
Jens Chr. Skous Vej
040
Aldersrovej
Torden
Fredrik Nielsens Vej
Otte Ruds Gade
Nordre Ringgade
Trøjborgvej
Barthsgade
030
Nørrebrogade
Niels Juels Gade
Trøjborgvej
Skt. Johannes Alle
Larsen-Ledets Gade
036
Bartholins Allé
037
Ole Worms Allé
039
Peter Sabroes Gade
Wilhelm Meyers Allé
Kirkegårdsvej
C. F. Møllers Allé
035
038
Nørre Boulevard
Vennelyst Boulevard
Kaserneboulevarden
Østboulevarden
Skovvejen
Høegh-guldbergs Gade
Fynsgade
Vennelyst Plads
Nørrebrogade
034
Østbane-torvet
Hjortholmsvej
Falstersgade
Samsøgade
Sjællandsgade
Knudrisgade
Molsgade
032
Hjelmensgade
Kaløgade
033
Sølystgade
Samsøgade
Hjarnøgade
Norsgade
031
Nørreport
Sverigesgade
Lollandsgade
Nørregade
Paradisgade
Kystvejen
Dalargade
Grønnegade
Mejlgade
Studsgade
Snevringen
Nørre Allé
Teglværksgade
Klosterport
Borggade
Guldsmedgade
Volden

D

039
038

Teknik & Miljø

D

Heiko Weissbach

Auditorium and Exhibition Building of the School of Architecture

031 D

Nørreport 22

Kjær & Richter, 1998

Owing to the steadily growing number of students since the foundation of the School of Architecture in 1965, new premises within various buildings on both sides of Nørreport, the main road, had to be rented. It was only in 1998 that a long-standing dream became reality: the long-awaited extension featuring a large auditorium and flexible exhibition space could be inaugurated. The royal building inspector, Niels Vium, designed the Blackbox with a white interior and spruce hardwood flooring for the Kjaer & Richter practice. The building was constructed from abstract black concrete elements and is more or less completely enclosed on three sides. The exterior sets itself apart from its heterogeneous neighbourhood spanning numerous epochs. The glass façade towards the south is furnished with large solar screening lamellae and is also a showcase for the work of 800 students. The large auditorium is located within the core of the building as a house within a house. The foyer, circulation areas and the double-height room featuring a circumferential gallery behind the auditorium host temporary exhibitions. A mobile partition between the auditorium and this workshop enables the joint use of both rooms. An alley evoking the medieval epoch in which the city centre emerged has been created between the historic existing building and the new one.

Thomas Pedersen og Poul Pedersen / Kjær & Richter

Thomas Mølvig/E+N Arkitektur

Mengel Tower, Apartment High-rise

032 D

Høegh-Guldbergs Gade 33
E + N Arkitektur
2013

The Mengel Tower residence, which is named after the investor Sten Mengel, contains a mere fifteen apartments. Accordingly, Mengel allowed "The smallest high-rise in the world's smallest city" to be engraved upon the bricks of the façade. Its slender form and location at the foot of Høeg-Guldbergs Gade lend it the appearance of a small high-rise. The trapezoidal site necessitated a particular approach, also requiring a response to the noise emission level of the main road, among other things. A building composed of slabs of masonry, which are interspersed with vertical strips of windows, thus emerged. The red exposed masonry is attributable to the so-called Flex System developed by the Egernsund Tegl brick factory, a series based on a Danish system from the toy industry comprising bricks in three different heights. These may be freely combined and render possible a multitude of different effects.

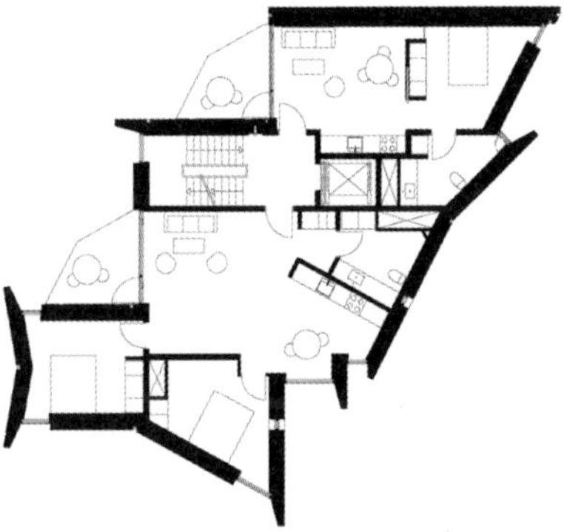

E + N Arkitektur

Heiko Weissbach

E+N Arkitektur

Casa Octagon, Residence 033 D
Thunøgade 14
E + N Arkitektur
2013

This small corner building in the island-street quarter draws its inspiration from the villa La Rotunda, a masterpiece of Renaissance architecture which was designed in the fifteenth century by Andrea Palladio and has a central dome above a symmetrical, cruciform floor plan. The building is situated directly on the street between three historic villas. Taking inspiration from Palladio, the design for an octagonal central room based on the juncture of two axes emerged. The stairwell is furnished on each floor with a glass eye that enshrines a targeted view of its vicinity. At the very top there is a panoramic lounge with a circumferential balcony affording sweeping views across the entire city. The building takes on something of the subdued scale and materiality of its environs while at the same time endeavouring to be a modern counterpart to the emergent urban quarter.

Lena Kondrup Sørensen

Residential and Commercial Building

034 D

Nørrebrogade 22–26
Hans Møller
1959

The architect of this residential and commercial building was trained at the Royal Prussian School of Architecture in Berlin, the subsequent Schinkel Academy of Architecture in 1914 before gaining his first professional experience on the imperial shipyard in Kiel and on the design for the new main station in Copenhagen. At about the same time as this residence, Hans Møller also designed the corner building at Klostergade and Gammel Munkegade in Aarhus. He created this finely detailed, five-storey building with a reinforced steel construction comprising prefabricated columns and beams on the sloping Nørrebrogade. The façade is clad in natural stone, while the window frames in natural wood are coated with a transparent lacquered finish. The recessed attic storey has continuous balconies which are now largely glazed to furnish the apartments with conservatories for winter gardens. The small balconies with white filigree railings are freely suspended from the facade and lend the large surface a correspondingly more lightweight structuring.

Lena Kondrup Sørensen

Heiko Weissbach

Hejmdal **035 D**

Peter Sabroes Gade 1
Rudolf Clausen, 1908
Gehry Partners LLP/CUBO/
Kristine Jensens Tegnestue, 2009

The consultation centre for cancer patients is located in the converted former gatehouse at the southern end of the community hospital (see 036). It was refurbished in the typical style of Frank O. Gehry – which some people refer to as deconstructivist – and is named after one of the most mysterious gods of Nordic mythology: Hejmdal, ascribed the power over sunlight and the safeguarding of human and spiritual values. Solely the exterior façades of the existing building remain intact. A new, solid wooden structure made of Douglas fir bears two storeys and the roof, although it is kept free from the raw masonry of the exterior walls. It has been inserted into this hollow shell in keeping with a pro-bono design by Gehry. The tree-like supporting framework filters the daylight penetrating through the fully glazed roof in a pleasant fashion, scattering it throughout the building. Mechanical solar protection prevents overheating and glare. In order to offer patients and their relatives a homelike setting, Hejmdal has been conceived as an open centre. The garden and an amphitheatre grant direct access to the art studio, the gymnasium and the lounge within the basement, merely half of which lies beneath the premises. Another lounge, a dining room and a shared kitchen are situated on the access level above. Conversational enclaves and common rooms lie on the second floor beneath the glazed roof.

Helene Høyer Mikkelsen/CUBO

Helene Høyer Mikkelsen/CUBO

Heiko Weissbach

Community Hospital

036 D

Nørrebrogade 44
Kay Fisker, C. F. Møller
1935/1994

The solid, but elegant, brick buildings of the community hospital were designed by Kay Fisker and C. F. Møller in 1931, readily bearing the stamp of both architects, who only recently had designed the university campus on the other side of Nørrebrogade. This involves homogeneous red structures without roof overhang and featuring slender white glazing bars, devoid of any identifiable ornamentation – pure functionalism! Although the university buildings are freely scattered across the campus, the hospital has been assigned a rigorous, linear axis of access running parallel with the main road along which, over the decades, T- or H-shaped buildings boasting their original architectural features have been added. Since 2004, the buildings have belonged to Aarhus University Hospital (AUH), the activities of which are pooled together within the new location in Skejby (see 073). Once the new building is completed, the inner-city sites will be decommissioned.

Heiko Weissbach

CUBO

Heiko Weissbach

Institute of Biomedicine ↑↓ 037 D
Wilhelm Meyers Allé 4
CUBO
2017

Owing to the merger of the Institutes of Anatomy, Medical Biophysics, Physiology and Biophysics, Human Genetics and Microbiology along with Immunology and Pharmacology, the existing Bartholin Building boasting a scenic location at the lakeside is undergoing renovation and expansion. The master plan for the new research and educational features of this super institute also proposes the construction of new buildings within the southern part of the university campus. Here, they blend together with the old buildings to create a single entity in the tradition of the university park dating back more than eighty years. The traditional gable motif of the campus is construed here in a semi-transparent model – a motif which CUBO had already developed in Building S of the commercial school (see 067). The overlapping of both new, elongated buildings, which are slightly offset in relation to each other, gives rise to a large panoptic central room. The offices and laboratories for the research units are distributed flexibly across the length of the narrow buildings. Of course, the new buildings are constructed from yellow exposed brickwork. Yellow brick is used as a flooring material both inside and outside. Inside, the traditionally white walls are augmented by oak details.

CUBO

CUBO

Steno Museum ↑→ 038 D
C. F. Møllers Allé 2
C. F. Møller Architects
1994

The museum named after the pioneer in anatomy and geology, Nicolaus Steno, is located at the southern end of the university park. The collection includes medicine and natural sciences and is the sole museum in Denmark to be engaged in the history surrounding the disciplines of mathematics and physics. The building oriented in a north-southerly direction consists of three parallel wings made of yellow exposed brickwork which are slightly offset in relation to each other – a familiar motif of the campus. A herb garden enclosed by a semi-circular wall occupies a central position between the three wings. To illustrate the rotation of the earth, a Foucault pendulum is suspended from the ceiling of the double-storey foyer. A planetarium featuring a projection dome is located on the upper floor.

Heiko Weissbach

Julian Weyer / C. F. Møller Architects

Natural History Museum 039 D

Wilhelm Meyers Allé 210
Kay Fisker/C. F. Møller/
Povl Stegmann, 1941
C. F. Møller Architects, 2000

The Natural History Museum occupies a central position on the campus, although it is not affiliated with the university. It is both a museum and a teaching and research facility. In accordance with the wishes of the building committee, this autonomy was to be marked by red roof tiles in lieu of the traditional yellow ones. However, the architect C. F. Møller also succeeded here in imposing harmony with the remaining buildings. The museum has been placed by the lakeside and encompasses three edifices of differing height which are offset in relation to each other. This staggered arrangement gives rise to a small forecourt with steps leading to the main entrance. According to Nils-Ole Lund, the museum is in keeping with that which Kay Fisker subsequently referred to as "the Danish functional tradition." The collection contains a myriad of stuffed animals and insects. In 2000 the museum underwent conversion and expansion on behalf of the C. F. Møller practice to include a larger hall for temporary exhibitions, where international traveling exhibitions are unveiled every now and then.

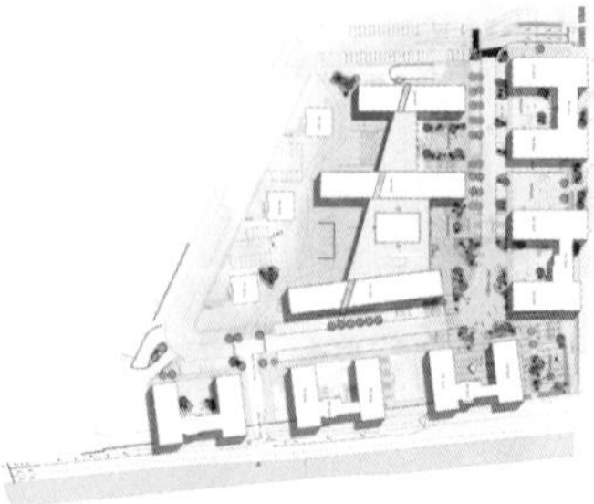

C. F. Møller Architects

Nobelparken ↙↘ 040 D

Randersvej/Nordre Ringgade
C. F. Møller Architects
2000

The campus named w is located at the corner of Ringgade and Randersvej on a site where there once stood a construction market for over 100 years – after which the site was named Barnow-Grund for a long time to come. Conceived as a city within the city, Nobelparken boasts a dense development with squares and streets in betwixt and between. In common with the rest of the city, Nobelparken also contains dormitories and classrooms of the university and other institutes, as well as rental space for offices and commercial property units. Five identical sets of six-storey blocks create a shield against the two roads with heavy traffic. In the middle, access towers, connecting bridges and glazed walls ensure noise protection and a high standard of living within the outside facilities. Apartments, such as those belonging to guest researchers, have been assigned to key buildings on the grassy areas of the site situated behind. Nobelparken is furnished with various artworks, some of which have been integrated into the buildings, such as a large glass artwork within the auditorium with portraits of the hitherto thirteen Danish Nobel Prize winners.

Heiko Weissbach

Heiko Weissbach

Christian's Church ↑↗

041 D

Frederikshaldsgade 13
Aage C. Nielsen
1958

Christian's Church composed of red brick was inaugurated in 1958 within the northern region of Aarhus. The free-standing, 32 m high belfry with a hexagonal floor plan dominates the urban landscape of the district. A much smaller church dedicated to King Christian X was located in the same place between 1913 and 1946. Although the competition for a new building had been held as early as 1937, it was only the crypt beneath the church – which was conceived as a parish room but was forced to serve as the actual church prior to 1958 – which could be built immediately. The striking building is entered through a low porchhouse containing the necessary auxiliary functions. It is adjoined by the prayer room featuring a bright, high ceiling and a seating capacity of 500 people. The striking, white concrete buttresses are visible as far as the ridge of the roof, awakening both modern and gothic associations. A horizontal strip of windows illuminates the church to the south, affording a view into the garden and is protected from sunlight owing to the roof overhang. The altar fresco representing The Last Supper is attributed to Frits Bruzelius.

Torben Eskerod/C. F. Møller Architects

Julian Weyer/C. F. Møller Architects

INCUBA Science Park 042 D

Inge Lehmanns Gade 10

C.F. Møller tegnestue, 2006

INCUBA stands for Innovation Network Centre for the University and Businesses of Aarhus and is a merger of four research institutes from 2007: Skejby, IT City Katrinebjerg, the University and Navitas (see 104). It is the first science park of its kind in Denmark which fosters partnerships between research and industry and aims to assist young researchers in setting up a business. The INCUBA Science Park is located at the campus of IT City Katrinebjerg and, as its name implies, places emphasis upon information and communication technologies. The building is composed of three elements: a glazed entrance hall facing the forecourt, an inner courtyard behind around which offices and classrooms are clustered and featuring a glazed roof. These are furnished with flexible spaces as required. In response to strong demand, a further section of the building has already been added which contains additional offices and conference rooms. The design for the framed, four-storey main façade of steel and glass is marked by adjustable solar protection lamellae. Access corridors on several storeys, from which small glazed workspace cubicles are suspended, are located behind the façade.

Julian Weyer/C. F. Møller Architects

Julian Weyer/C. F. Møller Architects

Gert Skærlund Andersen

IT-Hjørnet
Åbogade 34
Jørn Schütze
2016

043 D

The so-called IT Corner (IT-Hjørnet) is the second stage in the expansion of the Faculty of Informatics within the University of Aarhus. Quality classrooms for students at this satellite site of the university were created as early as the first construction phase (see 042). The five-storey new building denotes a consolidation of the micro-campus, containing both research institutions and classrooms. Furthermore, it is intended as an assembly point for the surrounding educational establishments. The building has no main entrance, but may be accessed via several entrances on the upper or ground floors. The various features are brought in line with each other via bridges, passages and interspersed recreational spaces on the ground floor and the second floor. A wide staircase connects the recreational areas. The body of the auditorium is clad entirely in maple wood both outside and inside and

Gert Skærlund Andersen

Gert Skærlund Andersen

Gert Skærlund Andersen

has a seating capacity of 240. It occupies a central position within the space encompassing the IT Corner. Reading balconies, a café as well as classrooms are clustered around the auditorium on three levels. The library nestles like an island upon the auditorium – the glass roof of which provides exposure to daylight. Administrative headquarters, conference rooms, laboratories and workshops have been placed on both of the upper floors skirting around the central glazed roof. Large windows lend shape to the façade which contains elements of laminated glass with a silk-screen pattern in front of the background white concrete elements of the supporting framework.

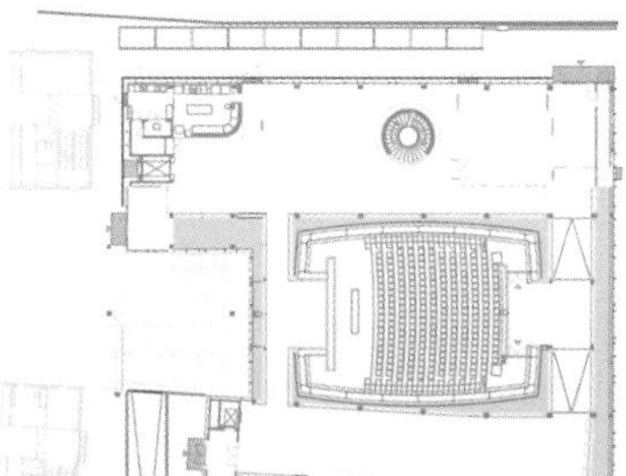

Gert Skærlund Andersen

043 D

Ge[illegible] Andersen/Jørn Schütze

The City Centre on the Left and Right of the Å

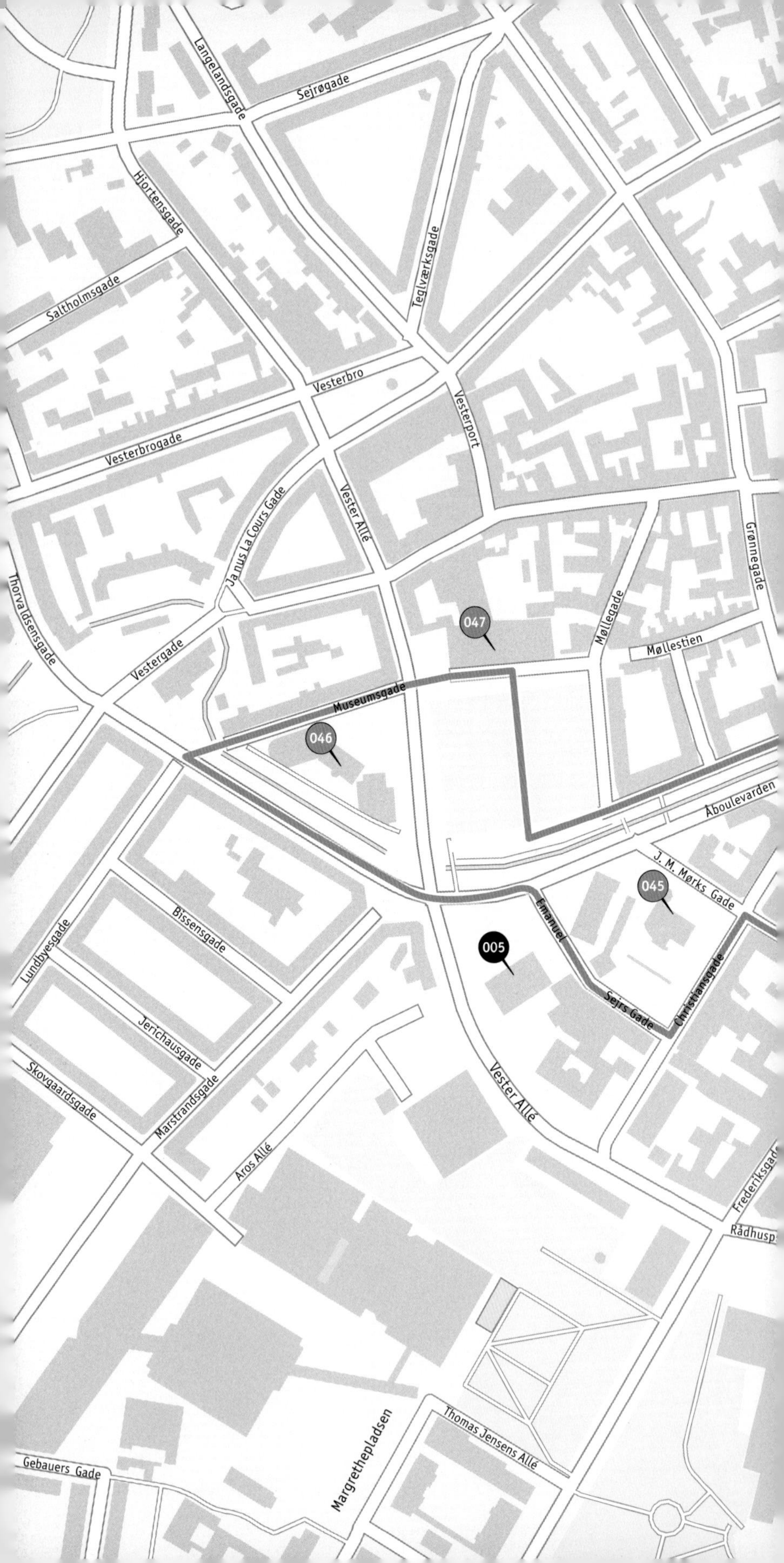
Langelandsgade
Sejrøgade
Hjortensgade
Teglværksgade
Saltholmsgade
Vesterbro
Vesterport
Vesterbrogade
Janus La Cours Gade
Vester Allé
Grønnegade
Thorvaldsensgade
047
Møllegade
Møllestien
Vestergade
Museumsgade
046
Åboulevarden
J. M. Mørks Gade
045
Emanuel
Bissensgade
005
Sejrs Gade
Christiansgade
Lundbyesgade
Jerichausgade
Skovgaardsgade
Marstrandsgade
Vester Allé
Aros Allé
Thomas Jensens Allé
Margrethepladsen
Gebauers Gade

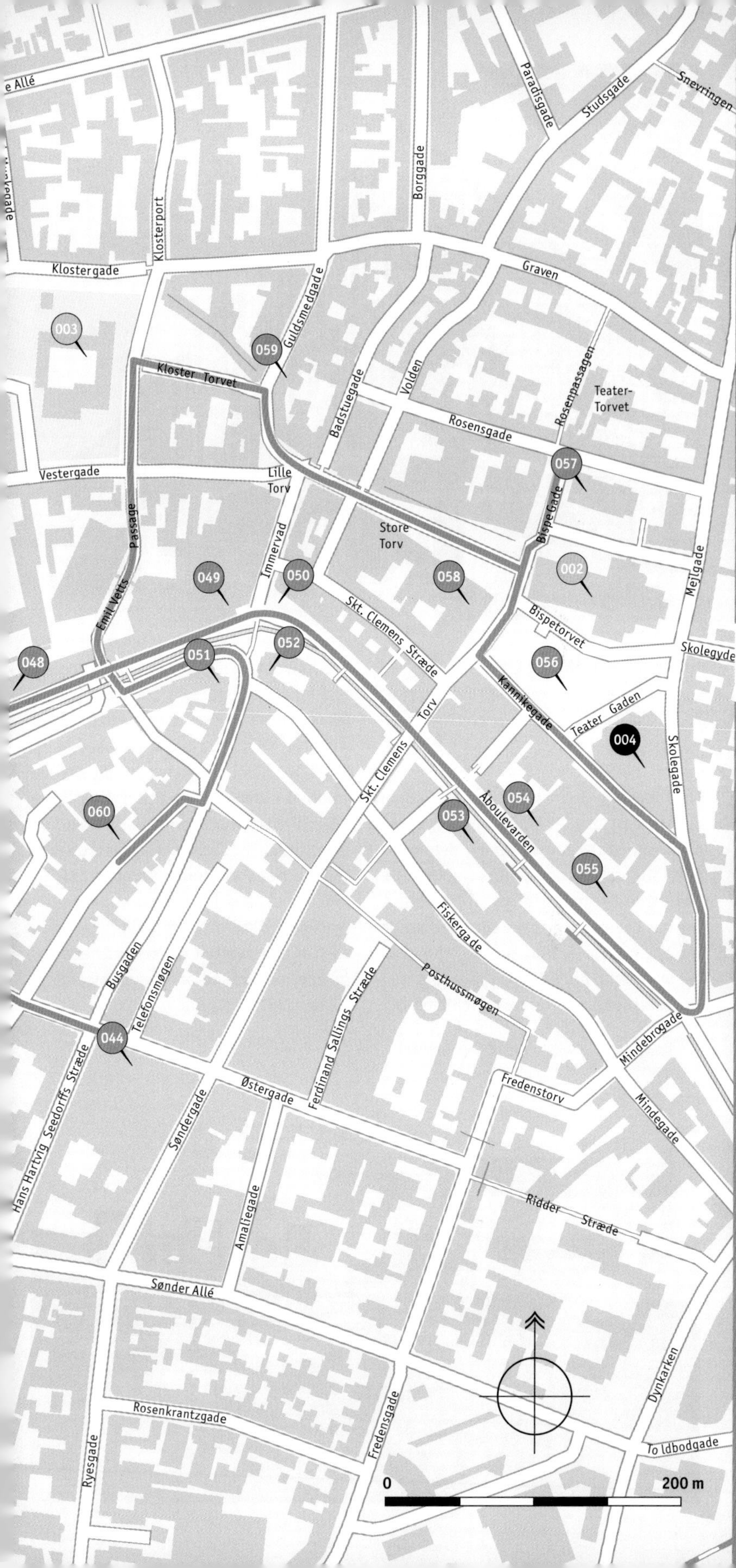

Snevringen
Studsgade
Paradisgade
Borggade
Klosterport
Klostergade
Graven
Guldsmedgade
Kloster Torvet
Volden
Badstuegade
Rosenpassagen
Teater-
Torvet
Rosensgade
Vestergade
Lille
Torv
Immervad
Emil Vetts
Passage
Store
Torv
Bispegade
Mejlgade
Skt. Clemens Stræde
Bispetorvet
Skolegyde
Kannikegade
Teater Gaden
Skolegade
Torv
Skt. Clemens
Åboulevarden
Fiskergade
Posthussmøgen
Mindebrogade
Busgaden
Telefonsmøgen
Ferdinand Sallings Stræde
Hans Hartvig Seedorffs Stræde
Østergade
Fredenstorv
Mindegade
Søndergade
Amaliegade
Ridder Stræde
Sønder Allé
Dynkarken
Rosenkrantzgade
Ryesgade
Fredensgade
Toldbodgade
0
200 m
002
003
004
044
048
049
050
051
052
053
054
055
056
057
058
059
060

E

AART architects

Hotel Scandic Aarhus City 044 E

Østergade 10
AART architects
2012

The inner-city branch of the hotel chain consists of one existing and one new building. Of the façade facing Østergade from the nineteenth century, solely the outer shell remains intact. A new building has been added at the corner, disrupting the historic proportions of the quarter in order to provide the space required for 228 rooms, conference facilities and a restaurant within a tapering penthouse spanning five storeys. The dark brown façade elements set out to mesh together with the neighbouring brick façades. At times one floor, at others two – in a vague colossal order intended to mitigate the visual impact of the complex – are marked by white bands. Corner rooms on the ground floor with glass façades extending the full height of the storey have been leased to a store. Sustainable elements, such as photovoltaic panels and beehives on the roof, round off the architectural sustainability concept.

AART architects

Torben Eskerod/C. F. Møller Architects

Kunsthal

045 E

J. M. Mørks Gade 13
Axel Hoeg-Hansen, 1917
C. F. Møller Architects,
1993 and 2003

Built in 1917, the Kunsthal bore formerly the name of Arts Institute and was established on the initiative of the Art Society of Aarhus in 1847. Today it is dedicated to national and international contemporary art. The original building consists of an L-shaped main part and an extension comprising an octagonal pavilion featuring white exterior walls and red tiled roofs. In keeping with the era of construction, the building includes stylistic elements of national romanticism, such as local materials, although its formal clarity lends it a neo-classical appearance. The free-standing building set amidst a small park underwent expansion on two occasions at the hands of the C. F. Møller practice. Since there was very limited space available to expand the front part of the site, the first extension has been built at the rear facing the south and the entrance relocated there. In order to subtly guide visitors around the building, the artwork entitled *Shaped Canvas Tracks* – a four-lane, curved running track by the Dutch artistic duo Jeroen Bouweriks and Linda Beumer – was subsequently added. Ten years later, the exhibition space underwent expansion below ground in a similarly subtle fashion in order to incorporate over 1,000 m². The new galleries within the basement are exposed to daylight via a large skylight and a glazed stairwell which is also used as an escape route and service entry. Since the inauguration of the new ARoS art museum, the Kunsthal primarily contains works of contemporary art from Denmark and abroad.

Heiko Weissbach

Torben Eskerod/C. F. Møller Architects

Helene Høyer Mikkelsen/CUBO

Atlas, Music Venue

046 E

Vester Allé 15
Kjær & Richter, 1989
CUBO, 2009

Both Atlas and VoxHall are extensions of the cultural institute, Huset (The House), which took up residence in the neo-classical villa as of 1972, although it has relocated in the interim to the site of the former freight depot (see 014). Huset was originally built in 1877 by the then court architect Vilhelm Theodor Walther to house the local art collection, thus serving as Aarhus' first art museum. Following the exodus of art, it was established as a house for youth featuring workshops and providing theatrical and musical activities. At the end of the 1990s there arose the need for a new concert venue for rhythmic music. This led to the establishment of VoxHall which was designed by Kjær & Richter and completed in 1997. The relocation of Huset to the new centre for cultural production, Godsbanen, was accompanied by a further venue called Atlas. Capacity thus increased to accommodate 700 spectators; in the meantime, the location has also attracted international names. The work entitled *Tonalities* by the artist Viera Collaro, a specialist in lighting installations, is projected at night on to the façade clad in expanded sheet material.

Helene Høyer Mikkelsen/CUBO

Helene Høyer Mikkelsen/CUBO

Heiko Weissbach

Central Library 047 E

Mølleparken
Alfred Mogensen/
Harald Salling Mortensen, 1934
Poul Lund, 1967, 1978
Lundager Landskab, 2007

The central library acts as a backdrop for Møllepark and was built in 1934 with the objective of focusing on national education. This red brick building featuring light-coloured window frames, symmetrical façades and a large inviting window looking towards the city embodies both classicist and modern traits. Clean lines and cube-like forms underline the sober, concrete public library. Public areas lay on both sides of the main staircase, the repository on the lower ground floor. The increasing demand for space prompted several renovations and expansions, thus giving rise to a complex sprawling from Møllepark to Vestergade. In 2015, the relocation of the central library into the new building Dokk1 (see 103) at the port meant that the historic building from the 1930s, worthy of preservation, was set aside for different purposes. In the coming years, a Library Hostel with 450 beds is to be fitted out within the former library and new residential buildings added. Furthermore, plans are underway to create a public access thoroughfare from Møllepark to Vesterbro Torv. In 2007, the grounds were revamped to connect the park of the library with the new promenade along the reopened riverbed. The kinetic sculpture entitled *Snake* was designed by Phil Price, an artist from New Zealand, in 2013.

Leif Wivelsted

Aagaarden, Residential and Commercial Building ↓

048 E

Åboulevarden 82–84
Ove Christensen, 1933

The first building made of reinforced concrete in Aarhus is also the first to be executed by the engineer Ove Christensen, who, upon completion, moved here himself with his family. *Funkis* – as international functionalism is affectionately referred to in Scandinavia – thus arrived in Aarhus. Light concrete in lieu of dark exposed brickwork, flat roofs instead of gabled ones, horizontal windows, an underground car park, refrigerators and an intercom system – all contributed to the modern fitting-out of the residences. The twenty apartments contained 100 m² to 200 m² of living space which at the time was considered to be a luxury. Today, apartments of this size are rented out to student housing cooperatives rather than families.

Heiko Weissbach

Magasin du Nord, Department Store ↗→

049 E

Immervad
Aage C. Nielsen / Poul Andersen
1971

Magasin du Nord is a cornerstone of the Danish retail industry. In 1894, the grand parent company at Kongens Nytorv in Copenhagen was built in the style of the French renaissance. Inspired by its Parisian counterparts – such as Bon Marché – the Wessel & Vett operators brought goods, sales methods and technological achievements, such as lifts and escalators, to Denmark. The growth during the years of economic boom propelled Magasin to Aarhus, where a series of historic buildings were forced to make way for the new building. The first stage took place in 1964; the new building was completed in 1971 on Åboulevarden. The department store constituted a considerable leap in scale at the time of its establishment. Today, the Å has been cleared and the neighbouring buildings have also increased in height. The sheer volume of the new building was given a uniform curtain wall façade composed of black anodised aluminium profiles as well as Eternit panels and glass producing various hues of dark green. The pillars of the arcade on the ground floor are clad in natural stone. In 2004, Magasin was purchased by the Icelandic property developers Baugut Group and sold on to the British chain Debenhams in 2009.

Leif Wivelsted

Tegningsarkiv Aarhus Kommune

Andreas Trier Mørch/KADK

Reopening of the Riverbed of the Å 050 E

Immervad/Åboulevarden
Stadsarkitektens Kontor/
Birk Nielsens Tegnestue,
1996

Everything points to the fact that Aarhus was founded by the Vikings circa. 770 where the river (Danish: Å) flows into the bay. There are only a few hundred metres separating the river estuary from the first port to the nearest ford. This ford, which served as a crossing centuries ago, is called Immervad. The origin of the name is not entirely clear. In the 1930s, the course of the river between Immervad and the estuary was laid within two concrete pipes beneath street level "on hygienic and traffic-related grounds". It was subsequently expanded into a four-lane transport artery leading towards the port: Åboulevarden. It was only in the 1980s that the significance of the course of the river to the city was acknowledged once more. Its reopening was thus decided upon to capitalise on its recreational potential. Work began in 1995 and was phased in in stages. The stretch of river between Immervad and Mølleparken was inaugurated in 2008, followed by the final leg from Mindebrogade to the estuary into the harbour in 2015. Through the use of ever-changing greenery, floor coverings and a custom-designed inventory for the city a coherent promenade of varying appearance was created from the old central library in Molleparken (see 047) to the Dokk1. (see 103) Birk Nielsens Tegnestue designed the initial phases in collaboration with the planning department of the municipality, while Kristine Jensens Tegnestue designed the last stretch around Europaplads and Dokk1 (see Essay 5). The area along the northern bank between Immervad and Clemensbro in particular has since become The Rendezvous area of the city with a vibrant nightlife, cafés and restaurants, thus drawing a considerable number of residents and tourists.

Thomas Sørensen Hermansen/

Leif Wivelsted

Aarhusgaarden, Residential and Commercial Building 051 E

Åboulevarden 41/
Frederiksgade 2
Alfred Skjødt-Pedersen, 1935
Heiko Weissbach, 1995

Aarhusgaarden is one of the most striking corner buildings in the city and ranks among the most beautiful from this epoch. This brick building, up to seven floors high, espouses expressive functionalism and occupies to dynamic effect the elegantly laid out corner of Frederiksgade and Åboulevarden opposite the massive building of the Magasin department store (see 049). Both streets meet at a corner tower bearing the name of the building. The masonry façades along the riverbed are broadly conceived in terms of rhythm and accentuated by balcony motifs. The ground floor contains a number of shops and access to the apartments. Here, the façade is consistently finished in white plaster and features large exhibition windows with nickel-plated steel frames. It is offset from the brick façade above by a baldachin. The optician's Lindberg is located on the ground floor of the corner building. Its minimalist interior design is modelled on the initial success stories of today's internationally recognised brand.

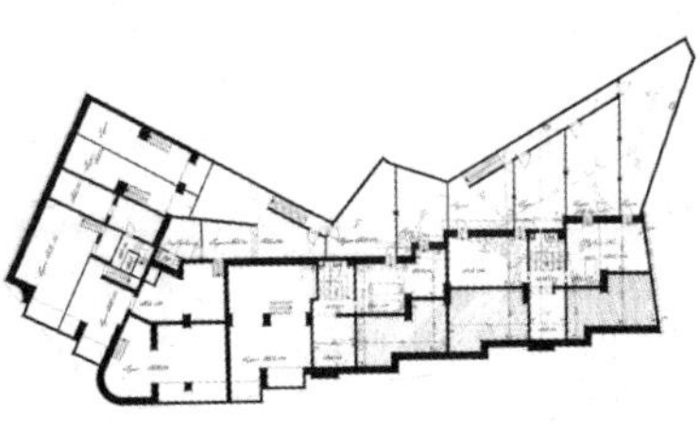

Tegningsarkiv Aarhus Kommune

Leif Wivelsted

Centrum, Residential and Commercial Building

052 E

Frederiksgade 1
Oscar Gundlach Pedersen/
Michael Stigaard, 1939

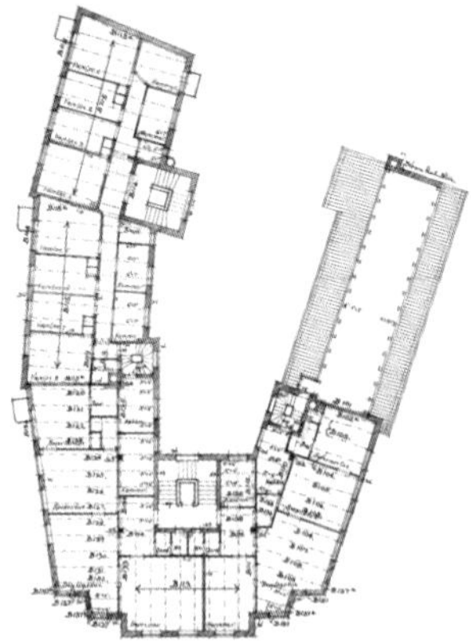

Tegningsarkiv Aarhus Kommune

The row of houses along Åboulevarden and Fiskergade – running parallel – culminates in the yellow Centrum building which has a V-shaped floor plan. Together with the Aarhusgaarden opposite, it marks the beginning of the pedestrian street Frederiksgade. A symmetrical, tripartite façade featuring a protruding and elevated central part arises facing Åboulevarden, while the two arms of the building behind pan out along the linear street or the curved course of the river. The lettering *Bo i Centrum* ("Living in the City Centre") is in evidence on the outline drawing, presumably intended to mark the uppermost point of this magnificent, seven-storey building in neon letters. This slogan is once again pertinent today.

Since the inauguration of the riverbed, the downtown residential area of Aarhus is in fierce demand once more. Regrettably, many apartments within this building had been converted for commercial use over the years and had to be "reconquered" for residential purposes. However, the structural criteria for marvellous views from the dwellings along Åboulevarden still exist.

Leif Wivelsted

also tapered back, thereby furnishing the penthouse apartments with terraces. It was not until 1990 that the architects had won a competition with the theme of streamlining construction (see 123). They were able to implement the construction system developed during the competition on Arosgård through the use of high-quality prefabricated concrete elements. Here, the façade elements are tinged with light red and the windows are framed in white. The entrance at the corner of the building, opposite a small bridge, is marked by the exposed lift shaft clad in dark tinted glass and polished black natural stone

Arosgaarden, Residential and Commercial Building ↑ 053 E

Åboulevarden 23–31
Arkitema Architects
1993

This building complex, which is oriented towards both the river and Fiskergade, situated behind, primarily contains office rental space and a handful of rooftop apartments. With a view to the reopening of the riverbed and the accompanying waterfront promenade, the ground floor of the building was given a special ceiling height and a colonnade positioned at the front. The attic storey was

House on the River ↑↓ 054 E

Åboulevarden 30
C. F. Møller Architects
2005

Since the reopening of the riverbed in the 1990s, this downtown waterfront location is again of relevance for the construction of apartments. This residential and commercial building is a plain white, modernist edifice. Its high ground floor contains two restaurants and the five upper storeys fifty-nine apartments. All dwellings facing the river incorporate full-height glazing and spacious loggias. These open up on to the city, restoring a sense of everyday routine to the quarter.

E

Julian Weyer/C. F. Møller Architects

Friis & Moltke

MOE (Former Bruun & Sørensen) 055 E

Åboulevarden 22
Friis & Moltke
1962

This six-storey building was originally constructed for the heating and electrical installation company Bruun & Sørensen at a time when the riverbed of the Å was laid out beneath the street and Åboulevarden served as a major transport artery in the direction of the port. Apart from workshops and offices, the building contains a rooftop apartment with a garden for one of the proprietors. The radical, horizontally structured, minimalist façade is composed of in-situ concrete cast in sandblasted wooden boards. Its sole ornamental element is the name of the company. Horizontal lamellae provided protection against the sun and privacy. Since the bankruptcy of the company circa 1980, the building has been let floor by floor, today to the engineering firm MOE and the architectural practice AART, among others. Only in the past few years has full-height glazing been incorporated into the former enclosed ground floor which today houses bars and restaurants. A relief by the artist Emil Gregersen, with whom the architects responsible often collaborated, remains partially intact in the foyer.

Heike Wairsbach

Leif Wivelsted

Univers ↓ 056 E

Asymptote Architecture
(Hani Rashid / Lise Anne Couture)
1997

The temporary tent roofs named Univers were mounted for the first time in 1997 at the central Bispetorv, right next to the Cathedral. The roofs covered the stages during the annual festival week at the end of August. These were designed in 1996 by the architectural studio Asymptote from New York and are intended to bring together architecture, theatre and media technologies, as well as promoting social interaction on the historic square. Looked at in the cold light of day this is a cost-effective and expedient, mobile structure evoking the parabolic edifices by Frei Otto. It has served the city as an event venue for twenty years, but now also crops up at times other than the festival and at other locations in the city, for example at the port.

Asymptote

Nykredit Financial Institute ↑ 057 E

Domkirkepladsen 1
Axel Berg, 1926
C. F. Møller Architects, 1989

This free-standing building north of the Cathedral is the former headquarters of the National Bank in Aarhus. It is the final design to be implemented by the prominent historical architect Axel Berg from Copenhagen and combines elements of the English Baroque with the Italian Renaissance. The façades are made of porphyry, while the base, cornicing, roof parapet and architraves consist of pink sandstone and the saddle roof is clad in copper. The marble floors, mahogany doors and brass handrails have remained intact. This branch of the National Bank was established as the first bank in the city as early as 1837. Since 1989, the listed building has been used by the mortgaging institution Nykredit. Adopting a respectful approach, its interior underwent restoration and conversion on behalf of the C. F. Møller practice for this purpose. This refurbishment was accompanied by the incorporation of a balcony to create new workspaces within the former banking hall. This is kept clear of the existing building on all sides; the inherent character of the building has thus remained overwhelmingly intact. Several years ago, archaeologists from the Moesgaard Museum (see 135) unearthed the remains of episcopal dwellings from the medieval ages and the twelfth century beneath the building which lies within the rampart of the Viking city.

Heiko Weissbach

Nordea Bank

058 E

Bispetorv/Store Torv/
Skt. Clemens Torv
Axel Høeg-Hansen, 1937
F.D.B. Arkitektkontoret, 1958
Tormod Jakobsen with Knud Blach Petersen and Herbert Jensen, 1960
Arkitema Architects/Atelier'et, 2011

Church and capital were and still are located – at least as far as architectural appearance is concerned – in close proximity to each other in Aarhus. The National Bank (see 057) was built north of the Cathedral in 1926. Three bank buildings that now belong to Nordea – arguably the largest finance group across Scandinavia – were built at the south-western corner of Bispetorvet between 1937 and 1959. The striking corner building marks the beginning of the pedestrian zone, which leads to the main railway station, and was built according to the plans of Axel Høeg-Hansen in red facing masonry as a reinforced concrete structure. With four normal storeys and one staggered storey facing both squares, it falls in line with the eaves height of the neighbouring building; a taller corner tower featuring a stairwell rises in the direction of the Cathedral. The building south of Skt. Clemens Torv was designed by the Copenhagen-based F.D.B. Arkitektkontoret for Aarhus Andelsbank and completed in 1958. The minimalist five-storey reinforced concrete building with a strong horizontal emphasis contains a branch of the bank on the ground floor. A Viking museum is situated within the basement at the location where the city was founded 1,200 years ago. The fact that the city centre remained at the same location throughout centuries is unprecedented in Scandinavia. The third building of the ensemble of banks is oriented towards Store Torv (Big Square). The four-storey reinforced concrete building was designed by the Copenhagen-based architect Tormod Jakobsen for the Landmandsbank and planned by the Aaarhusian architects Knud Blach Petersen (see 125) and Herbert Jensen. The ground floor was occupied by customers' areas related to banking as well as shops. Above are two storeys featuring office space as well as one staggered storey with an apartment. Bands of windows lend a horizontal structure to the façade which was originally clad in natural stone. The entrance to the banking hall had formerly been marked by a baldachin, although this was ousted within the framework of the façade renovation in 2011. Today, the ground floor is occupied by a textile and jewellery store –

Leif Wivelsted

the successor to the Hindelberg family business which had its address here for over five decades. The Thorup's Kælder tavern was located within the basement for over 125 years – a vaulted cellar built in the thirteenth century by Cistercian monks which is listed for preservation. Albert Thorup, the founder of the basement tavern, dressed his guests up in monks' habits at the beginning of the twentieth century. Regrettably, it is solely the shadows of the signage for Thorup's Kælder which are still discernible on the rehabilitated façade. The vaulted cellar has in the meantime been converted into a discotheque.

Heiko Weissbach

Arkitema Architects

Guldsmedhuset, Row of Shops 059 E

Guldsmedgade
Arkitema Architects
2002

The heterogeneous cityscape within the pedestrian zone is dominated by small-scale historical as well as contemporary buildings boasting large dimensions. The Guldsmedhuset (House of Goldsmiths) replaces four former buildings marked by vertical elements within the homogeneous façade. This comprises extensive glazed surfaces with dark brown aluminium profiles. Signage has been integrated into the façade and the shops are accessed via a common main entrance. Inside, customers can roam the three shopping floors freely. Offices are located on the floor above.

Arkitema, Headquarters → 060 E

Frederiksgade 32
Arkitema Architects
2002

The architectural practice Arkitema – formerly Arkitektgruppen i Aarhus – was founded in 1969 in Aarhus and is today one of the largest across Scandinavia with branches in Copenhagen, Oslo, Malmø and Stockholm. For the architects, it was a matter of course that the new headquarters at the heart of the city would be made subject to an internal competition and become a figurehead of their own work. The building is located between the pedestrian street Frederiksgade and Bødker Balles Gård, the circulation and delivery area for shops situated behind, thus forming the edge of a small square on the northern side. The building may be accessed on both sides via an alleyway. Retail space leased to third parties is located on the ground floor facing the pedestrian precinct, whereas storeys one to three are occupied by the architects' studios. A canteen has been provided on the rooftop. In keeping with traditional Scandinavian practice, the best location within the building has been made accessible to all employees as well as the roof terrace which is used in many different ways. A glass-roofed atrium at the centre of the building doesn't just provide a source of daylight, but also mediates over open, non-hierarchical communication between the studio levels. Visitors to reception on the first floor may follow project reviews or observe meetings within the prominent glazed rooms whilst awaiting attention.

Thorbjørn Hansen / Arkitema Architects

Arkitema Architects

The feel of a workshop imparted by the building is heightened by robust materials such as exposed concrete, galvanised steel, spruce wood and plenty of glass.

Vargo Nielsen Palle & ADEPT

The Good School* and the Architectural Milieu of Aarhus

014 A 031 D

Mogens Brandt Poulsen

Since 1754, Danish architects have been educated at the Royal Danish Academy of Fine Arts in Copenhagen. It was only in 1963 that the plan laying the foundation for a School of Architecture outside the capital was toyed with by the newly created Ministry of Culture under the auspices of which architectural education falls. The municipality of Aarhus provided the premises of a former estate at Nørreport to accommodate the forthcoming School.

The estate was still a construction site and everything – from paper and furniture to personnel – was still absent when the newly appointed rector, C. F. Møller as well as eight teachers, the majority of whom hailed from Copenhagen, and the Trustee greeted the first fifty-two students within the modest auditorium in October 1965.

Today, the school falls within the responsibility of the Ministry of Research, Innovation and Higher Education and caters for roughly 800 students – among which approximately 20 per cent are guest students from abroad – as well as 142 employees.

Over the years, existing buildings on all sides of the former estate have been incorporated into the school setting and transformed into a canteen, workshops, drawing studios, and auditoriums. In the more than fifty years since its foundation, the school has played an increasingly prominent role within the fabric of the city centre.

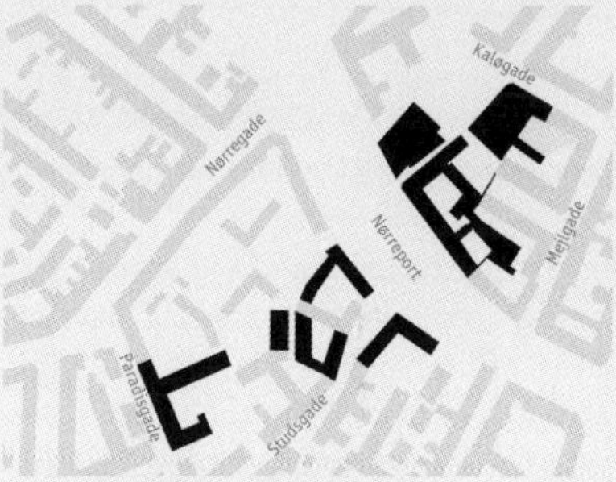

Arkitektskolen i Aarhus

Map of the School of Architecture

In future, the wide-ranging individual bodies across the city are to be merged into one new building. The design for the new building was determined on the basis of an international competition. A total of 230 teams from forty-seven countries were involved in the first phase, an open competition looking for ideas. The jury awarded prizes to three designs by Erik Giudice Architects, Atelier Lorenzen Langkilde and VARGO NIELSEN PALLE. These three teams competed against the prequalified participants SANAA from Japan, Lacaton & Vassal from France and BIG from Denmark. VARGO NIELSEN PALLE & ADEPT emerged triumphant in the competition and were commissioned with the planning in March 2017.

Although the School continued to be exposed to major changes and austerity measures, it has held on to a rich study environment where each student has their own workspace accessible twenty-four hours a day, seven days a week.

← NEW AARCH – competition for the New School of Architecture, interior view of the winning design by Vargo Nielsen Palle, Brian Vargo, Jonas Nielsen, Mathias Palle

Poul Petersen, Den Gamle Bys billedarkiv

Demonstration on 4 May 1977 against admission restrictions and in support of better facilities

The current objective of the School is to further research and artistic development efforts of the highest standards with a view to refining the training and practice of architecture as well as the public understanding thereof.

The teaching programme includes three approaches to the discipline equal in weight: aesthetic, academic and that based on practice. In keeping with the vision *Engaging Through Architecture*, the School is seeking to contribute to the remediation of societal challenges through courses focused on transformation, sustainability and integration.

At the same time, the School is committed to working with Chinese and Australian educational establishments. Beyond that it works in close collaboration with the numerous architectural practices in Aarhus. It is not least these collaborative efforts that the Ministry of Economic Affairs has underscored as an example of the fruitful interrelationship between an educational establishment and the economy, deserving of emulation.

Architectural Cluster in Aarhus

The year 2009 saw the publication of the findings of a research project under the title Architectural Cluster in Aarhus (*Arkitekturklyngen i Aarhus*), the content of which is concerned with an examination of the architectural milieu, its history and its present state. This examination includes an analysis of ten of the largest architectural practices in central Aarhus – the surrounds of which are home to a number of small to mid-size firms, as well as the School of Architecture. From a chronological point of view, this study spans 1965 to 2008. The year 1965 was chosen as a point of departure for the analysis since the foundation of the School of Architecture in this year created fertile ground for the development of a broad, locally based architectural milieu. In order to make the research relevant today, emphasis has been laid on the past decade.

The introduction to the report states: "Since the mid-1960s, Aarhus has become an important location for high-flying architectural bureaus, having won national and international competitions alike and constructed buildings. The collaboration between architectural practices during competitions and an extensive exchange of knowledge among them and with the School of Architecture seem to be factors in this development."

The seeds of this milieu – the distinguishing mark for the architectural cluster in Aarhus – were sown as early as the 1950s when architectural practices had a lot to do and in their free time employees participated in numerous competitions held during these years. As well as competing in competitions, they also worked together on the establishment of a new School of Architecture earmarked for Aarhus.

Børge Venge, Den Gamle Bys billedarkiv

← The first teachers in front of the entrance at Nørreport 20: Sven Hansen, Niels-Ole Lund, Søren Abrahamsen, Hans Bondo, Johan Richter, Johannes Exner and the administrator Arne Sørensen, 1965

As described above, teaching staff convened for the first time in the autumn of 1965. Teachers had six weeks to prepare for the new course of studies and the arrival of students. The renovation of the School buildings was then a long way off. At first, teachers met each other at their homes. This created a special solidarity among those teachers present from the outset. These chaotic conditions called for forbearance and pandered to solidarity among all those involved – students, teachers and employees in equal measure. A sense of camaraderie, which has since shaped the school, panned out under these circumstances.

In 1969 the first students began to stand out: Lars Due, Michael Harrebek, Ole Nielsson, Erling Stadager and Helge Tindal won several competitions and were dubbed the *Golden Boys* in the newspapers. They founded the practice Arkitektgruppen i Aarhus (today's Arkitema Architects) in the following year. Their organization of the bureau with a circle of partners who can be regarded as proprietors in day-to-day matters became commonplace among architectural practices in Aarhus.

Following a somewhat disorienting period in the first half of the 1970s – a time of dispute among traditionalists and political theoreticians – the community at the School evolved anew. This arose from

Kjær & Richter / Arkitektskolen i Aarhus

Model of the new auditorium and exhibition building which was inaugurated in 1997

social crises and accompanying austerity measures, but also from internal professional debates and the changes within the multi-faceted and unique study environment mirroring international disarray within architecture. Despite all contrarian stances and spirited debates – particularly among post-modernists and neo-rationalists – there lay an unconscious solidarity amidst all this diversity in that everyone acknowledged the key significance of the ongoing development for the School and the profession.

This period heralded the beginning for many talented students who have subsequently exerted an influence in a number of ways on the architectural scene in Aarhus and on courses of study. The open and inquisitive ambience gave rise to close professional ties and friendships of major importance for the development of "old" practices and for forming the basis of new practices founded in the coming decades. These were primarily architectural practices, such as Poulsen & Terkelsen (today's P+P), Schmidt, Hammer & Lassen (today's Schmidt/Hammer/Lassen), 3 x Nielsen (today's 3XN), Pluskontoret and CUBO. This is accompanied by landscape architects, such as Kristine Jensens Tegnestue, Preben Skaarup Landskab and design agencies such as DesignIt and 3part.

Thus, office environments began to grow and the contour of today's cluster emerged – a positive outcome for architects from Aarhus on the basis of proximity and the network between the practices.

The research report outlines the three main factors behind this success: "The architectural practices lie close together and there is a clear interplay between companies from a commercial, professional and social perspective." It goes on to say: "This form of collaboration and the general flow of labour among architectural companies secures the existence of social and professional development processes." "The School of Architecture in Aarhus is finally serving as a repository of knowledge in its immediate vicinity." "The foundation of the School of Architecture in 1965 is the main factor behind this development. A study among practices unanimously confirmed this, for if they did not have continuous access to a highly qualified workforce, they would not be in Aarhus."

Spring 2015

As fate would have it, the School of Architecture in Aarhus was brought into being during a period of major change, yielding a decisive influence on university courses – not least on architectural education. In the initial years education quickly acquired its form and content on the primary basis of the newly established group of teachers and their experience gained in the School of Architecture within the Academy of Fine Arts in Copenhagen. A few years later, with the unrest in 1968, the first curricula were discarded, new curricula adopted and the subsequent period was beset by change.

Therefore also the beginning of the new millennium was marked by radical restructuring. Social development, university budgets, policy demands and professional development have had a lasting effect on studies which is arguably something necessary.

The change of government in 2011 saw the transfer of architectural schools from the portfolio of the Ministry of Culture to the Ministry of Education and Research, although fresh vigour may be detected in professional activities when entering the School today.

This sense of professional growth may be attributed to the fact that time was available to introduce and develop new opportunities and routines – introduced in 2011 – in a leisurely fashion such as, for example, the decision to bring in teachers and researchers from multiple social platforms, to nurture them and give them space to expand. The history of the school has demonstrated that restructuring needs time and that some candour is necessary in order to develop a professional environment which not merely takes time to inform the necessary aspiring students, but also lends the School the opportunity of delivering the correct response to short-term market thinking. This is a prerequisite if the School of Architecture in Aarhus is to fulfil a major role within the city's architectural cluster looking ahead.

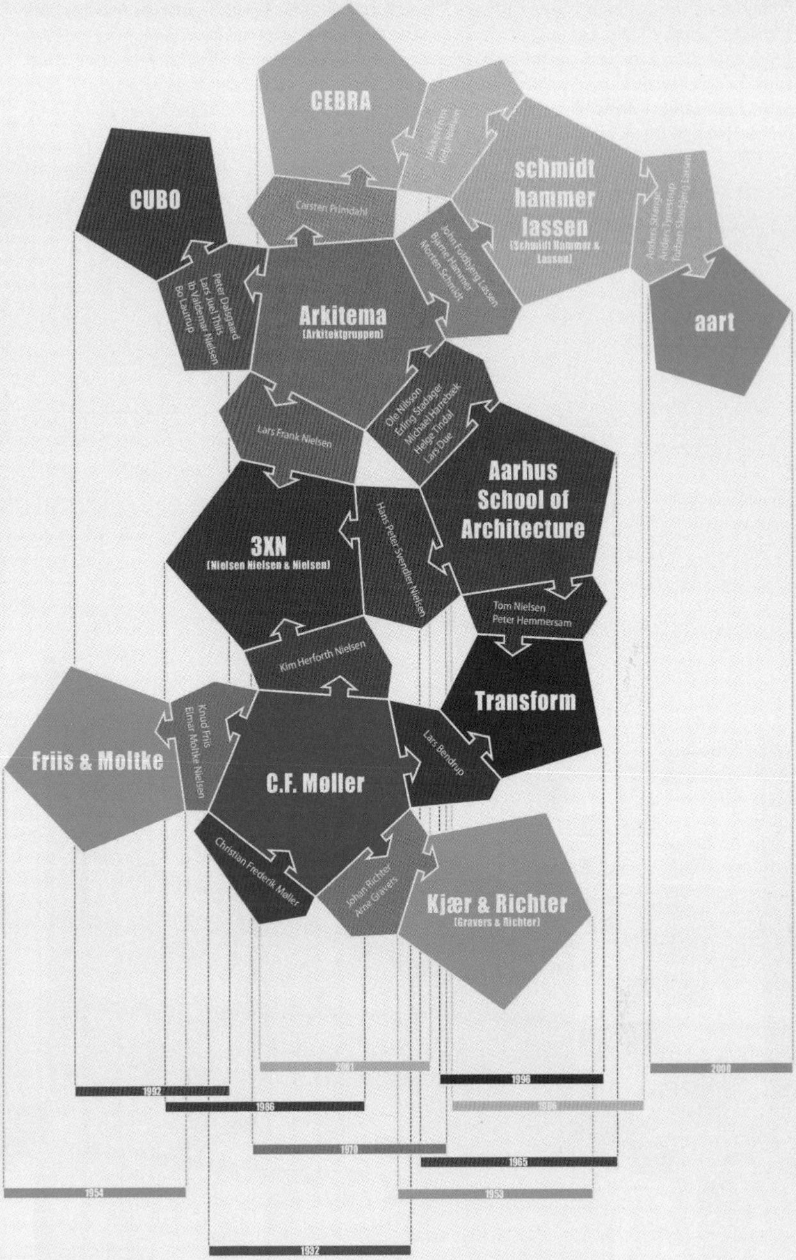

Family diagram of the Architectural Cluster in Aarhus, 2011 – more offices have been added since

CEBRA

Resumé from *Den Gode Skole – og arkitektmiljøet i Aarhus* by Morgen Brandt Poulsen, Arkitektskolens Forlag, 2015, issued to commemorate the fiftieth anniversary of the School of Architecture.

**Den Gode Skole i Aarhus* (The Good School in Aarhus) was a denomination which Henrik Steen Møller, the architectural critic of the Copenhagen daily broadsheet newspaper *Politiken*, gave to the School of Architecture in the 1980s.

Further information has been provided by Lena Kondrup Sørensen.

From the architects' project description: "The New School of Architecture will become a part of a broader urban vision, a unique link between the formal and informal development of the city. The school should connect the informal landscape of the Green Wedge with the formative urban spine of Carl Blochs Gade. By addressing both conditions, the school will become a natural anchor point in the area. An anchor point that highlights the heritage of the site and helps shape the urban vision of the neighbourhood."

Perspective of the New School of Architecture facing the streetscape

Perspective of the New School of Architecture facing Carl Blochs Gade
Bottom left: design sketch (formal – informal)
Bottom right: perspective longitudinal section

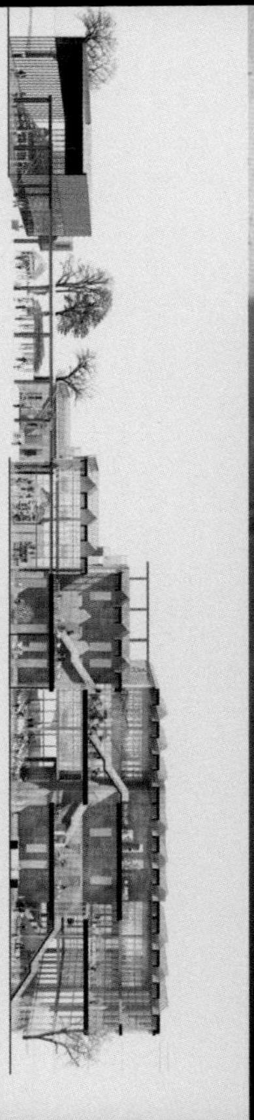

Vargo Nielsen Palle & ADEPT

From the River Valley through the Botanic Garden to the Western Cemetery

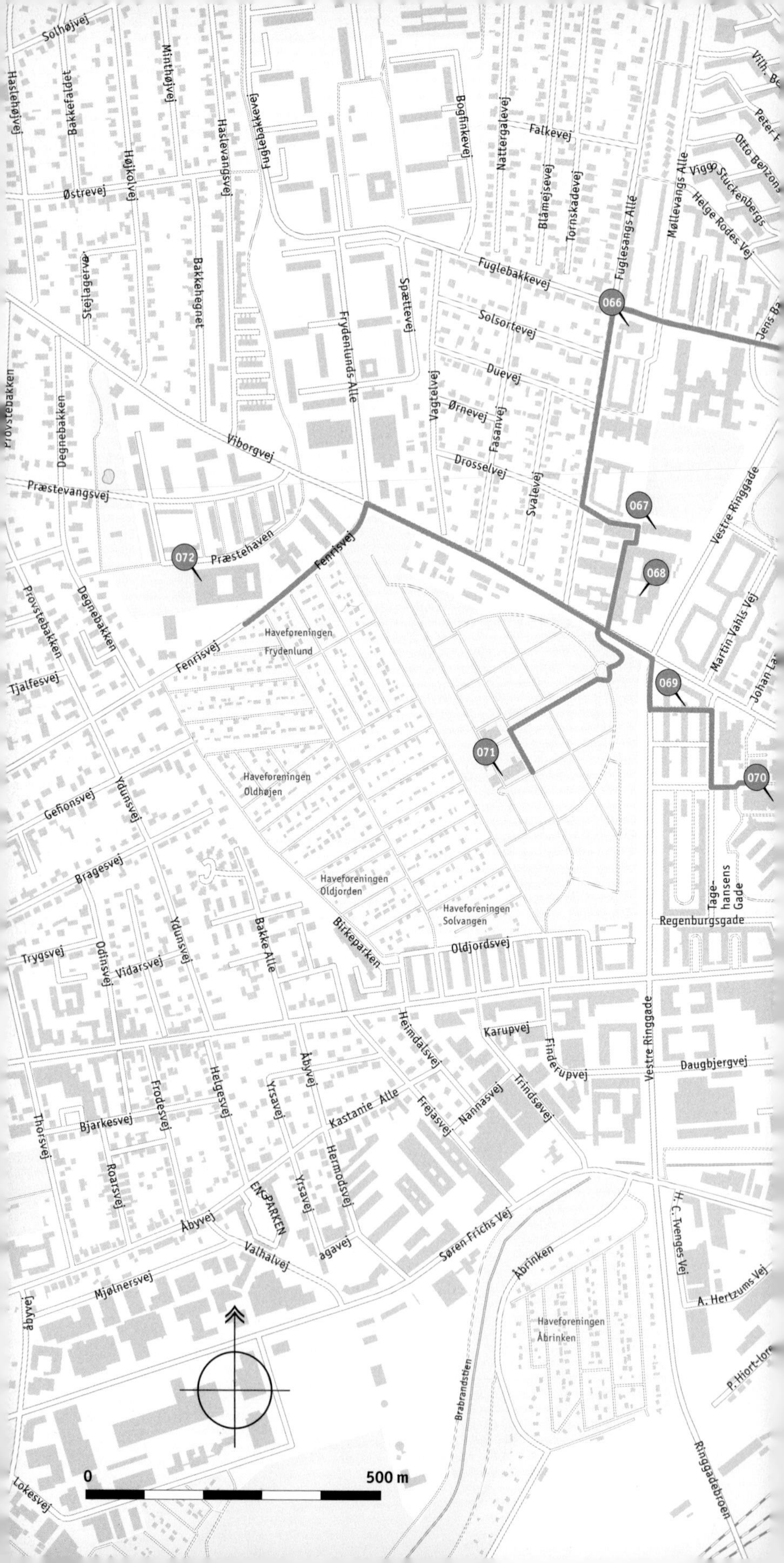

Solhøjvej
Haslehøjvej
Bakkefaldet
Minthøjvej
Højkolvej
Haslevangsvej
Fuglebakkevej
Bogfinkevej
Falkevej
Nattergalevej
Blåmejsevej
Tornskadevej
Fuglesangs Allé
Møllevangs Allé
Viggo Stuckenbergs
Otto Benzons
Helge Rodes Vej
Østrevej
Stejlagervej
Bakkehegnet
Spættevej
Frydenlunds Allé
Solsortevej
Duevej
Ørnevej
Vagtelvej
Fasanvej
Drosselvej
Svalevej
Vestre Ringgade
Martin Vahls Vej
Provstebakken
Degnebakken
Viborgvej
Præstevangsvej
Præstehaven
Fenrisvej
Haveforeningen Frydenlund
Tjalfesvej
Haveforeningen Oldhøjen
Gefionsvej
Ydunsvej
Bragesvej
Haveforeningen Oldjorden
Haveforeningen Solvangen
Regenburgsgade
Tage-hansens Gade
Trygsvej
Odinsvej
Vidarsvej
Bakke Allé
Birkeparken
Oldjordsvej
Heimdalsvej
Karupvej
Finderupvej
Daugbjergvej
Thorsvej
Bjarkesvej
Frodesvej
Helgesvej
Yrsavej
Åbyvej
Kastanie Allé
Hermodsvej
Frejasvej
Nannasvej
Trindsøvej
Roarsvej
ENGPARKEN
Valhalvej
Søren Frichs Vej
Åbrinken
H. C. Tvenges Vej
A. Hertzums Vej
Mjølnersvej
Haveforeningen Åbrinken
Brabrandstien
P. Hjort-Lorenzens
Ringgadebroen
Lokesvej
066
067
068
069
070
071
072
0
500 m

Victor Albecks Vej
Jens Baggesens Vej
Vestre Ringgade
Karl Verners Vej
Gustav Wieds Vej
Ole Worms Allé
Bartholins Allé
Paludan-Müllers Vej
Emil Aarestrups Vej
Wilhelm Meyers Allé
Ny Munkegade
C. F. Møllers Allé
Ærøgade
Vennelyst Boulevard
Poul Martin Møllers Vej
Vestervang
Kaserneboulevarden
Langelandsgade
Falstersgade
Fynsgade
Høegh-guldbergs Gade
Vennelyst Plads
Samsøgade
Sjællandsgade
Vestervang
065
Peter Holms Vej
Sølystgade
Samsøgade
Hjarnøgade
Norsgade
Lollandsgade
Grønnegade
064
Sejrøgade
Nørre Allé
Møllevejen
Hjortensgade
Langelandsgade
Teglværksgade
Klosterport
Guldsmedgade
Viborgvej
001
Mønsgade
Vesterbrogade
063
Vestergade
Ringkøbingvej
Herningvej
Thorvaldsensgade
Vester Allé
Møllegade
Grønnegade
Immervad
Museumsgade
Ceresbyen
062
Åboulevarden
061
Ceres Alle
Bissensgade
Christiansgade
Busgaden
Lundbyesgade
Marstrandsgade
Østergade
Frederiksgade
Vester Allé
Søndergade
Amaliegade
Aros Allé
Carl Blochs Gade
Rådhuspladsen
Sønder Allé
Sonnesgade
Rosenkrantzgade
Margrethepladsen
Frederiks Alle
Park Alle
Ryesgade
Eckersbergsgade
Valdemarsgade
Ny Banegårdsgade
Banegårdsgade
Søgade
Kriegersvej
Hallssti
Hallssti
Værkmestergade
Jægergårdsgade
Ankersgade
Jægergårdsgade

F

070
Teknik & Miljø

030
065
064
001
063

Thomas Mølvig/E + N Arkitektur

Folkestedet 061 F

Carl Blochs Gade 28
Heinrich Wenck, 1902
Stadsarkitektens Kontor, 1994
Exners Tegnestue, 2005

Today's so-called People's Place denotes the building's current use as a railroad station on the line to Hammel. It was created in 1902 according to the plans of the architect Heinrich Weck, who has also designed countless other Danish stations. In 1994, when this train service had long been suspended, it was converted into the city's local history museum and enhanced by an extension in 2005. However, as early as 2011 its role as a museum was usurped by the open-air museum Den Gamle By

Thomas Mølvig/E + N Arkitektur

(The Old Town) and the building, in keeping with the new concept behind the former railway grounds Godsbanearealet (see 014), was converted into the community centre. A double-storey building correlating with the elongated character of the grass strip along the river was made available for the expansion of the museum. A glass corridor connects the old building with the new one – the latter set back from the street so that the ensemble forms a small forecourt with parking spaces. The street façade composed of light red exposed brickwork is enclosed with the exception of the glazed entrance and several small windows while the masonry is designed with ornamental associations. The rectangular solid structure opens out on to the park-like setting on both sides of the riverbed via a double-height glazed loggia clad in ornamental wooden lamellae – providing protection against the sun and acting as a light filter. Since 2012, the former museum café has been run as a soup kitchen by residents of the neighbourhood.

E + N Arkitektur

Arkitema Architects

VIA University College, Campus City
062 F

Ceresbyen 24
Arkitema Architects, 2015

Today, VIA University College is an integral part of the new central district named Ceres City and lies on a plot of land covering 140,000 m² between Viborgvej, Silkeborgvej and the Å. Ceres Brewery was founded in 1856, although it was forced to cease production activities in 2008, following 152 years of brewing beer. Almost nothing remains intact from this industrial historic building complex which has had such a profound influence on the development of the city. The brewery and its premises underwent urban development as of 2012, giving rise to apartments, commercial space and educational establishments, as well as a public park along the Å. VIA University College is the largest technical college in Denmark. The City Campus consists of several buildings under the auspices of the so-called Center for Educational Services which

Niels Nygaard / Arkitema Architects

has approximately 6,000 matriculated students. The new buildings form an independent urban structure within the heterogeneous urban environment. The campus is composed of four elements which the architects refer to as Knowledge Square, Learning Street, Culture House and the Learning Clusters. These encompass a comprehensive programme in terms of space allocation, ranging from traditional classrooms and lecture halls to sports and leisure facilities. This is to establish an open and informal ambience befitting a house of culture. The many different courses under one roof are intended to facilitate the exchange of expertise between branches of education – which have hitherto been physically separated from each other on an academic basis – and create new synergies from an economic and a pedagogical point of view. The outcome of a competition for ideas is the concept behind this building which was subsequently refined in close collaboration between architects, technical planners, occupants, the main contractor and the property owner.

Niels Nygaard / Arkitema Architects

Prismet High-rise 063 F

Silkeborgvej 2

Friis & Moltke/

Schønherr landskab, 2001

Heiko Weissbach

This 63 m high building is the first high-rise measuring more than 50 m in Aarhus and lies next to Den Gamle By (The Old Town), within the triangle between Viborgvej and Silkeborgvej. It was against a backdrop of finding space for high-rise building, as demanded by investors, that this harbinger of the trend toward greater heights – particularly on the new waterfront – took shape. The building is called Prismet (Prism) owing to its triangular floor plan and the sloping roof area. The slender, transparent glazed tower of the design stage ended up as a rather solid structure. The glazed façade, which appears almost black in daylight, is in stark contrast to the neighbouring clinker brick buildings from the *Gründerzeit* period. It emits little light in the evening. Furthermore, the tower casts Den Gamle By – the open-air museum opposite – in shadow, something which sparked controversy in the press and disquiet among the museum directors during the construction of the high-rise – not least because it shatters the illusion imparted by the open-air museum's interior of finding oneself within a medieval town. Full occupancy of the office space was a long time coming. It was only with the development of the new district on the site of the former Ceres Brewery opposite – where the new campus VIA University College (see 062) was built, among other things – that the location and demand showed positive trends. The high-rise and its three-storey plinth building have been fully let since 2015.

Friis & Moltke

Heiko Weissbach

Greenhouses within the Botanic Garden

064 F

Peter Holms Vej
C. F. Møller Architects
1970/2014

Heiko Weissbach

Both greenhouses within the Botanic Garden are designed by the same practice. The first, from the year 1969, was built in steel and glass on a helical floor plan. The old palm house underwent restoration together with the establishment of a new tropical greenhouse and was converted into a Botanical Centre. The new greenhouse is a 18 m tall, translucent construction. Two by ten slender steel arches form a uniaxial symmetrical cupola with an elliptic floor plan which is covered with 124 square ETFE-foil air cushions, ninety of which are double-layered on the northern and western side and thirty-four triple-layered in a south-easterly direction. The layers are serigraphed for shading. By varying the pressure of the air within the cushions, the position of the layers may be adjusted in relation to each other in order to manipulate the intensity of sunlight. Hence, a dynamic façade cladding regulates the indoor climate. The fascinating minimalist construction, the bridges between the treetops and the new overall concept have renewed interest in the Botanic Garden, bringing it some element of fame.

Science Museerne / VisitAarhus

C. F. Møllers Architects

Julian Weyer / C.F. Møller Architects

Vestervang, Settlement ↑↓ 065 F

Vestervang 35–45
Friis & Moltke, 1971
Niels Noach, 1986

From the outset, the construction of residential housing was a core discipline of the Friis & Moltke practice which preferred to design single-family homes in the early years, but later included multistorey residential buildings as of 1962. In 1970 the first two high-rise blocks named Vestervang were built in the immediate vicinity of the Botanic Garden, featuring approximately 600 apartments. This was accompanied by a further 350 apartments in the mid-1980s. Its central location on a hill and the view across the city centre and the bay led to the rapid popularity of the settlement. Each apartment has a large balcony or a terrace facing a south-westerly direction as an extension of the residential space. Pedestrians have been separated from car traffic in line with the ideals of the era. The tall development acts as a shield against traffic noise, while parking spaces have been laid out beneath the elongated, terraced building. The green spaces are free from traffic and very inviting.

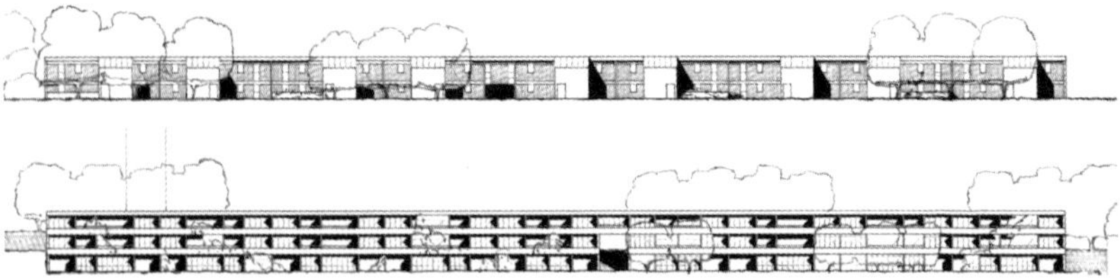

Friis & Moltke

Julian Weyer

Møllevang Church

066 F

Møllevangs Allé 49
C. F. Møller, 1958
Mads Møller, 1969/1978

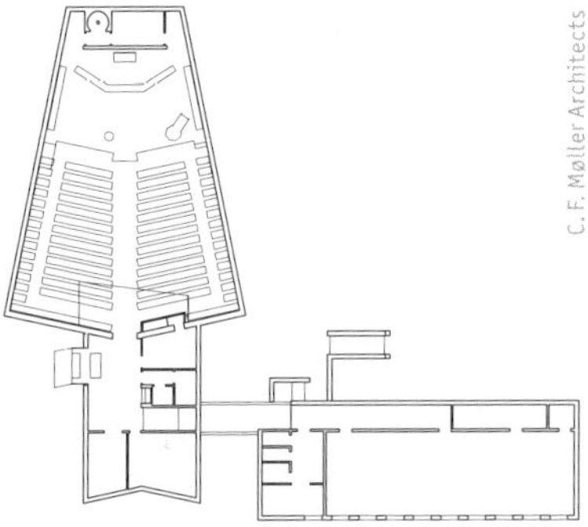

C. F. Møller Architects

This church ranks among the first sacred buildings of the post-war period in which C. F. Møller sought to combine traditional elements with modern ones. The church sits on a simple fan-shaped floor plan and has a large projecting gabled roof which dips towards the altar and the font at the narrow end of the room. A small circular window on the south-facing roof provides the sole source of daylight within the church. The exterior walls and roof are composed of red brick. The church has whitewashed walls and is dominated by the symmetrically open wooden roof construction evoking an upturned boat. The altar wall is free-standing. The eastern façade situated behind has masonry recesses in cruciform arrangement, allowing pooled sunlight to penetrate the room to striking effect. The crucifix above the altar is attributable to the sculptor Erik Heide. It wasn't until 1969 that the 25 m high belfry in a free-standing position beside the church was created according to a design by C. F. Møller's son Mads Møller. The crypt was subsequently also added as well as a lower storey featuring parish spaces, confirmation rooms and offices, made possible by the sloping terrain. A new parish hall was built in 1978.

Jesper Rais/AU Kommunikation

College of Commerce, Building S

Fuglesangs Allé
CUBO, 2012

067 F

In terms of urban development, the extension of the Handelshøjskole Aarhus University (HAU) for the School of Business and Social Sciences falls in line with the existing building stock and forges a connection between the main street named Ringgade and the internal buildings of the College of Commerce (see 068). This gabled building featuring a pitched roof contains a large hall with a seating capacity of up to 1,000 which may be used as a canteen on an everyday basis, but can also host events of all kinds. The ground floor of the new building is completely glazed. Administration offices, seminar rooms, workspace and a lounge for up to 600 students are located on the four storeys above. Brick in six different nuances has been used for the façades – the yellow and red colour scheme of which is intended to harmonise with the neighbouring clinker brick buildings from the 1960s. The masonry on the gable facing Ringgade uses an open bond, allowing sunlight to penetrate to the glazed façade behind and ensuring protection against the sun during the day. Conversely, artificial light from the interior penetrates the perforated masonry in the evening and at night, bestowing the building with a certain lightness.

Martin Schubert/CUBO

C. F. Møller Architects

C. F. Møllers Architects

College of Commerce

068 F

Fuglesangs Allé 4
C. F. Møller Architects
1968–2010

The College of Commerce (Handelshøjskole) was inaugurated in 1968 as an independent training institution and has since undergone continuous expansion and renovation. In 2007 it became a faculty of the university. C. F. Møller is also committed to the continuous use of brick in the design for the College of Commerce; red and yellow flamed brick for the façades and red roof tiles are in evidence here. The simple architectural vocabulary is thus continued in the clear-cut structures and roofs with a pitch of 30 degrees, in common with the university campus and other buildings on Fuglesangs Allé: the 4. Maj Kollegiet (student residence), the Musikkonservatorium (Music Conservatoire) and Møllevang Church (see 066). Although the university buildings stand as solitary islands within the park, the buildings of the College of Commerce are arranged in a structuralist configuration. Those with one or two storeys lie slightly offset in relation to each other at inner courtyards and atria, along internal streets and passages connected by glass corridors, catering for recreational spaces. Options for extension were addressed from the outset. The homogeneous character and the intimate scale of the complex have hitherto remained intact.

Heiko Weissbach

C. F. Møller Architects

Aarhus Arkitekterne

Ringgaarden, Settlement 069 F

Vestre Ringgade 72–82
Thomas Nielsens Gade 4–6,
Tage Hansens Gade 27–33
Salling Mortensens tegnestue, 1940
Aarhus Arkitekterne/Vibeke Rønnow, 2015

The oldest settlement owned by the Ringgaarden housing association was built at the end of the 1930s in the heart of the city. The settlement underwent complete renovation and expansion between 2010 and 2015. Formerly small and unilaterally oriented apartments have been converted into bright, modern ones. The remodelling was declared a demonstration project, allowing a radical approach. Only those façades worthy of preservation remain intact; everything else, including the floor slabs, has been removed. The exterior of the buildings in red exposed brickwork with red tiled roofs facing Vestre Ringgade has scarcely changed. However, a metamorphosis is discernible as soon as one steps between the housing blocks. Extensions with a steel structure design containing balconies and oriels have arisen as an expansion of the residential space facing the inner courtyards. The former drying rooms beneath the roof have been converted into apartments, thus forming a communal room as well as a roof terrace affording a view across the city for all occupants. The new apartments covering between 62 m² and 118 m² obtain exposure to daylight on both sides.

Heiko Weissbach

District Hospital 070 F

Tage-Hansens Gade 2
Axel Høeg-Hansen, 1935
Salling Mortensens tegnestue, 1963, CUBO/Fich & Bengaard, 2002

The district hospital (Amtssygehuset) was founded as an institute as early as 1880. This was accompanied two years later by the inauguration of the first building on Kroghsgade which was however quickly found to be too small. The municipality commissioned the renowned architect Axel Høeg-Hansen with the design for the new building. The planners were called upon to design a pragmatic building. The tight budget exerted a positive influence in terms of creativity. Høeg-Hansen developed a groundbreaking complex where the medical department and the patients' wing are kept strictly separate. It was intended that sunlight would pierce inside the 200 m long, four-storey building made of red and yellow exposed masonry – which is oriented in an east-westerly direction – at all times of the day in order to promote healing. The patients' wing was connected to the treatment building at the centre. Roughly four million clinker bricks were used and great amounts of earth moved in order to get the site ready for the hospital and parklands. The inscription above the main entrance reads "Cure, palliate, comfort" (*helbrede, lindre, trøste*). The hospital underwent extensive expansion in 1963 and 2002. Owing to the restructuring of the Danish healthcare sector, the days in which it continues to serve as a hospital are numbered. With the new building of the largest Danish hospital in Skejby (see 202), the municipality of Aarhus is taking possession of the district hospital in order to develop a new urban district here.

Leif Wivelsted

Henning Larsen

Vestre Kirkegård 071 F

Viborgvej 47 a
Frederik Draiby, 1927
Henning Larsen, 1969,
1995 and 2011 (expansion)

The "western cemetery" is one of two cemeteries in Aarhus covering an area of roughly 17 ha. The cemetery contains two chapels: a large one with 250 seats, designed by Aaarhus' first city architect, Frederik Draiby – built in 1927, as well as a small one with fifty seats and an adjoining crematorium, designed by Henning Larsen and built in 1969. Today, both chapels have no religious affiliation. Several tombs of fallen soldiers and resistance fighters are located at the cemetery, in addition to a memorial wall to those citizens of Aarhus who died in German concentration camps during the Second World War. Among the prominent persons whose tombstones are located at the cemetery are the architects Harald Salling-Mortensen and C. F. Møller, whose tombstone has been built in yellow brick – in common with his magnum opus, the City University which is only a few hundred metres from here. The original chapel by Frederik Draiby

Henning Larsen

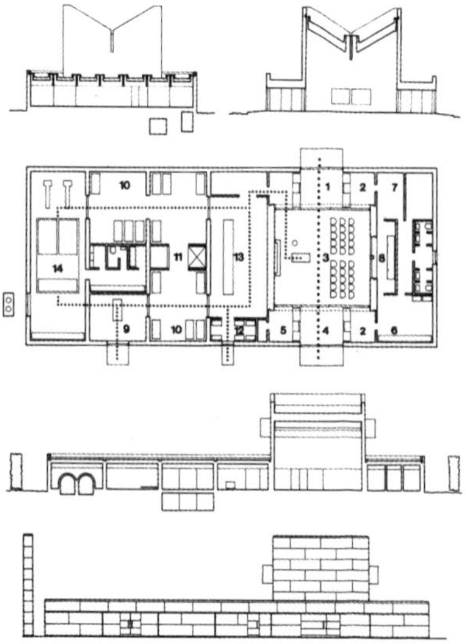

Henning Larsen

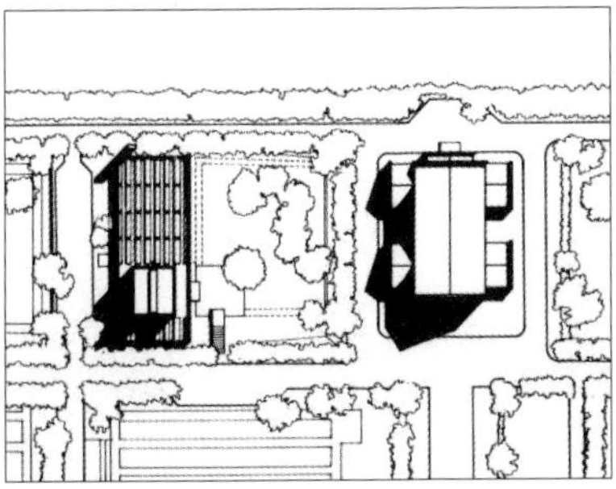

Henning Larsen

Villy Fink Isaksen

is situated at the end of the elongated access route of the cemetery and – drawing clear inspiration from Grundtvig's Church in Copenhagen – has been built solely from yellow clinker brick. Only a few metres south of the expressive, large chapel, Henning Larsen designed this small but significant early composition which is considerably more introverted, comprising a chapel and the adjoining crematorium. Both buildings have been constructed in smooth exposed concrete, with the outlines of the formwork serving as the sole ornamental feature. Furthermore, the walls within the hall are clad in tombac extending to the height of the door. The cuboid hall of the chapel has an inverted gable roof which juts out into the room and is supported by a concrete beam at the centre. Both the beam and the roof areas have been kept clear of the exterior walls via glazed slits through which daylight penetrates into the hall, lending a striking and atmospheric effect. The hall is in turn furnished with forty chairs which have been custom-made for this location. It became necessary to create a new vestibule and recreational spaces on the northern side for practical reasons. A few years later, the furnace system required modernisation and was augmented by a modest extension facing west. Both extensions were designed by the Henning Larsen practice.

Leif Wivelsted

Kjær & Richter

Kjær & Richter

Aarhus Statsgymnasium 072 F

Fenrisvej 33
Arne Gravers/Johan Richter, 1958, GPP Arkitekter, 2013, Kjær & Richter, 2015

This secondary school was the first edifice by the architects Arne Gravers and Johan Richter (the subsequent Kjaer & Richter practice) to be executed on a larger scale and was declared a listed building as early as 2003 since it features "particularly prominent architectural qualities". The building is situated on a hill, affording views across the city and surrounding landscape. All rooms are arranged around a square inner courtyard and rendered accessible via two corridors. The classrooms are oriented outwards and the technical rooms inwards. Materials of no perceptible colour include exposed concrete, grey limestone from Gotland and aluminium windows. Standing in stark contrast to this is the richly coloured wall mural by the artist Asger Jorn, which extends across the overall length of the foyer (27 m). A tapestry by Jorn and Pierre Wemaëre within the ceremonial hall of the secondary school accounts for further artwork in the building. Its modernisation spanning several years was completed in 2013, involving the refurbishment of the building envelope and technical installations as well as the design for an extension. New classrooms have been attached to the existing building via a glazed corridor and the canteen enhanced to form the new centrepiece of the secondary school.

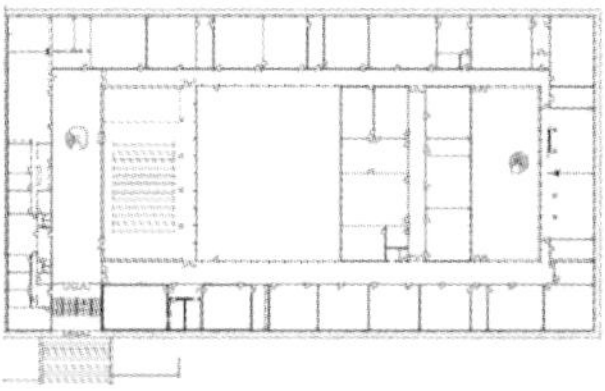

Kjær & Richter

Teknik & Miljø

Aarhus Ø and the Urban Development over the Past Decades

Gøsta Knudsen

The Lengthy Run-up

In terms of architecture, Aarhus in the mid-twentieth century was more commonly only known for the sharply defined, brick-lined homogeneity of the university buildings, the modernist town hall and the concert venue (Musikhuset) inaugurated in 1982. This stepmotherly approach towards architecture was finally abandoned in the 1990s with the dawn of the new century.

International interest in the efforts of Leon Krier and Aldo Rossi to create anew urban life and the spatial structures of the European city – something they had articulated in the 1980s – also had some impact in Aarhus in the 1990s. Here the municipal council adopted an ambitious development plan for the city centre. The objective was the promotion of trade and tourism by significantly enhancing architectural quality within the public realm. An exhaustive commitment followed this heroic decision.

Together with Frederiksgade and the labyrinthine street network layout of the Latin Quarter, the upmarket pedestrian and retail streets Søndergade and Ryesgade acquired new surfaces composed of heavy, solid and imperishable granite from China. The historic squares at the Cathedral – Bispetorv, Store Torv and Sankt Clemens Torv – likewise acquired new surfacing as well as stylish, high-amenity street furniture custom-made for this purpose. This large-scale architectural renewal has yielded lasting success. Following its rehabilitation, the city centre has become an inviting setting for urban development. Buoyed by this success, the municipal council went a stage further and in 1994 adopted a large-scale plan for the reopening of the riverbed which since the 1920s had been laid out with concrete sewers beneath Åboulevarden in order to make way for heavy traffic heading towards the port. This plan was initially met with scepticism. Without Åboulevarden as the main access route to the port, wouldn't

← View over the eastern station at the interface of the city centre and Aarhus Ø

Port at the mouth of the river (today's Europaplads), ca. 1892

the traffic system collapse? Would trade within the city centre fall off owing to the lack of parking spaces? And wouldn't the grey, murky waters of the river smell unpleasant?

The execution of this project was a thundering success, silencing the critics. Visitors from near and afar, both national and international, flocked to the new riverbanks, the self-evident merit of which led to the establishment of highly frequented cafés strung together like a string of pearls, where everything from Café Latte to potent cocktails is on offer.

The enhancement of architectural quality in the 1990s lent Aarhus a new identity and self-confidence. This was embodied within the plans for the new millennium where the municipal council set out new, visionary goals devoted to urban development. This new self-confidence can be deduced from the new perception of Self: the old slogan City of Smiles (*Smilets By*) turned into the self-confident ambition to become the new powerhouse of the whole of western Denmark, or the World's Smallest Big City. The objectives of this new vision are to meet the following growth targets by 2030:

- 75,000 new residents,
- 50,000 new flats,
- 50,000 new jobs,
- 15,000 new university places.

These growth forecasts are accompanied by strategic planning. Key themes therein include mobility – with the construction of a new light-rail line – and the upgrading of road infrastructure, coastal security, new water storage facilities (the keyword being climate change), CO2-neutral urban development and new urbanisation to the north near Lisbjerg with an approximate population of 25,000 and to the south near Beder/Malling with an approximate population of 18,000. The transformation of former industrial sites into residential and commercial areas as well as densification has moreover rendered possible a newbuild floor area covering roughly three million square metres within the realm of the city centre.

The positive experiences gained from architectural tweaks that have already been implemented and the unique opportunity to remodel and extend the city centre are weighty criteria. This is accompanied by a desire to solve the conflict involving the heavy traffic of the container port and the functional and visual barriers arising from port operations in order to restore the rapport between the historic city centre, the bay of Aarhus and the cultivated landscapes on the Mols peninsula. Accordingly, it goes without saying that the municipal authority is placing emphasis on the transformation

Visualisation of the boulevard at Aarhus Ø

of the inner dock areas and the northern container terminal into a new urban district: Aarhus Ø.

The Master Plan

The opening salvo for this ambitious metamorphosis – intended to turn the container terminal into a new urban district with 8,000 residents and 12,000 jobs, as well as restoring the route between the city centre and the bay – was the decision of the municipal authority in 1997 to hold an open, urban planning competition for ideas. Here, the land from Europaplads via Nørreport to Pier 4 at the marina and the entrance to the port was to be taken into account.

This open procedure for a new urban use of the dock area took place in 1999. It met with significant interest – more than 150 designs from Denmark and abroad were submitted. Ultimately the jury awarded first prize to the design by the Copenhagen-based architects Knud Fladeland and Per Teglgaard Jeppesen.

Visualisation of the new light-rail line at Dokk1

Teknik & Miljø

Aerial view over the harbour front and the bay in a northerly direction, spring 2016

The winning design translates the visions of the municipal authority into a vibrant, multifaceted and attractive urban district featuring flats, retail opportunities, cultural facilities and recreational oases with a flourishing urban life of which residents could be proud. At the same time, the design flags up Aarhus both nationally and abroad as a dynamic city of architecture which somewhat "lies dear to our hearts" regarding the development of the new harbor quarter underpinned by two comprehensive urban development strategies.

The first principle of the urban plan is a sharply defined, symbolic segregation of the dock area, created by man-made infilling, from the natural coastline which assumes the form of a new canal along a recreational promenade for pedestrians and cyclists, spilling out from the forested area of Risskov in the north all the way to the Marselisborg forests in the south.

This demarcation between natural and cultivated land illustrates the dividing line between old and new. At the same time, it paves the way for the new urban model at the inner harbour and Aarhus Ø.

The second principle of urban planning involves the restoration of the rapport between the city centre and the water. This includes, on the one hand, the reopening of the riverbed beneath Åboulevarden between Mindebrogade and Europaplads and, on the other, the establishment of an open port encased by water and the new bastions – the Dokk1 cultural centre and the Navitas education centre – affording a view upon the reflective expanse of the bay in widescreen format. But that was not all: in front of Dokk1, Warehouse 13 and Hack Kampmann's Customs House building, the quayside is designed in a credible manner as a tremendous flight of steps making contact with the water surface. Irrigated incisions aim to strengthen still further the sensation of water when traveling along the waterfront on the same latitude as Mindebrogade and Skolegyde. With a little imagination, the dock area – that is the inner harbour and Aarhus Ø – may be perceived as a vast, curved comb. The lower part of the spine of the comb is the existing peripheral development along the streets of Havnegade, Skolebakken and Kystvejen. The upper part of the spine of the comb follows the dead straight Bernhard Jensens Boulevard stretching for kilometres. Dokk1, Navitas and the Bestseller headquarters may be interpreted as the teeth of the comb along the inner harbour. The teeth along the new boulevard consist of the islands of the former piers 3 and 4 defined by the new canals. In the allotment of Aarhus Ø, the master plan proposes that the densely

Aerial view over the harbour front in a southerly direction, spring 2016

built-up backbone of the dead straight Bernhard Jensens Boulevard, the open canals, the multifaceted interpretation of the islands as urban blocks and the recreational urban squares and park-like settings team urban density with openness and memorable views over the surrounding landscape in an elegant fashion.

Aarhus Ø and Challenges Posed by the Economy

Following a public debate on the proposal of the master plan for the inner harbour and Aarhus Ø, the municipal authority resolved upon a quality manual in 2002 in close collaboration with the architects and took a stand on the strategy regarding the scheduling and future use of the land. In 2007, the municipality of Aarhus took possession of the first areas at Pier 4 of the port, while the first competitions for the land along the new boulevard were held. The architectural quality of the designs is high – striking projects such as the Lighthouse or Z-Huset have received international acclaim. Driven by the tailwind of a buoyant economy, the groundbreaking ceremony for Z-Huset and the construction of the two-storey parking deck in reinforced concrete took place in 2008. Owing to the international financial crisis, the works came to a standstill shortly thereafter. The clients of the proposed new buildings – with the capital of Icelandic banks as a guarantee – were forced to shorten sails and activities in Aarhus Ø reached an impasse. However, the municipal authority did not resort to panic-stricken solutions. The attitude is and remains that the parameters of the master plan and the quality manual must be observed. With this reassurance on board, the department of land development within the Municipality for the Environment and Technology set in motion an extremely arduous working process to find new investors. An old Danish proverb states there is nothing so bad that it is not good for something. Born out of necessity, the pause during the construction schedule piqued interest in temporary activities which might shape Aarhus Ø into a place with new forms of urban living. While construction activities were resumed with the help of local investors and large Danish pension funds, a highly frequented beach bar has been kitted out in Aarhus Ø where up to 1,000 visitors enjoy exotic cocktails, play beach volleyball, soak up the sun or dance in the open air on a daily basis. Aarhus Ø also features the largest expanse with Urban Farming, where the young hipsters of the city cultivate organic salad in small flower beds. The beautiful waterfront

Top: aerial view over the harbour and the city in a north-westerly direction, September 2016

promenade with an artificial subaqueous reef is the place to be if one is keen to fish for herring, cod, mackerel or sea trout. The 500 m long swimming lane conceived within the bay is also pleasant, imparting a potential open-ocean feeling. Further elements which mark Aarhus Ø off as something special are, for example, the forthcoming water sculpture by the artist Jeppe Hein at the harbor, Dorte Mandrup's observation tower or BIG's harbor pool at Bassin 7 donated by the Salling Fund.

Aarhus Ø 2016

A mere eight years following the financial crisis, the greatest part of the initial construction phase saw Aarhus Ø being built upon with construction sites at the marina, Pier 4 and along Bernhard Jensens Boulevard. Further areas along the streets Kystvejen and Skovvejen are currently being developed. In a nutshell, things are going well here. The names of the buildings – for example Lighthouse, Z-Huset, Kanalhusene, Pakhusene and SHIP – shed light on the role of architecture as an important parameter for identity and branding. This is a development which differs from the proposed urban districts of the early twentieth century, such as, for example, on Ingerslevs Boulevard where aesthetically pleasing urban space emerged owing to the material homogeneity of the block perimeter development in red exposed masonry.

Next double page: aerial view over Aarhus Ø, September 2016

The homogenous element in Aarhus Ø is diversity which is a corollary of the form of tender and the architects' intense thirst for immortality through architecture striving for greater heights and boasting a high degree of recognisability. Whether or not one agrees with this development is a matter of taste, but from a great height Aarhus Ø is dominated by ambitious and thorough planning, by density and scale introducing new principles for inner-city development and by architecture "with heart and soul". In spite of these convincing qualities, several city architects have not refrained from delivering critical comments. The absence of material homogeneity has undergone discussion along with the scale and obtrusiveness of the architecture. In other words, these critics may be hankering after robust, unsentimental and readily comprehensible port architecture such as the old corn silos in a region with a harsh coastal climate, in lieu of architecture espousing filigree glass inspired by Malaga. Go ahead and experience Aarhus Ø. There are ample opportunities here to gain exposure to memorable architecture at close quarters, intriguing excursions with splendid views across the reflective expanse of the bay and the new canals as well as of the spires of the cathedral – which acts as a focal point of the city centre – and a congenial blend of well-established and temporary activities alike.

Teknik & Miljø

Skejby

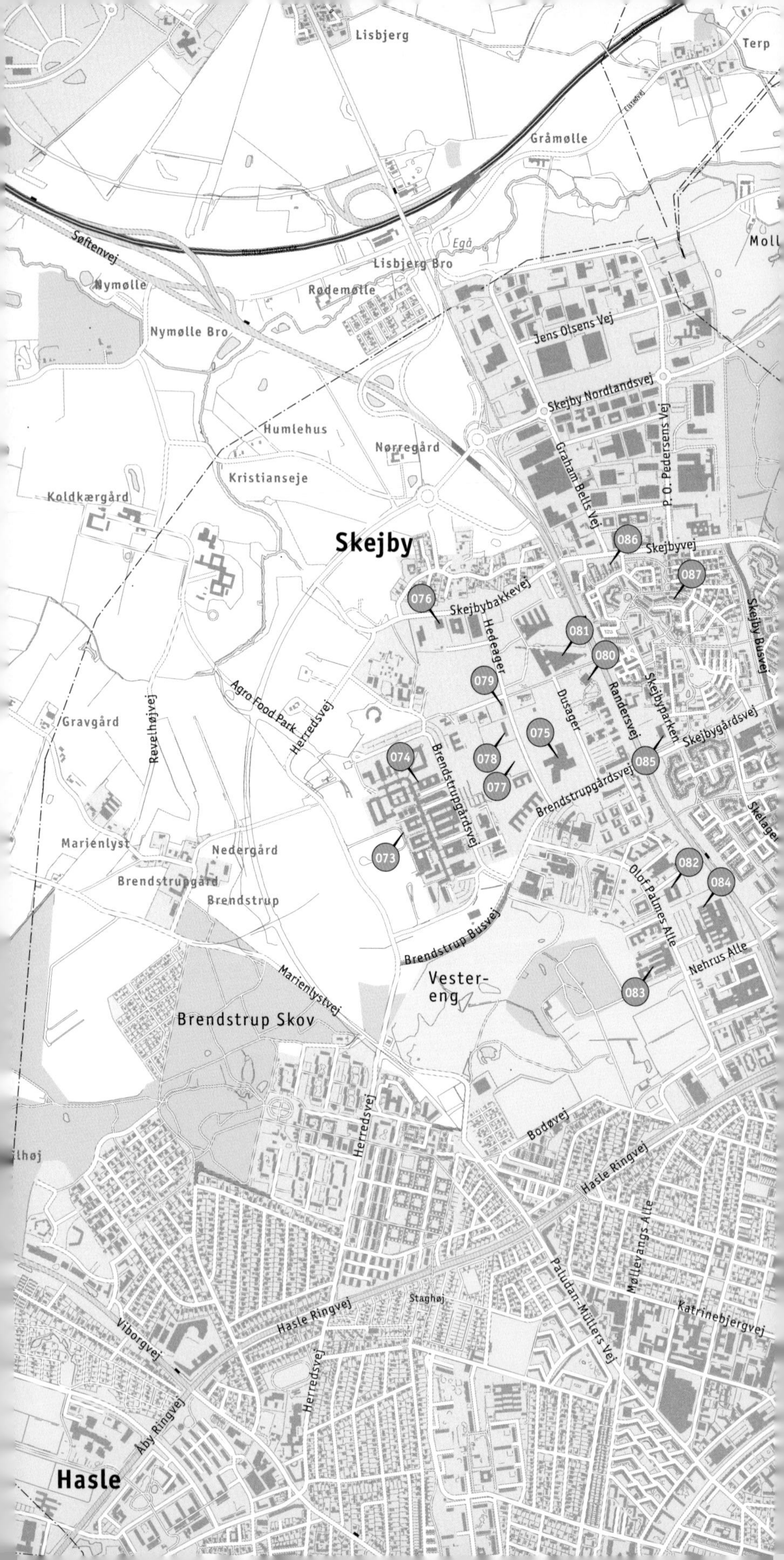
Lisbjerg
Terp
Gråmølle
Moll
Egå
Søftenvej
Nymølle
Lisbjerg Bro
Rødemølle
Nymølle Bro
Jens Olsens Vej
Skejby Nordlandsvej
Humlehus
Nørregård
Kristianseje
Koldkærgård
Graham Bells Vej
P. O. Pedersens Vej
Skejby
086
Skejbyvej
087
076
Skejbybakkevej
Skejby Busvej
081
080
Hedeager
079
Agro Food Park
Herredsvej
Dusager
Randersvej
Skejbyparken
Gravgård
Revelhøjvej
075
Skejbygårdsvej
074
Brendstrupgårdsvej
078
085
077
Brendstrupgårdsvej
Skelager
Marienlyst
Nedergård
073
082
084
Brendstrupgård
Brendstrup
Olof Palmes Alle
Brendstrup Busvej
Nehrus Alle
Vester-
eng
083
Marienlystvej
Brendstrup Skov
Herredsvej
Bodøvej
Hasle Ringvej
Møllevangs Alle
Paludan-Müllers Vej
Staghøj
Hasle Ringvej
Katrinebjergvej
Viborgvej
Herredsvej
Åby Ringvej
Hasle

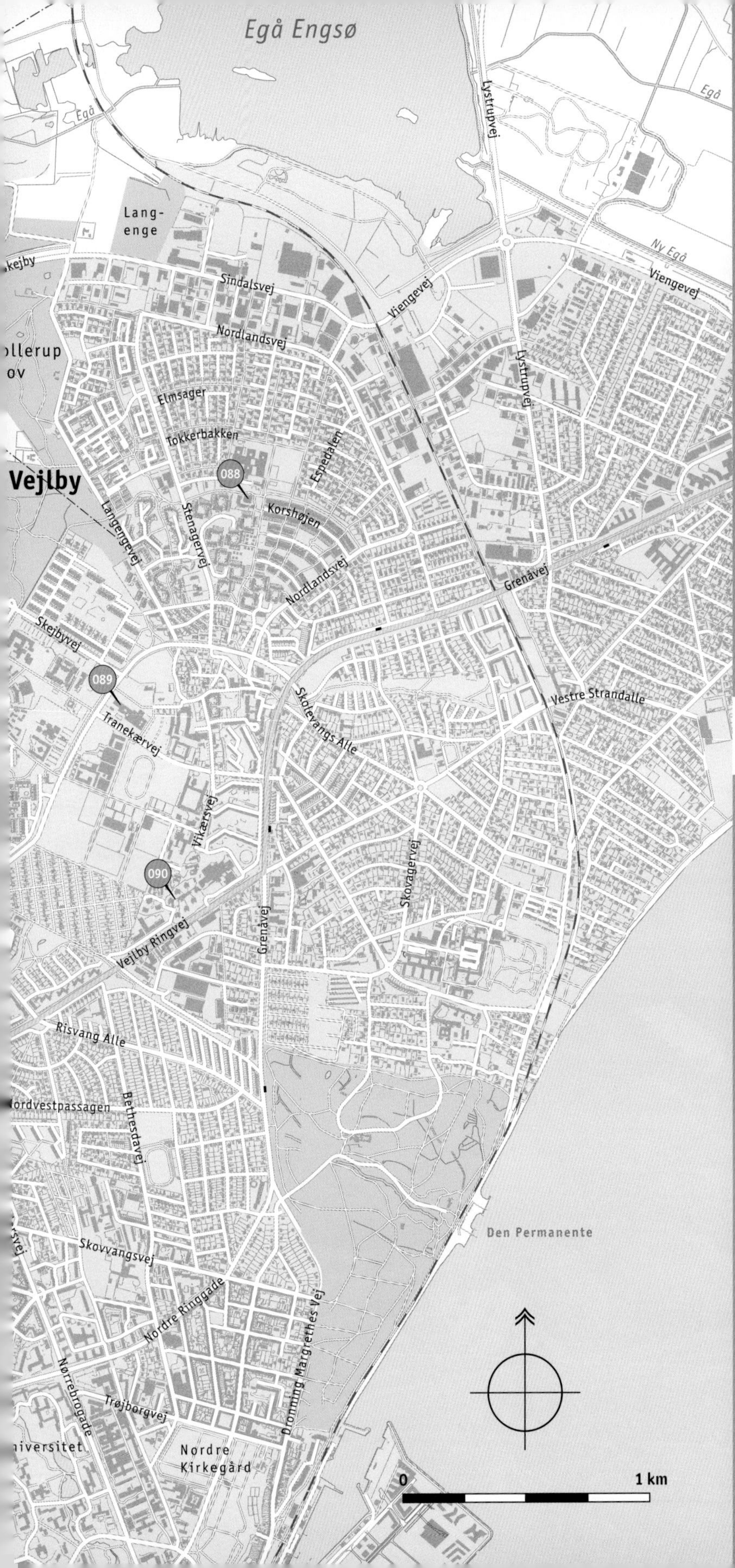

Egå Engsø
Egå
Lang-enge
Sindalsvej
Nordlandsvej
Elmsager
Tokkerbakken
Vejlby
Langengevej
Stenagervej
Korshøjen
Espedalen
088
Viengevej
Lystrupvej
Ny Egå
Grenåvej
Skejbyvej
089
Tranekærvej
Skolevangs Alle
Vestre Strandalle
Vikærsvej
090
Vejlby Ringvej
Grenåvej
Skovagervej
Risvang Alle
Nordvestpassagen
Bethesdavej
Skovvangsvej
Nordre Ringgade
Dronning Margrethes Vej
Den Permanente
Nørrebrogade
Trøjborgvej
Nordre Kirkegård
0
1 km

G

073
074
077
083

094
086
085
081
087
076
080
075
082
084
Teknik & Miljø

C. F. Møller Architects/CUBO

C. F. Møller Architects/CUBO

DNU, The New University Hospital in Aarhus

073 G

Palle Juul-Jensens Boulevard, Skejby
C. F. Møller Architects/CUBO/Schønherr Landskab/Tegnestuen Havestuen, 1987/2007–2020

The largest hospital project in the history of Denmark has been executed on the site of the existing university hospital in Skejby in order to arrive at a single hospital complex covering 400,000 m² – roughly corresponding in size to a Danish provincial town. At the same time, it is set to be the largest workplace in the whole of Aarhus. The gigantic complex has also been organised in a manner befitting a city and features a hierarchy of neighbourhoods, streets and squares which lay down the basis for a multifaceted and dynamic green municipal area. This construction project is also a cultural project incorporating various branches of science and art. Apart from its role as a university hospital, the complex is also intended to serve as a regional centre and hospital catering for the basic care of local residents. It is designed to deliver a flexible response to future developments in technology, treatment and working practice.

Aarhus Arkitekterne

Danish Centre for Particle Therapy 074 G

Skejby

Aarhus Arkitekterne, 2015–2018

The Danish Centre for Particle Therapy is the only one of its kind throughout Denmark. The design reflects its purpose both inside and outside. The façades are intended to relay the history of the precise art of radiotherapy. The structure emerges as a concrete mass cast with a volume of up to 14,000 m^3 and walls with a thickness of up to 4 m. The building will boast an overall length of 70 m and contain three storeys. This heavy construction renders the building unique. The centre has been conceived by adopting an exceedingly functional approach from the inside out in order to create optimal patient turn-around. An atrium brings daylight into the "backbone of the building" – a route providing access and orientation leading to the treatment rooms. Pleasant materials and hanging gardens are intended to impart a friendly, professional ambience. The façade owes its unique appearance to the three overlapping architectural elements which the architects denote as the lighting, the concrete structure and the façade; the latter will consist of corten steel.

Adam Mørk / Schmidt/Hammer/Lassen

VIA University College
Hedeager 2, Skejby
Schmidt/Hammer/Lassen
2011

075 G

With 2,000 employees and 20,000 students, VIA University College is one of eight Danish polytechnics offering courses of study in the sectors of social welfare, technology and health care at a wide range of locations throughout Jutland. Owing to its proximity to the university clinic in Skejby, the primary focus at Campus North is training within the health sector. It is at the same time the administrative headquarters of the third largest educational institution in Denmark. The floor plan of the building consists of four windmill-sail wings, of which three stand orthogonal to each other and the fourth is positioned obliquely to mark the entrance. A multi-storey atrium with a glazed roof is located at the point of intersection and provides a circulation space which may give rise to chance encounters. Core features, such as lecture halls, media spaces and canteens, as well as recreational enclaves, are accessible from here, whereas study cells for individuals and groups, administrative departments and other features are arranged within the wings. Strips of windows lend horizontal structure to the façades featuring projections and mouldings clad in rust-coloured corten steel, while complementary balustrades and balconies have been adorned with greenery. The approach towards materials is simple and robust in order to maintain the day-to-day routine. Inside, striking touches of colour on surfaces, fittings and furniture lend contrast to the exposed concrete walls.

Mikkel Frost / CEBRA

Elbek & Vejrup, Headquarters 076 G

Tangen 6, Skejby
CEBRA
2011

Elbek & Vejrup is a software systems supplier with 140 employees at six locations throughout Denmark and numerous customers within the private and public sphere. A building conveying reliability and digital high-tech was sought for the new headquarters in Skejby. The architects designed the first of two buildings on the same site as a traditional, square patio house with a diagonally rotated circulation system. The leitmotif of the architectural concept is based on the combination of bricks and pixels which brought forth the hybrid term *Brixels*. In common with digital photographs composed of small coloured squares, a building is constructed from building blocks. Glazed bricks of various colours have been installed here with a "digital twist" – without bonding – as pixelisation in square fields at the entrance. This motif is continued right through to the tiles of the sanitary facilities with figures from Space Invaders. Even the different types of vegetation on several interior walls are assorted in such a manner that gigantic pixels are formed. The carpets denote the name of the firm via the binary numbers 0 and 1.

Mikkel Frost / CEBRA

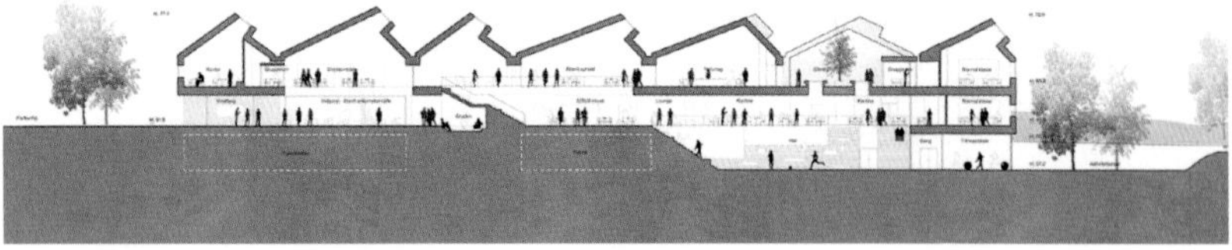

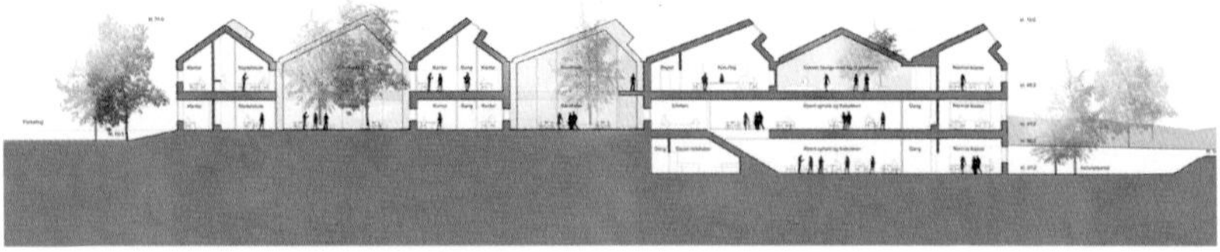

CUBO

SOSU, Vocational School for Social and Health Education 077 G

Hedeager 33, Skejby

CUBO/Møller & Grønborg, 2015

The development of the urban district of Skejby, which has emerged on former farmland since the 1980s, is primarily composed of free-standing solitary buildings with a wide range of scale, functions and materials. The vocational school lies between the business quarter along the main road, Randersvej, and the new complex of the New University Clinic, the largest hospital in Denmark. It is therefore surrounded by firms and institutions with similar target groups. The architectural concept behind the school building seeks to counter the urban clutter in the neighbourhood with an island of tranquillity and is based on seven elongated buildings with shed-like roofs set out in a row. The building has several peripheral entrances. The connecting corridors,

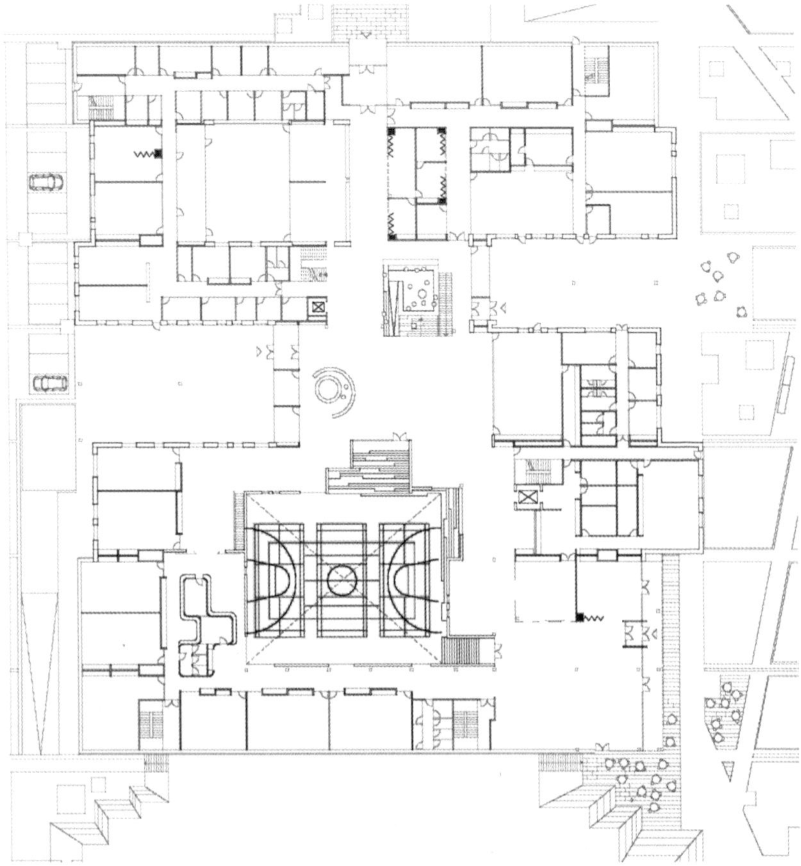

CUBO

Martin Schubert/CUBO

located centrally, run together and widen out into a square-like forum. The various domains of administration, education and sport as well as the canteen lie around this square, scattered over three storeys. Small, thoughtfully designed inner courtyards receive exposure to fresh air. The façades consist of light grey clinker. Inside, light surfaces with individual splashes of colour, as well as wood, linoleum and other local materials, create a pleasant ambience. Acknowledging that new technologies will exert a growing influence on the health sector and that pedagogical approaches are developing in step with societal transformation formed the basis for the physical concept behind the school building. Accordingly, it boasts a flexible design in order to facilitate future conversions and accompanying structural changes or even extension buildings – all without throwing doubt on the original concept. The building offers up possibilities of the most varied kind for the use of space both internally and externally. Everywhere, daylight streams through the asymmetrical roof ridges criss-crossed by bands of skylights. The offset storeys and differing ceiling heights create an open, friendly and dynamic ambience in which students may freely roam in their pursuit of knowledge and information, as well as fully capitalising on the opportunities for mutual learning. Two other buildings by the architectural practice CUBO boasting a similar typology are located in the immediate vicinity (see 078 and 079).

Martin Schubert/CUBO

Helene Høyer Mikkelsen/CUBO

Aagaardklinik
Hedeager 35, Skejby
CUBO
2009

078 G

The building contains a specialised clinic for gynaecology and fertility whose customers demand discretion, intimacy and security. The architecture is akin to the already existing headquarters on the northern neighbouring plot (see 079) and the vocational school bordering to the south (077) built subsequent to this. Both buildings have been designed by the CUBO practice. The clinic somewhat reiterates several architectural principles of the headquarters. Once again, there is a longitudinal building oriented in a north-southerly direction with a steep roof covered with zinc and a circulation area containing a car park on a plinth. This time the circulation area is located on the eastern side of the single-storey building in light grey clinker. A band of skylights, which are also oriented eastwards, allows daylight to flood the entire length of the building and makes its presence felt on the gables via an asymmetric incision. The reception side opens up to visitors with a glazed façade containing black sun protection lamellae, while the narrow band of windows on the western façade offers protection from too much sunlight. The interior of the clinic is white, while black doors and fixtures present a contrast. The clinic anticipates the subsequent school building in its materiality and outer form. One could argue that the architects have created a cohesive architectural vocabulary which permits extensions and amendments to functions. In this context, it is a matter of circumstance whether the individual building houses a firm, institution or something completely different.

Helene Høyer Mikkelsen/CUBO

Helene Høyer Mikkelsen/CUBO

Unisense, Headquarters
079 G
Tueager 1, Skejby
CUBO
2007

This dark grey longitudinal building was originally designed for a manufacturer of prefabricated housing. The challenge lay in creating prestigious premises for the parent company across an area of no more than 1,300 m² in an environment comprising much larger firms and institutions in Skejby. The originally rural territory served as inspiration and from this a former agricultural building type was derived: a longhouse on a plinth oriented in a north-southerly direction which assimilates the uneven terrain and forms the base of the building. The building seems to rise up out of the plinth and indeed both the podium and the building appear cast from the same mould since each is constructed using the same dark clinker. The spine of the roof clad in anthracite-grey zinc has almost been raised to the third floor and the ridge opened up via a band of skylights providing daylight. The facades differ on each floor. The façade on the ground floor facing the west has been sliced up towards the forecourt. A revolving door in a striking shade of orange has been set into the glazed façade of this groove. The opposite side of the building facing the streetscape has a more enclosed façade which is animated by bay windows jutting out in a northerly direction on the upper storey to the same rhythm as that of the ground floor facade. The interior with bright wooden floors and rooms which open on to the roof gable stands in stark contrast to the dark exterior appearance. Today, the building is used by the firm Unisense, a market-leading manufacturer of microscopes and measuring instruments.

Helene Høyer Mikkelsen/CUBO

G

078 G

079 G

Helene Høyer Mikkelsen/CUBO

Thomas Mølvig / Schmidt/Hammer/Lassen

NRGi Headquarters

080 G

Dusager 22, Skejby
Schmidt/Hammer/Lassen
2007

In common with many of the buildings along Randersvej, Denmark's fourth largest electricity company sought to draw attention to itself with a slanted building. With its diagonal location on site, creased façade and cladding in triangular reflective aluminium and glass panels boasting golden hues, the three-storey building dissociates itself from the solitary neighbouring development devoid of context. At the same time, this energy-smart building with maximum daylight and shade is intended to mitigate electricity consumption and cooling requirements. A central atrium builds visual alignments between the rooms. The atrium is covered with a 144 m^2 large ETFE-foil air cushion. In the event of any change to the airflow within the cushion – the printed pattern of which reduces the volume of sunlight – there is an increase in thermal insulation. The relocation to the new building was accompanied by the fact that almost all employees now work in open offices. Only significant features calling for discretion are accommodated within individual offices or enclosed conference rooms. Inside, the load-bearing elements are left as exposed concrete which is contrasted with white walls, industrial parquet flooring and red items of furniture.

Thomas Mølvig / Schmidt/Hammer/Lassen

House of Vestas
Hedeager 42, Skejby
Arkitema Architects
2009/2011

081 G

Vestas is a market-leading Danish manufacturer of wind turbines which relocated its headquarters from Randers to Aarhus. The administrative department as well as a research and development centre for 500 employees were built in two construction stages in Skejby. A sustainable concept was developed since the production of alternative energy is its primary focus. In 2010, the building was awarded LEED Platinum certification since, among other things, it was able to reduce total energy consumption to roughly 50 per cent in comparison with traditional administrative buildings through Denmark's largest geothermal energy plant. Both tracts differ in their outer form, circulation and choice of materials, but are ultimately to be perceived as one entity. The initially constructed development centre has a façade composed of partially transparent, partially dark tinted glass panes as well as fixed or movable lamellae which

Thorbjørn Hansen / Arkitema Architects

Thorbjørn Hansen / Arkitema Architects

provide shade depending on the position of the sun and lend the façade a dynamic touch. The development centre is placed on the uppermost point of the site in order to expose it to Randersvej. A multistorey atrium with a skylight and a "vast landscape composed of steps" occupies a central location within the building. This room is criss-crossed by steps and bridges spurring informal encounters and leading to exhibition space, dwelling areas, conference rooms and a library. The head of a wind turbine on the uppermost storey has been converted into a "3D cavern" where product presentations take place. The spacious administrative building with a tessellated façade composed of dark tinted, movable glass planes is configured as a comb structure along a circulation thoroughfare where all outward-facing features are located, such as conference rooms, auditoriums and the caféteria. The concept behind the office space denotes an extremely flexible design: party walls may be moved within a grid of 3 m in order to provide up to twenty people with office space at short notice.

Thorbjørn Hansen / Arkitema Architects

Schmidt/Hammer/Lassen

Schmidt/Hammer/Lassen

Martin Professional, Showroom ↑↗ 082 G
Olof Palmes Allé 18
Schmidt/Hammer/Lassen
1999

The headquarters of the Martin/Harman firm specialising in light installations – at rock concerts for example – emerged on a square floor plan. The three-storey building encompasses an atrium partially located inside, partially outside and featuring a continuous water basin. The dark tinted glazed façade with an entrance marked red on the ground floor – observers may discern the abandoned showroom clad in enclosed steel sheeting from the outside – is intended to lend the building a somewhat mystical touch. Up to 100 customers may be swayed by the possibilities that lighting design has to offer within the multi-media theatre.

Danish School of Media and Journalism ↓→ 083 G
Olof Palmes Allé 11
Kjær & Richter/Sven Hansen/
Preben Skaarup, 1973/1984/1993

As with the subsequent design for the Musikhuset (see 011), the architects cleverly capitalised on the sloping nature of the construction site in order to make room for the planned area of the fledgling college. Visitors enter the building via an understated entrance on the lower floor and make their way upwards via flights of stairs on an inner thoroughfare with a glass roof. Classrooms and offices facing west as well as technical premises, television studios, auditoriums, canteens and a library facing east are located within four separate wings which stand on individual landscaped terraces orthogonal to this halled transition area. Exposed concrete,

Kjær & Richter

Heiko Weissbach

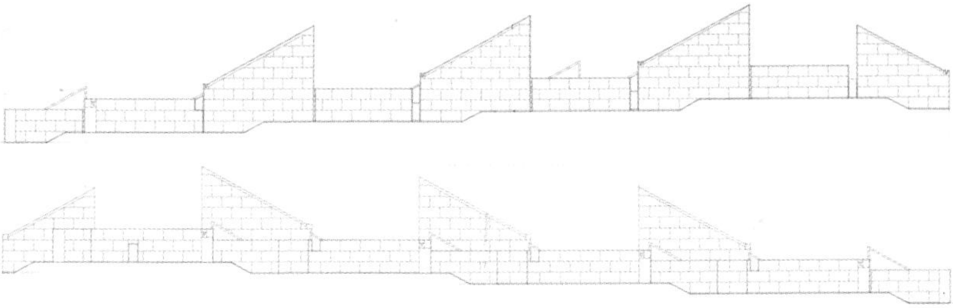

Kjær & Richter

cast to form a smooth membrane with varying seams, dominates both the interior and the exterior. Regrettably, the exterior façade has been given a lick of paint. Together with the terraced somewhat austere gardens by the landscape architect Sven Hansen, the School of Journalism ranks among the most prominent experimental edifices of Brutalism. The sculptor Jørgen Haugen Sørensen created the cluster of sculptures on the forecourt. The university underwent expansion in 1984 and 1993. In 2019 it will be relocated to a new building on Campus Katrinebjerg.

Kjær & Richter

084 G

Torben Eskerod/C.F. Møller Architects

Torben Eskerod

C. F. Møller Architects

DR, Denmark's Broadcasting Corporation

084 G

Olof Palmes Allé 10

C.F. Møller/Sven Hansen, 1981/2010

Scarcely any other design has inspired so many architects internationally than that by Candelis, Josic and Woods for the Free University in Berlin, which emerged triumphant from the competition held in 1963 and was executed prior to 1973. The structuralist principle of designing buildings which can be customised and which are expandable was also drawn upon for the building of the Danish state-owned radio and television broadcaster – DR for short – which was built in several construction stages over a period of twelve years. These buildings which house administration, the library, workshops and storage halls as well as video and recording studios are interconnected via a rectangular area of circulation. In common with a city, the width of the major roads and glass-roofed side streets is varied. A number of squares emerge at intersection points. The street motif is underscored by floors covered in shale and paving stones and everywhere comes up against exposed concrete walls forming a coarse outer skin with rounded corners and built-in furniture. The pipes of the building services are exposed and colourfully painted. The building complex lies on an artificial plateau built on a steeply sloping site and is closed off to the south and west by a ridge covered in cobblestones. The atriums between the individual buildings have each been given an individual design by the landscape architect Sven Hansen who bestows a unique ambience upon each address within this sprawling building complex, thus facilitating orientation. Furthermore, the building is richly furnished with works of art.

Torben Eskerod/C. F. Møller Architects

Heiko Weissbach

TV 2 Eastern Jutland 085 G

Skejbyparken 1
Schmidt/Hammer/Lassen
1999

The breaking of the state's monopoly over the media in 1988 was accompanied by a series of regional television channels, including the channel TV 2 – the first channel financed by advertising. The new channel carved out a strong architectural presence in northern Aarhus. Between two wings of differing width and composed of brown exposed masonry – which incorporate all auxiliary functions – there stands a third glazed building with reception, news studio and editorial offices over which the canteen hangs within a box clad in galvanised steel panels. The interior is host to the central, double-storey newsroom which is connected to the editorial department above via a circular opening featuring a diameter of 7 m. The news programmes of TV 2 are recorded against this backdrop. Today, a novel feature at the time continues to be commonplace in news programmes worldwide – the presenter in sharp focus in the foreground, whereas the blurred editorial staff actively work in the background.

Heiko Weissbach

Five Fingers,
Housing Development

086 G

Ladefogedvej 2–84
Vandkunsten, 1994/2002

Ecological, social and sustainable housing is the prime discipline of the Copenhagen-based practice Vandkunsten since its foundation in the 1960s. In 1989, the practice was awarded first prize in a competition with the topic of *The Northern Terraced House*. The Five Fingers housing estate in northern Aarhus is an enhancement of the competition design. The five parallel buildings, of which this social residential development is composed, lie diagonally to the land levels as they run. The buildings have two or three storeys owing to a slope measuring 5 m, as well as a continuous roof ridge. The elegantly unadorned edifices clad in grey Eternit feature low gable roofs which are visually elevated from the façade owing to a band of windows. Double-storey passages lend structure to these buildings, providing access to collectively used courtyard gardens and the community centre. The façades have been conceived with wooden window frames in lacquer and feature galvanised steel staircases and balconies.

Vandkunsten

Andreas Trier Mørch/KADK

Eco-houses, Settlement 087 G

Skejbytoften 106–182
Vandkunsten
1998

Originally named Eco-house 99, this estate of terraced housing is the outcome of a competition held under the slogan *Ecological Housing of the Future* by the Danish Ministry of Housing in collaboration with one of the largest housing cooperatives, KAB. Four slightly angled rows of two- and three-storey housing clad in black Eternit and wooden lamellae with mono-pitched roofs are placed on to the elongated plot. Both the gables of the end terraced houses and the northern façades are almost fully enclosed. The living rooms featuring sloping glazed façades and photovoltaic panels open up towards the south. Behind the large panes of glass, natural stone flooring and solid concrete walls absorb sunlight during the day and emit sunlight to the living rooms at night. Many ecological concepts have been adopted – from recycled building materials to the use of rainwater for toilet flushing, from the passive use of solar energy to the production of electricity through photovoltaics, from heat exchangers to the automated control of the room temperature. However, subsequent analyses by the Danish Building Research Institute SBI yielded the fact that the interiors of the highly insulated residential buildings develop moisture, afflicting the constructive wooden elements. Similarly, the extensive glazing of the double-storey living space is a blessing and a curse: on hot summer days, the solar thermal input is sometimes high in a manner that makes things ungovernable, overheating the living quarters into the night – contrary to this, the demand for heating increases in winter. Electricity savings are negligible in the overall balance. Although critics, armed with this information, referred to these eco-houses as a "failed experiment", they do offer their residents well laid-out, flexible living space.

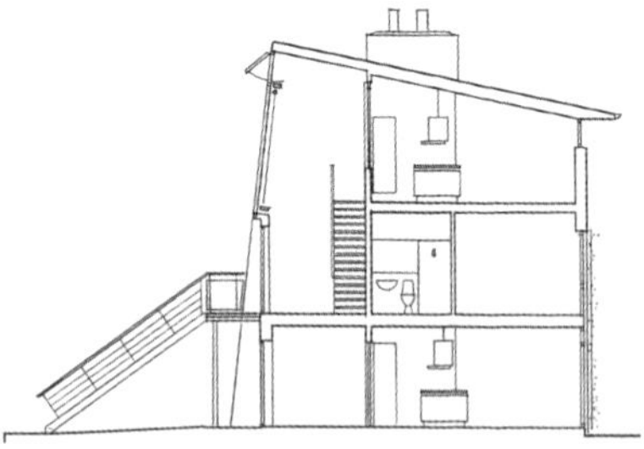

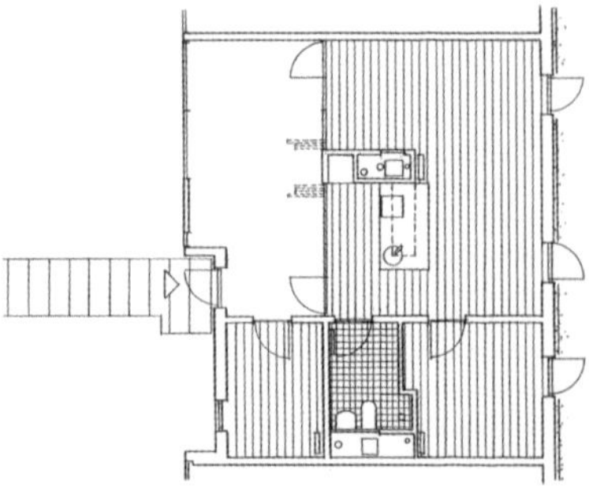

Vandkunsten

Friis & Moltke

Ellevang Church

088 G

Jellebakken 14, 8240 Risskov
Friis & Moltke/Sven Hansen
1974

In common with traditional Danish village churches – including the nearby Vejlby Church – Ellevang Kirke has also been built in whitewashed masonry. However, the choice of materials seems not to be the sole historical reference of the church which has a modern, traditional and puritan look about it. This is the first new church to be built by the architects. In contrast to both the interior and exterior white walls, raw wooden boards painted dark blue have been selected as ceiling lining and the floors are furnished with large exposed aggregate concrete slabs. The altar, baptismal font and pulpit were designed by the sculptor Erik Heide in granite and iron. The main room of the church lies between two abstract building volumes incorporating all auxiliary functions as well as the organ. Several roof or ceiling surfaces spanning these "cheeks" are slightly offset in relation to each other and filter the sunlight which is channelled to the altar. The body of the church may be divided asymmetrically via a partition in order to cater to various purposes. As with the naves of the basilica, adjoining rooms housing offices, conference facilities and confirmation rooms have been simply attached to both load-bearing structures. The free-standing belfry is located next to it, marking a small, slightly elevated forecourt.

Heiko Weissbach

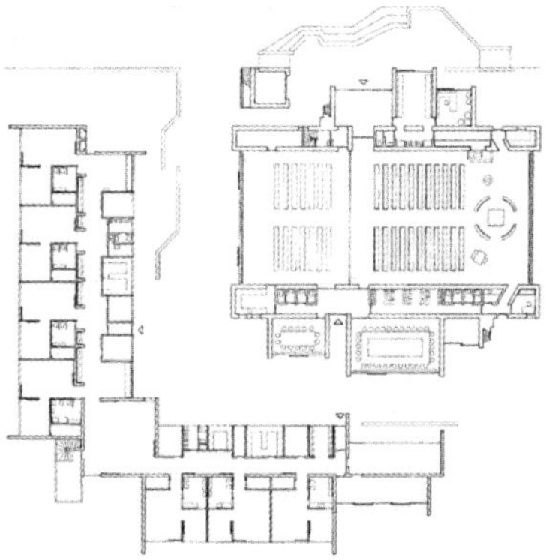

Friis & Moltke

G

Heiko Weissbach

Risskov Gymnasium

089 G

Tranekærvej 70
Friis & Moltke/K. Mejer Jensen
1969

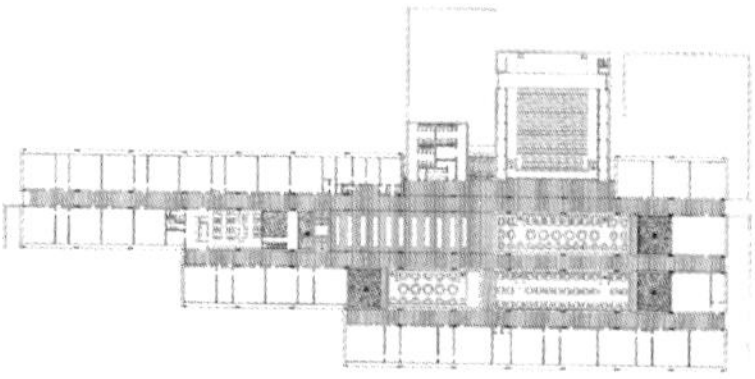

Friis & Moltke

The 1960s and 1970s ushered in a flourishing period of pedagogy in Denmark which had a knock-on effect on architecture. In comparison to pre-war architecture, the structural modifications to schools were revolutionary. Thus, traditional classes were abandoned and so-called specialist classes established, among other things. The first secondary school to be executed by the architects Knud Friis and Ivar Moltke is a reflection of this. It consists of various, individually furnished specialist classrooms between which students commute throughout the day. This imparted great significance to the design for the central circulation space. In common with subsequent buildings by the architects, this secondary school is configured in a manner befitting a small village. The four parallel wings with frame constructions comprising exposed concrete supports and beams – which, in common with a truss, may be filled by non-load-bearing facing masonry – are connected by glass-roofed arcades. The arcades furnished with concrete tiles lead to the carpeted classrooms and the central square which is also home to the canteen and the auditorium.

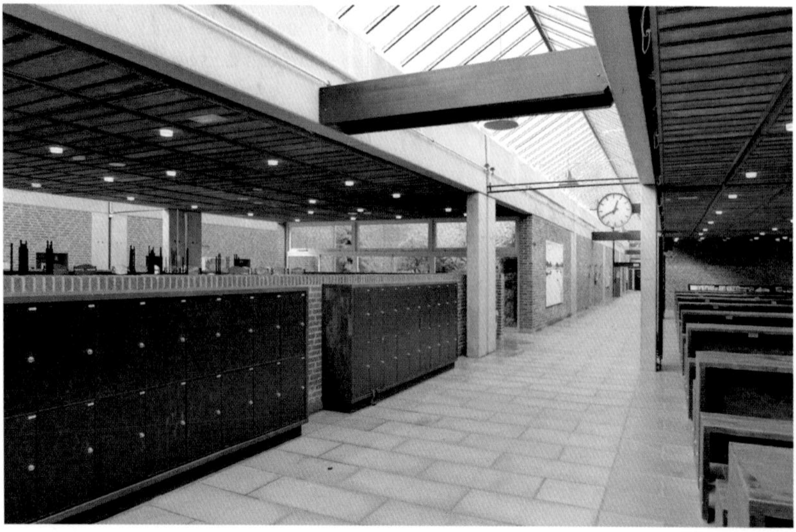

Heiko Weissbach

Børglum, Student Residence 090 G

Børglumvej 2, Risskov
Harald Salling-Mortensen/
Paul Erik Niepoort/
Jørgen Arevad-Jacobsen, 1967

The Børglum student residence is in many ways contrary to the traditional student housing complex from that period. It was constructed from yellow masonry with the architectural inspiration clearly hearkening back to buildings by the Finnish architect Alvar Aalto. In lieu of elongated, straight corridors with numerous rooms and communal kitchens and bathrooms, the architects have created an organic structure featuring seven four-storey residential blocks and a central communal building connected by roofed corridors. At the same time, these counterbalance the differences in level on the site through ramps. The communal building (*fælleshuset*) is arguably the most important meeting place within the residence since it is not only encompasses the main entrance, reception and the administrative headquarters, but also the letterboxes, a bar, fitness rooms and guestrooms. The residential blocks are virtually identical with ten to twelve apartments featuring one or one-and-a-half rooms on each floor. These are clustered around a central common room with a kitchen and a balcony facing south. The fan-shaped arrangement and the polygonal geometry lend each apartment an individual touch.

Heiko Weissbach

Heiko Weissbach

090 G

Heiko Weissbach

Northbound:
Egå – Lisbjerg – Lystrup – Løgten

Spørring
Risvangsvej
Hårup
Mejlbyvej
Spørring Å
Bøggildsvej
Hæstvej
Hæst
Todbjerg
Randersvej
Pannerup Mose
Pannerupvej
Pannerup
Elsted
Vennemindevej
Elev
Koldkilde
Lystrupvej
Langagervej
Ølsted
094
Randersvej
Ølstedvej
093
Lisbjerg
Elevvej
091
Djurslandmotorvejen
Egå Engsø
092
Søftenvej
Vejlby
Skejby

Balle
Segalt
Vorre
099
Grenåvej
Løgten
Brandstrup
Hesselballe
Grøttrup
Skødstrup
Åstrup
Kankbølle
Hjortshøj
096
Lystrup
097
Kankbøllevej
Svinbo
Djurslandmotorvejen
Mejlbyvej
Hjortshøjvej
Grenåvej
100
Skæring Hedevej
Hovmarken
Skæring Hevvej
Skæring
Mejlbyvej
Koraldybet
Egå Mosevej
Egå
Grenåvej
Tålfor Strand
Egå Strandvej
Egå Strand
101
Egå Marina
Ny Egå
Grenåvej
Nordre Strandvej
102
Risskov
0
500 m
1 km

H

Teknik & Miljø

Lystrup
Egå
Risskov

Helene Høver Mikkelsen / Kjær & Richter

Helene Høver Mikkelsen / Kjær & Richter

Heiko Weissbach

School in Lisbjerg

091 H

Lisbjergvej 13
Kjær & Richter / GBL Landskab
2008

Sølvbjærg Fotografi / Kjær & Richter

In 2001, the urban development plan for the new urban district of Lisbjerg Bakke was adopted by the municipal authority; a corresponding urban design competition followed between 2002 and 2003. A core feature of the development plan arising therefrom was the establishment of a school. This was commissioned as early as 2008 and is located in the immediate vicinity of a stop belonging to the new regional railway track. The school building consists of four assembled edifices clustered around a central atrium. Both northern wings contain classrooms and workshops; the more urban south-western one features musical and multi-functional rooms. A communal centre, a health centre and premises catering for after-school programmes are located within the fourth wing of the school.

H

Heiko Weissbach

RUBOW Arkitekter

Plus-energy Houses

092 H

Elmehøjen 90–184,
Lisbjerg Bakke
RUBOW Arkitekter/
GBL Landskab
2017

With the design for a new (residential) community, the architects are seeking to ensure common ground and forge a common identity irrespective of individual preferences. Well-defined alleys are intended to lend structure to the sloped terrain of the settlement. Each road consists of six to eight terraced houses offering varying types of dwelling. The slab-like buildings are oriented so that they provide shelter from westerly winds and fully capitalise on the sunlight. The six clusters of houses clad in larch wood give rise to an intervening green clearance which will be known as *Heartlands* and is in visual alignment with the new urban district of Lisbjerg Bakke and the landscape. Cars are parked north of the settlement; laundry facilities and parking spaces for bicycles have been established close to the buildings. The green heart is also the social hub of the settlement, spurring informal encounters among residents. Living space tailored to all generations – including young families, patchwork families, family collectives and senior citizens – is to be created within the complex. The energy concept delineates a compact design, photovoltaic system and smart home control technology to ensure that the settlement produces a surplus of energy beyond the passive house standard.

RUBOW Arkitekter

Vandkunsten

Sustainable Housing Development

Lisbjerg Bakke
Vandkunsten, 2014–2017

093 H

The model housing estate in Lisbjerg Bakke aims to contribute to the development of "the future of social housing" and is thus ecological, social and sustainable. This applies to living quality, the community and economics as well as structural engineering. The complex encompasses two building typologies – terraced and apartment houses – within four groups of dwellings, each with twenty flats around a communal centre. Motor vehicle access is confined to the drive at the communal centre. The wooden design is called Smart-Low-Tech. The operating expense is to be offset by the "reinvention of the roof overhang" and the "replacement of a coat of paint with patina". The interior fittings of the apartments have been ceded to residents in order to enable participation by them and scale back the initial cost. It will continue to be interesting to observe whether this does become "the future of social housing."

Vandkunsten

Friis & Moltke

Waste Incineration Plant ↑↓ 094 H

Ølstedvej 20–36, Lisbjerg
Friis & Moltke
1978/2004

Waste incineration to produce energy has a long-standing history in Denmark. Accordingly, a custom has evolved in which designs for buildings are placed in the hands of good architects. Competitions from previous years have yielded spectacular designs, such as that by BIG featuring a ski slope on the roof. Not only is the architecture ambitious, but also the technology: with the extension in Lisbjerg, up to 30 tonnes of incinerated waste per hour is intended to cover roughly 20 per cent of the heating requirements in the city of Aarhus. The new building in concrete, steel and glass encases the old building dated 1978. The façade composed of profile glazing gives the building mass a façade appearance which changes depending on the wind and the weather.

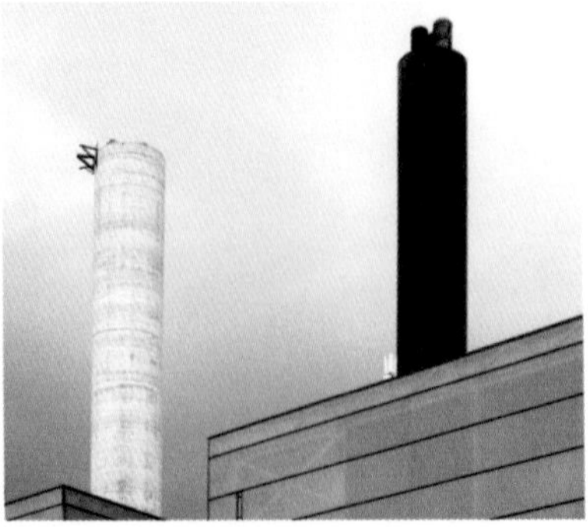

Heiko Weissbach

Lærkehaven, Housing Development ↗ 095 H

Lærkehaven 1–65, Lystrup
Schmidt/Hammer/Lassen, 2010

The largest passive house settlement in Denmark may be found at the Larch Garden address: departments 33 and 35 of the Ringgaarden housing cooperative. Department 35 consists of four by eight double-storey terraced houses covering 100 m^2 to 110 m^2 of living space and a community centre. The international competition stemmed from the EU initiative *Sustainable Housing in Europe*. Here an attempt was made to reduce energy consumption and C02 emissions through a compact building form with a highly insulated envelope surface and heat recovery. Therefore, the buildings are not connected to the district heating grid. Furthermore, the grey energy footprint of the building materials is optimised and the construction period shortened owing to the use of wooden prefabricated elements. The vertical windows and their orientation towards the sun enhance daylight usage. All recreational spaces are oriented towards the west; the main living quarters on the upper storey capture the southern rays via a tower-like construction. Each building along the joint access route, also facing south, has a small inner courtyard with storage space. The compact development forges an autonomous presence outside the city, bearing no relation to its surroundings.

Heiko Weissbach

Lærkehaven,
Housing Development ↓↘

096 H

Lærkehaven 2–102, Lystrup
Thomas Herzog, 2008

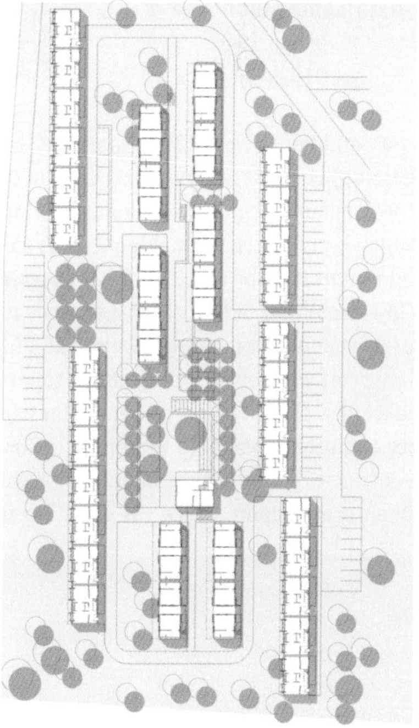

Thomas Herzog Architekten

In 1998, the Munich-based architect Thomas Herzog was awarded the Danish Association of Architects' Green Needle for his sustainable architecture. One decade later, fifty climate-friendly terraced houses were completed in northern Aarhus subsequent to his triumph in an international competition. The prefabricated one- and two-storey wooden buildings clad in larch wood aim to ensure a healthy interior climate and low energy consumption through passive use of solar energy, highly insulated façades featuring low-energy windows and ceiling elements featuring integrated phase change materials, among other things. Each flat has a terrace or a garden, as well as access to a common pavilion.

LIF (Lystrup Idrætsforening), Sustainable Clubhouse ↑
Lystrupvej, Lystrup
CEBRA, 2013

097 H

The clubhouse of LIF (Sports Club Lystrup) posits itself as a contribution to the community-wide Climate Action Plan which is committed to making Aarhus carbon neutral prior to 2030. Both passive (low-tech) and active (high-tech) measures aimed at ensuring a minimal CO2 footprint were enforced. In order to mitigate the consumption of heat, electricity and other operating expenses, unconventional construction methods have been drawn upon. Since the building is primarily used in summer, circulation spaces are located outside beneath a large roof overhang that shields the façade from rain and overheating and reduces cooling requirements. Heat-accumulating sand is used as an in-fill and as a drainage layer. The triple-layered windows are bordered by composite frames. Partitions have been constructed from recycled brick or phase change materials. Photovoltaic elements are installed on to the roof. As a one-storey wooden building with a kinetic roof structure and a roofed outdoor rest and relaxation space, the architecture is not solely idealistic and technical, but also creative and of high quality in terms of its functional role.

Mikkel Frost/CEBRA

Lystrup Church ↓↘ 098 H

Lystrup Centervej 80, Lystrup
Arkitektgruppen Regnbuen
1989

This church building stemmed from a competition held in 1984 which the architects won with a traditional and, at the same time, modern design. The whitewashed masonry building with a red tiled roof rises on an old burial mound in a traditional fashion, affording far-reaching views across the bay. The spatial configuration is modern: visitors roam in a diagonal direction across orthogonal rooms from the entrance to the altar. An octagonal porch forges a transition between the church hall, municipal meeting hall, administration and confirmation room. Light pink limestone with teakwood details lies on the floor. The benches consist of light ash wood with black cushions. The altar, altarpiece and colour scheme are attributed to Hans Berg, whereas the pulpit, baptismal font and the church silver were designed by Bent Exner.

Preben Bager/Lystrup Kirke

Hans Boas/Lystrup Kirke

099 H

C. F. Møllers Architects

Siloetten

099 H

Krajbjergvej 8, Løgten
Christian Carlsen/
C. F. Møller Architects, 2010

Everywhere in Denmark one sees numerous silo facilities, of which many are no longer in use although they continue to visually dominate their surroundings. Upon the development of the central square in the small town of Løgten into a new town centre near a stop belonging to the new regional railway track, the 36 m high concrete silo has been converted into a "high-rise within the countryside", proceeding to become a sculptural emblem for Løgten. One half of the silo was blown up and the remaining part has been converted into a service tower featuring stairs, a lift and bathrooms. The roof terrace affords sweeping views across Kaløvig, the bay of Aarhus and the hills of Mols. The apartments were conceived as a steel structure and integrated into three sides of the silo, creating recesses and cantilevers for large recreational terraces. Together with a subtle colour scheme featuring hues of blue, yellow and red, this new landmark is assigned a varied appearance on all sides. All twenty-one apartments are structured in various ways. These have one or two storeys and between 92 m^2 and 221 m^2 of living space. The building introduces a new type of dwelling which sets a precedent for similar conversions throughout the country.

E+N Arkitektur

Skæring Church
Skæring Kirkevej 1, Egå
Exners Tegnestue
1994

100 H

Villy Fink Isaksen

This church is located in a region with traditional single-family homes lined by hedges; it itself is bordered by a circular hedge and apple trees. Exterior walls in the same red exposed masonry featuring rough joints and striking elements glazed blue blend into the surrounding settlement. The far cantilevered roofs are clad in zinc. The church hall throws the visitor a curve with its light-coloured exposed concrete walls adorned with triangular, sound-absorbing stainless steel cassettes and the floors, also comprising triangular concrete elements which are almost black. As a matter of principle, primary geometric shapes – such as circles, squares and triangles – have been drawn upon for the design in order to imbue the church with a solemn, modern, venerable and laid-back appearance. Daylight is cast in a theatrical role, spilling from a skylight into the room, primarily above the altar. Further bands of narrow windows, indirectly filtering the light, are located at the upper end of the six load-bearing concrete walls. A large abstract chandelier with 216 incandescent bulbs and the diagonally positioned benches fashioned from light wood for roughly 100 churchgoers complement the minimalist interior design. The altar and the baptismal font are made of Norwegian Porsgrunn marble. A gilded cross with embedded gemstones – the work of the silversmith Bent Exner – is located on the altar. Many have condemned it as "ugly", but a church which "looks just how it should" may be easily overlooked. It is necessary to enter an ugly church in order to ascertain whether it is also effectively "ugly" inside. "See for yourself", wrote the pastor of the church on its website. The rectory north of the church was also designed by Inger and Johannes Exner and was built in 1993.

Ole Hein/CUBO

Ole Hein/CUBO

Egå Gymnasium

101 H

Mejlbyvej 4, Egå
CUBO/Kristine Jensens Tegnestue and Schønherr Landskab
2006/2012

This two-storey building of the secondary school in the suburb of Egå lies like an abstract white disc, visible from afar in the open field. At first sight, it might be confused with a company domicile. It was constructed from concrete, steel and glass and deliberately placed as an "island" amidst its rural surroundings. The hilly terrain incorporates various levels within and around the building. Inside, the circular Knowledge Forum is

Thomas Mølvig/CUBO

Ole Hein / CUBO

reached directly from the entrance. This is the most important room in the building featuring a library, laboratories and numerous open workspaces. All other functions are visible from here and fully accessible. Steps and lifts are consciously exposed in order to facilitate orientation. This is accompanied by bridges, galleries and recreational enclaves to promote encounters and interaction. Classrooms and administrative offices lie within the wings of the building around the forum. The sports hall and the canteen have been integrated into the structure, opening up on to the forum and the landscape. In 2012, an extension featuring music classrooms was added to the northern side.

Åkrogen, Housing Development ↓

102 H

Åkrogs Strandvej, Risskov
Arkitema Architects
2006

Eighteen double-storey terraced houses composed of whitewashed masonry are situated not far from Egå Marina, at the narrowest spot of the bay of Aarhus. The buildings are arranged in a U-shape, thus enframing a communal area and rendering possible a similar orientation towards the sun and the bay all round. Its location on the hill of a natural embankment accounted for the design with offset levels. Carports and adjoining rooms

Heiko Weissbach

have been arranged on the lower ground floor. The principal residential level situated above is accessible inside via a staircase or from the outside at ground level. The floor plans of the buildings are narrow with an approximate depth of 20 m. The living room with an open kitchen is large and bright, affording a view across the bay in a south-easterly direction. A balcony capturing the afternoon and evening sun is situated at the other end of the building.

Thorbjørn Hansen/Arkitema Architects

Return of the City to the Water!

Heiko Weissbach

Aarhus is a city which was founded at the water's edge. The history of the city is closely associated with the river and the sea as lifelines and transport routes for people and goods. Of course port facilities played a role from the outset. This once small river port at the mouth of the bay was deemed to be a coastal port for the first time in the mid-nineteenth century. It continued to expand into the bay, proceeding to become the largest workplace of the city in the twentieth century. The increasing size of ships was accompanied by the incessant growth of port space, creating a physical and visual barrier between the city and the bay. As a result the city turned in on itself. Rather than taking a stroll along the waterfront in downtown Aarhus, people became accustomed to swerving to the north or south when seeking a panoramic view, sea air, the beach or the sun. In 1996 a new master plan was presented to the public, pursuant to which the total area of the port facilities was to expand by a further 150 ha to cover a total of 260 ha and almost 10 km of quayside. The port authorities perceived this development as a matter of course since this area – by historical and statistical standards – has doubled roughly every thirty years, although the number of jobs has fallen steadily owing to the rationalisation and automation of loading mechanisms. In compliance with the latest EU-wide regulations, the master plan was made subject to an environmental impact assessment and was presented for discussion among the general public in the hearing phase. For the first time in history, hundreds of individual citizens, stakeholders, associations and institutions put forward a written objection to the proposed development and expressed vocal concern during public debates, for example in the town hall. Points of criticism centred on:

- Density of delivery traffic by truck amidst the city
- Noise exposure, air pollution and the risk of accidents
- Health risks posed by the production and handling of dangerous goods in close proximity to residential areas
- Physical prevention of urban development on the waterfront

Despite massive resistance, the municipal authority adopted the master plan in 1997 and it has been largely implemented over the subsequent twenty years. Owing to extensive, detailed and ongoing criticism among citizens and environmental groups, two promises have been given on behalf of the municipal authorities and port administration: firstly, funds were to be earmarked for tunnelling the main transport artery to the port, Marselis Boulevard, in the longer term, so as to ensure that at least the immediate environmental footprint which thousands of vehicles passing through densely populated suburbs give rise to each day is capped. Despite repeated studies and planning approaches, the tunnel is yet to be built.

← View across the periurban port areas and Aarhus Ø

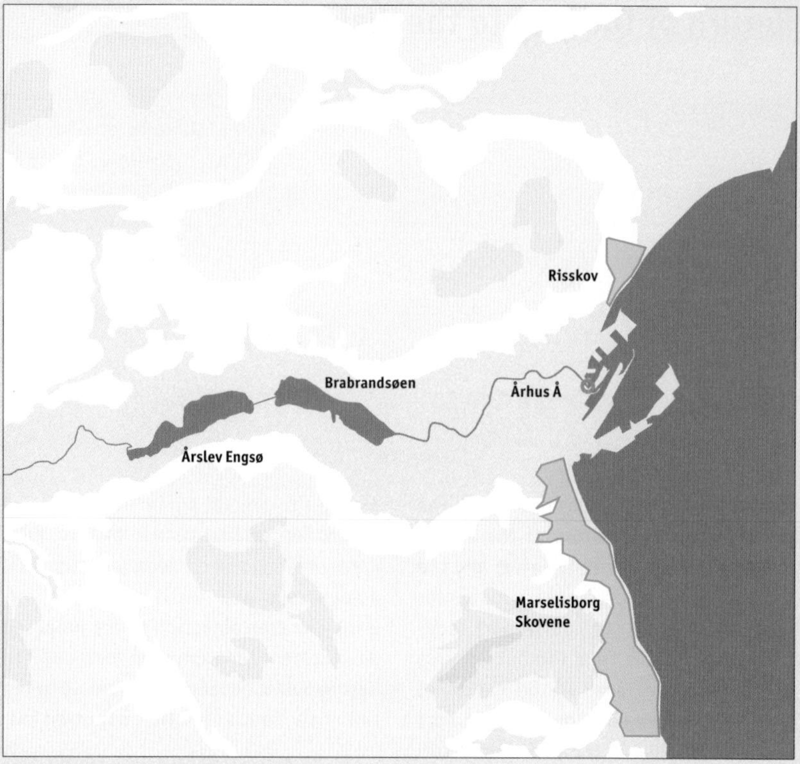

Heiko Weissbach

Diagram of the coastline featuring the port, the forests, the river and its estuary

The second promise to citizens concerned the execution of an urban planning competition for the development of port areas on the periphery of town. The construction of a vast new container port and further complexes meant that the port could no longer uphold its obligations toward the oldest, most run-down stretches over the long-term. Therefore, Aarhus was given the unique opportunity to create urban recreational areas again, at least on the port space adjacent to the city centre. The open urban planning competition involving 150 practices from Denmark and abroad took place in 1999. The winners of the competition were the Copenhagen-based architects Knud Fladeland Nielsen and Peer Teglgaard Jeppesen. The design essentially seeks to restore the city's access to water. Numerous sketches, plans, models, diagrams and descriptions portray an in-depth analysis of the history and visualise prospects for the future. This wealth of competition materials was further embellished and incorporated into town-planning guidelines within a short period of time.

In the autumn of 2003, the municipality published an overarching plan for port areas peripheral to the town as a basis for comprehensive urban redevelopment regarding the central, southern and northern parts of the port. The essential aspects outlined therein are:

- To bring the city, the harbour and the bay closer to each other,
- To create new correlations between the city and the water through the construction of a central, open, multifunctional harbour immediately in front of and aligned with the scale of the city centre, among other things,
- To establish a coherent promenade for cyclists and pedestrians along a canal between the wooded areas in the north (Risskov) and the south (Marselisborg),
- To create development opportunities which on the one hand preserve the port atmosphere but on the other take care not to curtail its operations,
- To pool together the commercial activities of the harbour within the new southern and eastern harbour,

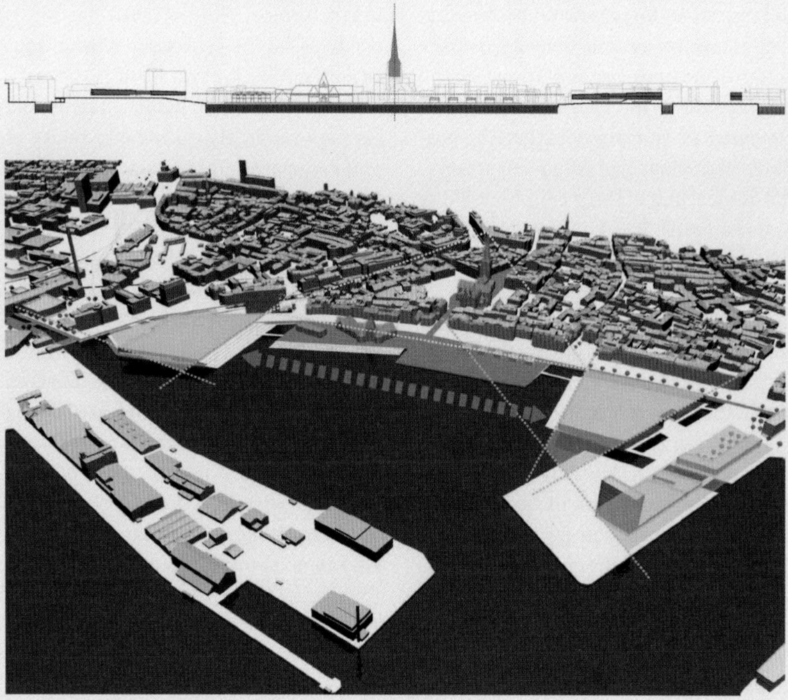

Knud Fladeland

Master plan for the periurban port areas by Knud Fladeland

- To create a framework – such as canals and infrastructure, plots and building heights, open spaces, and much more besides – as a common thread for the conversion of periurban port areas.

These objectives were fleshed out in the *Quality Manual for Periurban Port Areas* which was published in January 2008. The architect Knud Fladeland served as continuous advisor on the elaboration of all planning foundations and became the permanent consultant to the city. In 2007, the city took possession of the first areas of the port and the first construction projects were set in motion. The first occupants moved in a mere five years subsequent to this. In 2013 the cumbersome term *periurban port areas* was discarded and the new urban district within the former container port was rechristened Aarhus Ø. The Danish vowel Ø on its own means "island", although it is also the abbreviation of the cardinal point "east". It is precisely this which the new name seeks to encapsulate: a new urban district east of the centre imparting the nature of an island. The very first sketches by Knud Fladeland outlined the basic concept of separating the natural coastline from the port space which had been artificially filled in in stages – both in an emblematic and concrete manner through the construction of a canal, accompanied by a promenade for pedestrians and cyclists – the so-called recreational link

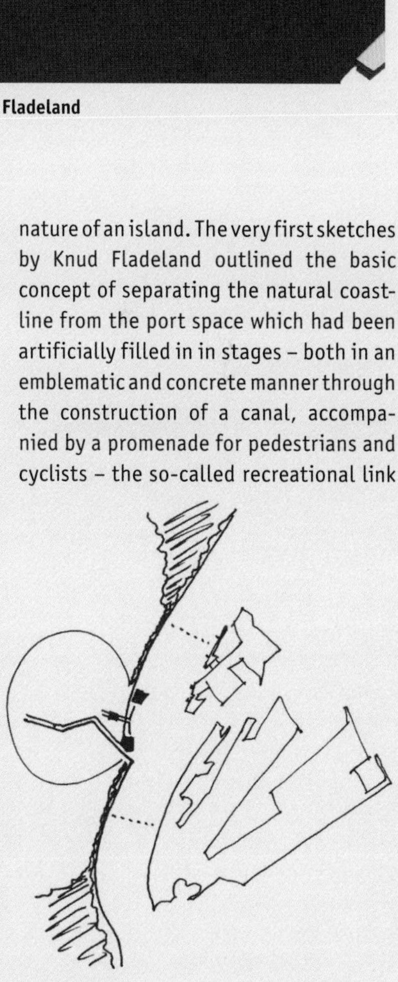

Knud Fladeland

Sketch demarcating the natural coastline and the port space

between the Risskov forest to the north and Marselisborg forest to the south. It was crucial to forge new urban rapports with the water (which went beyond the demarcation line). Vistas of the water and the expanse of the bay were to be foregrounded in as many locations as possible, assuming overriding importance. The dismantling of the pier in front of the Customs House building was decided on and carried out in order to create a vast coherent expanse of water.

Two bastions, between which the new port was set to emerge, clearly marked off and delineated this new expanse of water within the city centre.

The southern bastion, boasting a prominent location in the immediate vicinity of the river estuary and reopened riverbed, emerged in the form of the new complex Urban Media Space under the name of Dokk1, which is both a major traffic hub, public underground car park, library, municipal office, new venue and urban terrace. The northern bastion is occupied by the centre for science education and innovation Navitas, beneath which there is also a public underground car park to largely rid the city centre of parking spaces. The new urban harbour space spans over 400 m between both bastions and delineates the new interface between the city and the inner harbour basin. The practice owned by the landscape architect Kristine Jensen followed the underlying concepts outlined in the master plan by Knud Fladeland and developed new urban spaces as a "robust ground" comprising light-coloured concrete. This is laid out in large elements with a human dimension of 40 cm x 200 cm x 25 cm at various levels and in various patterns and finishes. This vast expanse is to be used as a "realm

Photo of a model of the new urban harbour space

of opportunity" on tranquil working days as well as for concerts and events of all kinds. Therefore, it is supplied with electricity and internet access and is connected to the water supply and drainage network. A series of lighting masts illuminates the area, one of which is to act as a sun dial during the day. A series of elongated wooden benches are strategically located (that is to say, in places affording generous views and ample exposure to the sun). Furthermore, 150 trees are being planted anew along the esplanade. However, before the architectural design could be implemented it was firstly necessary to assimilate the profile of the once busy coastal road – situated in front of the historic row of buildings, including the palace, schools and hotel – to its future setting. This involved scaling back the rail tracks to make way for the track bed of the new regional railway, cycle paths, the promenade and the canal, with the aim of separating the city from the harbour – both symbolically and in real terms. The greatest challenge lay arguably in the lifting of all those physical barriers between the city and the water which had hindered a spontaneous stroll along the waterfront until a few years ago. It goes without saying that ships will be able to moor here in future, such as, for example, that of the Queen. Together with her prince consort, she traditionally spends a part of the summer in Aarhus each year. Painstaking and detailed development plans have been compiled for the new urban quarters in the north – drawing inspiration from and based on experience gained in other European port cities, such as Oslo, Hamburg and Barcelona – in order to lend definition to overarching and sustainable concepts which can be implemented in detail. The quality manual by

Kristine Jensen

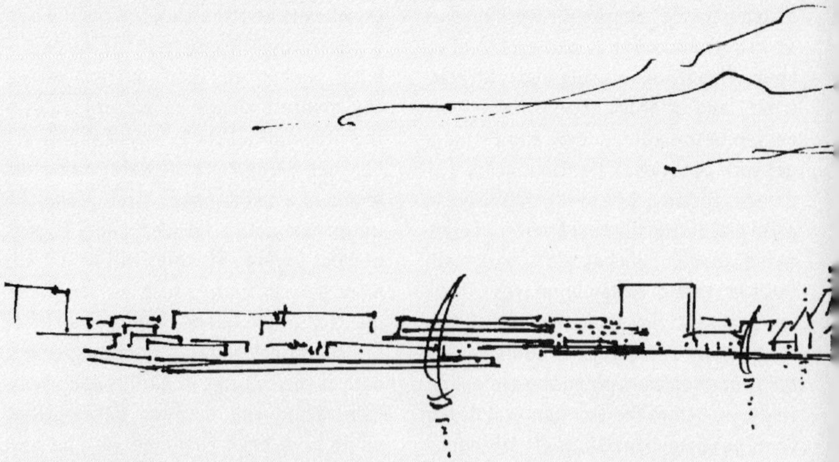

Sketch of the city silhouette from the water – an arrival drawing comparisons to Venice

Knud Fladeland provided balanced guidelines for sustainable development – from the large-scale profile of the boulevard and transport infrastructure to the definition of different forms of (mixed) use as well as details regarding the design for open spaces or the quayside.

Although the underlying concepts of the development plan, which was adopted in 2003, should be commended for lasting at least three legislative periods, it cannot be left unsaid that the financial crisis of 2008/2009, among other factors, slowed down implementation and led to the neglecting of several principles. Urban planning regulations on prominent sites were softened for financially sound investors seeking to build and create jobs. For example, the headquarters of the Bestseller fashion house are located at one of the places where vistas overlooking the water were to be created. Both Bestseller and the neighbouring scientific centre for innovation Navitas not only disrupt the framework conditions of urban planning, but also the scale of the adjacent historic urban perimeter featuring buildings with four to five storeys.

Critics also regard the much-lauded and award-winning Dokk1 as not merely an asset, but a foreign body. They impugn its interplay with the urban infrastructure and the – absence of – dialogue with buildings of historic significance, such as the Customs House building by Hack Kampmann, which is not merely the first port of call on the waterfront, but which also draws inspiration from the municipal coat of arms in its design. Mixed uses and public functions were assigned to the ground floor for new buildings within the new urban district of Aarhus Ø, but

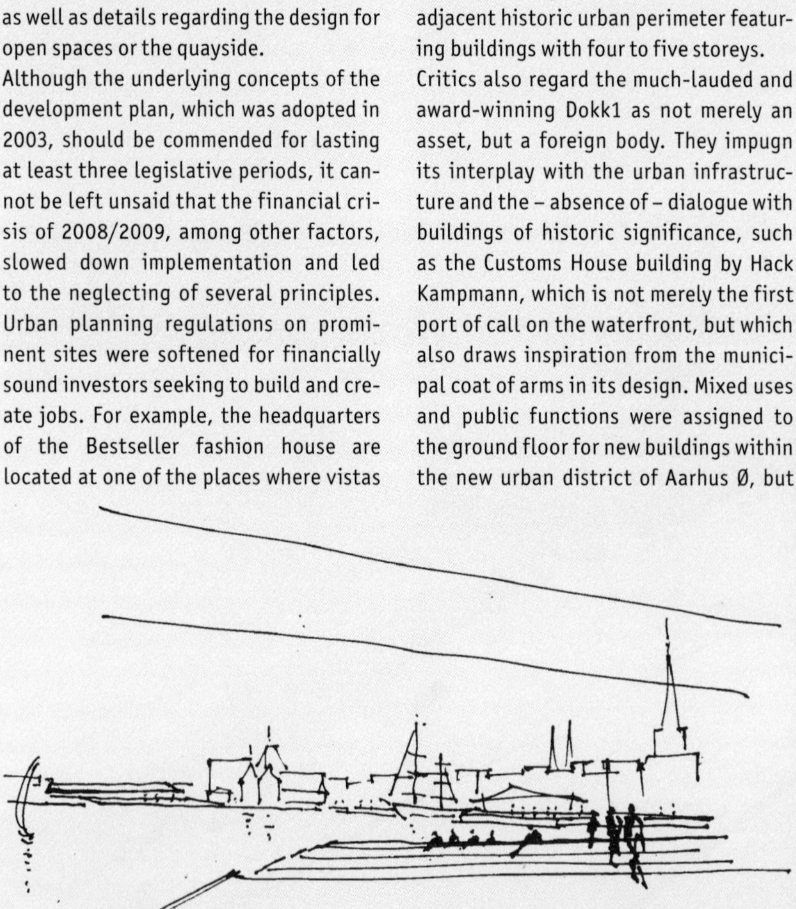

Sketch of the new harbour in the direction of the Customs House and the Cathedral

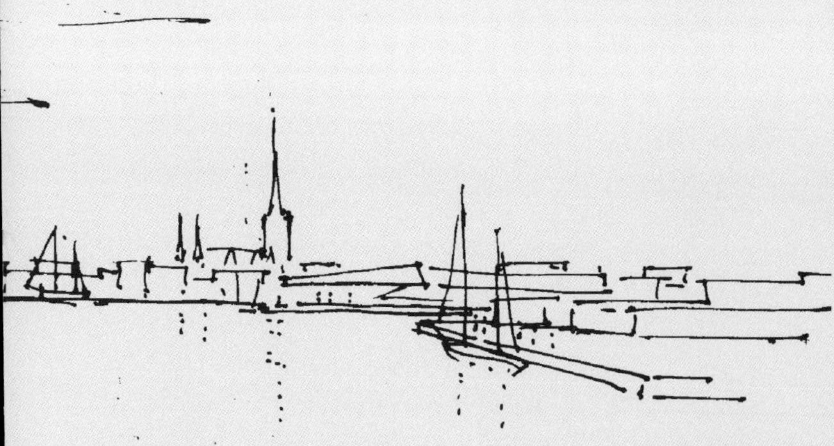

Knud Fladeland

requirements were not strictly met. Standards with little lasting effect were also couched in terms which go beyond the scope of currently valid building regulations and those promoting energy efficiency, although several architects and clients have voluntarily planned and built in a more sustainable manner. Only time will tell whether a completely new urban district created from scratch and almost exclusively composed of residential buildings is fundamentally viable over the long term. Fresh hopes – but also concerns with regard to the originally proposed visual axes between the city centre, the new harbour and Dokk1 – are pinned on the designs for the development at Bassin 7, where dynamic project developers and renowned architects are planning at least one intermixed urban district. In addition to countless luxury flats which are sold at unprecedentedly high prices even before being mapped out, a harbour pool and other public functions are also set to emerge.

The southern harbour holds great potential for the future of Aarhus. Countless throwbacks to the former industrial premises continue to be visible here, as well as among others the so-called Coal Crane Bridge (*kulkranbroen*), which, inspired by the High Line in New York, is to be preserved and remodelled. Trailblazers demonstrating creative potential have already moved into the old vacant slaughterhouse and other abandoned industrial halls. Developers are giving architects full rein to draw up the initial designs for new buildings. Maybe there will be an integral urban district boasting a mix of old and new with historical traits and a vision of the future.

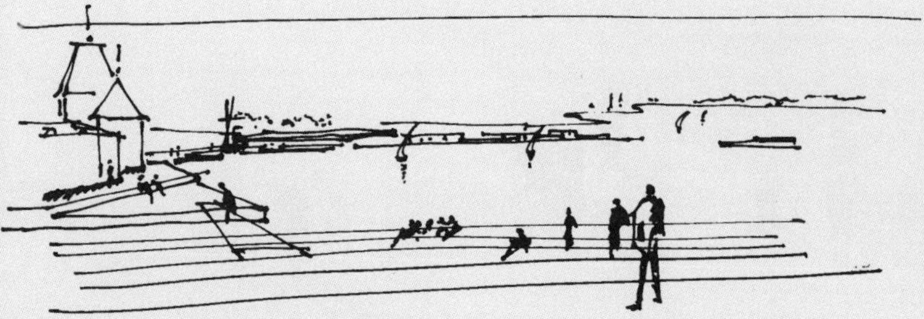

Knud Fladeland

Sketch of the new harbour from the southern bastion in the direction of Aarhus Ø

Visualisation of the new harbour with the Royal Yacht Dannebrog on the quayside

Arkitekt Kristine Jensens Tegnestue / 0003A

Periurban Port Areas and Aarhus Ø

Stjerne-
pladsen
Lyøgade
Jordbrovej
Tåsingegade
O.H.A.
Haveforening
Jens Chr.
Skous Vej
Finsensgade
Louis Hammerichs Vej
Herambsgade
Langelandsgade
Fredrik
Nielsens Vej
Nordre Ringgade
Nørrebrogade
Trøjborgvej
Barthsgade
Aldersrovej
Willemoesgade
Ivar Huitfeldts Gade
Peder Skrams Gade
Skjoldsgade
Herluf Trolles
Tordenskjold
Otte Ruds Gade
Niels Juels Gade
Trøjborgvej
Skovvan
Victor Albecks Vej
Karl Verners Vej
Ole Worms Allé
Bartholins Allé
Skt. Johannes
Alle
Larsen-Ledets
Gade
Peter Sabroes Gade
Wilhelm Meyers
Allé
Ny Munkegade
C. F. Møllers Allé
Ærøgade
Vennelyst Boulevard
Nørre Boulevard
Kirkegårdsvej
Kaserneboulevarden
Høegh-guldbergs Gade
Østboulevarden
Langelandsgade
Falstersgade
Fynsgade
Vennelyst
Plads
Nørrebrogade
Østbane-
torvet
Samsøgade
Sjællandsgade
Knudrisgade
Molsgade
Kaløgade
Hjelmensgade
Sølystgade
Samsøgade
Hjarnøgade
Lollandsgade
Norsgade
Nørregade
Nørreport
Kystvejen
Sverigesgade
Grønnegade
Paradisgade
Studsgade
Snevringen
Mejlgade
105
Sejrøgade
Nørre Allé
Klosterport
Guldsmedgade
Borggade
104
Hjortensgade
Langelandsgade
Teglværksgade
Volden
Vesterbrogade
Vester Allé
Vestergade
Rosensgade
Mejlgade
Skolebakken
Møllegade
Grønnegade
Immervad
Bispetorvet
Museumsgade
Kannikegade
Åboulevarden
Skolegade
007
Åboulevarden
Havnegade
Bissensgade
Christiansgade
Busgaden
Fiskergade
Mindebrogade
Hack Kampmanns Plads
Marstrandsgade
Vester Allé
Frederiksgade
Østergade
103
Aros Allé
Søndergade
Amaliegade
Mindegade
Europa
Plads
Rådhuspladsen
Sønder Allé

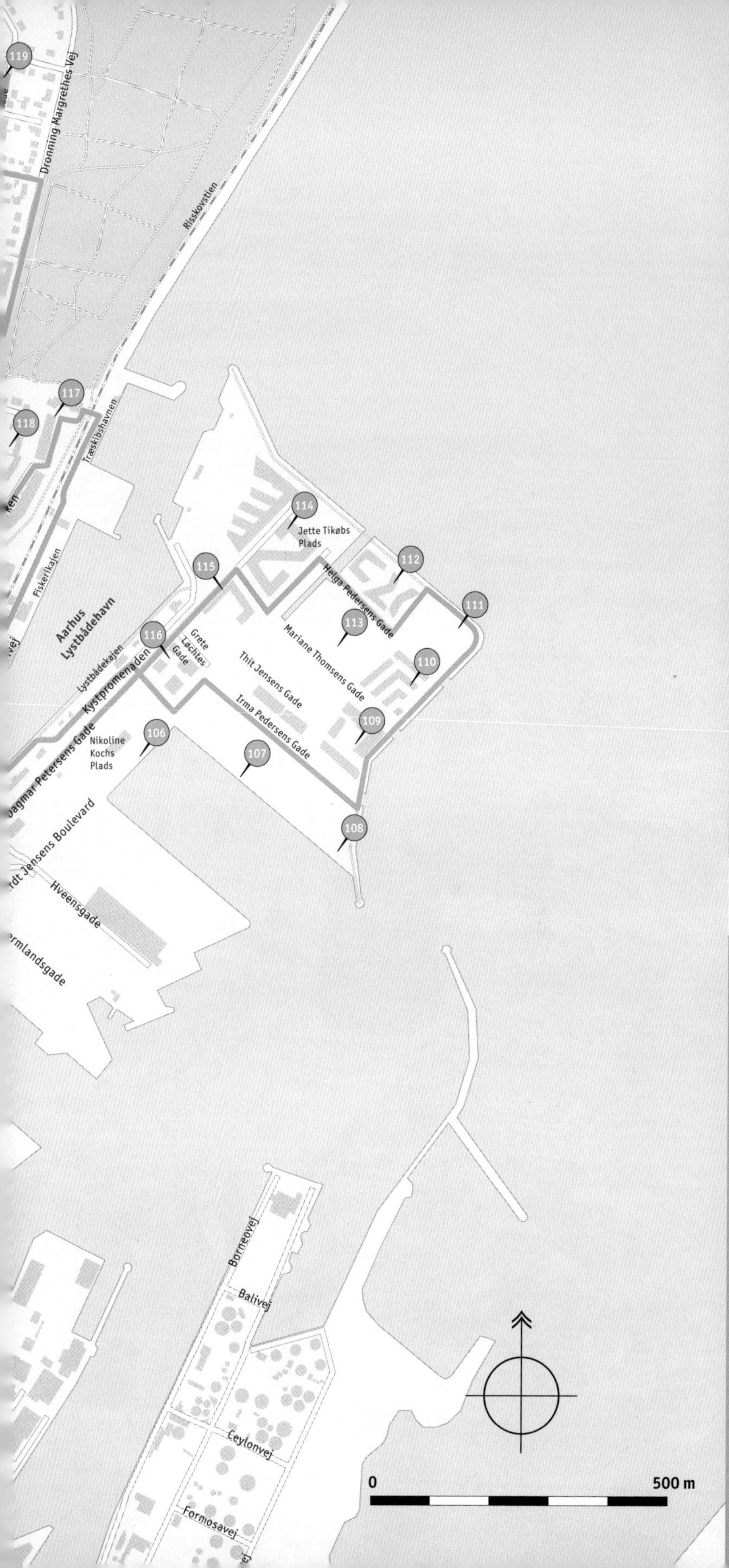
119
Dronning Margrethes Vej
Risskovstien
117
118
Træskibshavnen
114
Jette Tikøbs Plads
112
115
Helga Pedersens Gade
111
113
Fiskerikajen
Aarhus Lystbådehavn
116
Grete Løchtes Gade
Mariane Thomsens Gade
110
Lystbådekajen
Kystpromenaden
Thit Jensens Gade
109
Irma Pedersens Gade
Nikoline Kochs Plads
106
107
Dagmar Petersens Gade
108
Hveensgade
Borneovej
Balivej
Ceylonvej
Formosavej
0
500 m

I

116
114
112
110
109
Bassin 7
105
104
007
103
017
020
018
016
015
Comwell

056
021
dlg
dlg

Adam Mørk / Schmidt/Hammer/Lassen

Dokk1

103 I

Hack Kampmanns Plads 2
Schmidt/Hammer/Lassen/
Kristine Jensens Tegnestue,
2015

The building named Dokk1 (pronounced *Dokk-en*) lies on the estuary leading into the bay and is one of the two bastions at the crossing-point between city and harbour which are laid out in the master plan by Knud Fladeland for the harbour area adjacent to the city (see essay no. 5). With 36,000 m² of floor space, it is said to be the largest public library in Scandinavia. This multi-functional building contains the former central library (see 047) as well as the municipal archives, the city administrative headquarters and office rental space. The ground floor, being at street level, serves traffic and provides access. This is where a stop for the new regional railway and an automated underground car park for approximately 1,000 vehicles is located. Any cars entering disappear into elaborately designed and well-illuminated lift cars. Pedestrians seek out public functions on the storeys above via internal stairs and lifts or via four large, spacious external stairs visible from any orientation. The steps facing west towards the river promenade and the city centre are seen to be extending a welcoming gesture toward citizens. The harbour's new esplanade runs around the block at street level; large concrete surfaces fan out like ice floes, inviting one to linger by the river or port. The first and second upper storeys have square floor plans and fully glazed façades. The uppermost storey features a polygonal floor plan projecting above those below. Likewise, the circumferential terrace on the first upper storey is

Adam Mørk / Schmidt/Hammer/Lassen

Adam Mørk / Schmidt/Hammer/Lassen

polygonal and cantilevered. The library is an open space supported by pillars with various levels and ceiling heights, organised in a broad-meshed grid featuring ceiling voids for skylights and confined areas for subsidiary functions. The so-called media ramp is centrally located in the building, beneath a large skylight. This has five different platforms catering to various functions and leads to the second floor, where the children's and young adults' library is to be found. The rented office space on the third floor has an unimpaired view of life in the library. The interior of the library also has two event rooms lacking in daylight: a smaller one for seventy people and a larger one for up to 300 people. The building has been constructed from robust materials such as concrete, steel, glass and wood. The façades and cantilevered ceilings are clad in expanded metal. The main rooms and areas have been assigned specially chosen colours and surfaces – such as, for example, the wooden cladding of the main hall. In order to meet the 2015 Danish energy criteria for buildings, approximately 2,400 m^2 of photovoltaic panels have been installed on the roof to produce self-renewable energy. In addition, seawater is used for cooling.

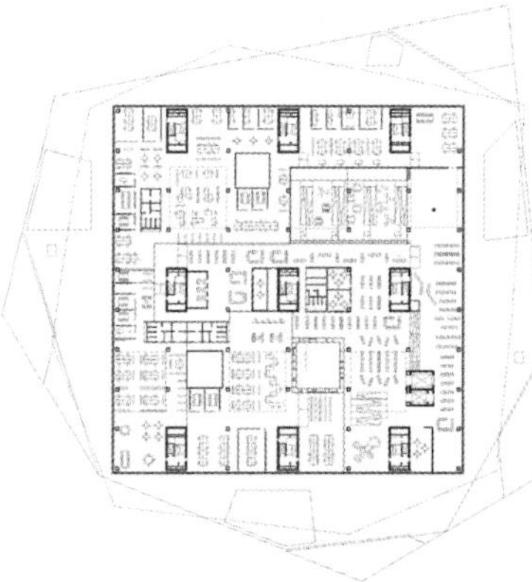

Schmidt/Hammer/Lassen

Adam Mørk / Schmidt/Hammer/Lassen

DOKK
POST-
EUROPE

103 I

Adam Mørk / Schmidt/Hammer/Lassen

Adam Mørk / Kjær & Richter

Navitas,
Scientific Innovation Centre

104 I

Inge Lehmanns Gade 10
Kjær & Richter/
Christensen & Co./
Marianne Levinsen Landskab, 2014

The star-shaped Navitas building is one of the two "bastions" outlined in the master plan by Knud Fladeland for the peri-urban port areas (see Essay 5). In terms of urban development, the centre disrupts the scale of the four- to five-storey historic buildings situated behind along Kystvejen owing to its horizontally layered façade composed of black, white and transparent glass sheets. Navitas unites the engineering disciplines of the University, Aarhus School of Marine and Technical Engineering and the INCUBA Science Park on an area covering 38,000 m² to boost collaboration among higher education, research and business. The expertise of the institutions lies in the field of energy and environmental technologies. This low-energy building

Heiko Weissbach

with photovoltaic panels is itself an illustrative laboratory owing to its innovative technical and structural approaches. Apart from numerous offices, it contains classrooms and conference rooms, a canteen, fitness rooms and a café. Imparting an inviting presence, vast recreational spaces covered with wood are oriented towards the south and the water. The lower storeys provide 685 parking spaces, 450 of which are for the public – these were co-financed by the city of Aarhus in order to free up the city centre.

Lars Ditlev Pedersen / Kjær & Richter

Adam Mørk / C.F. Møller Architects

Bestseller, Headquarters

105 I

Inge Lehmanns Gade 2
C.F. Møllers tegnestue
2015

In terms of urban development, the new domicile of the Bestseller fashion company occupies a prestigious position in front of Nørreport street on the new waterfront and is encircled by water basins and canals. The daily work environment catering to roughly 750 employees covers a space of 22,000 m². The building complex has been conceived as a city within a city, containing exhibition space, presentation rooms, offices, studios and a canteen. Five structures with up to ten storeys rise above an elevated ground level. The natural stone façade is an orthogonal grid and frames large glass panels of equal size. The interior also contains large surfaces of Sicilian stone in the form of stairways, floors and wall panelling. The pale stone sets up a play with the dark oak, exposed concrete and metal surfaces. The building is arranged along an inner corridor on the first floor to allow room for a covered delivery area on the ground floor. The entrance bridge affords sweeping views across all building storeys. The internal connecting axis culminates in the company restaurant which is separated into set area of disparate size and design – with access to a recreational outdoor area commanding views over the bay and the city, of course.

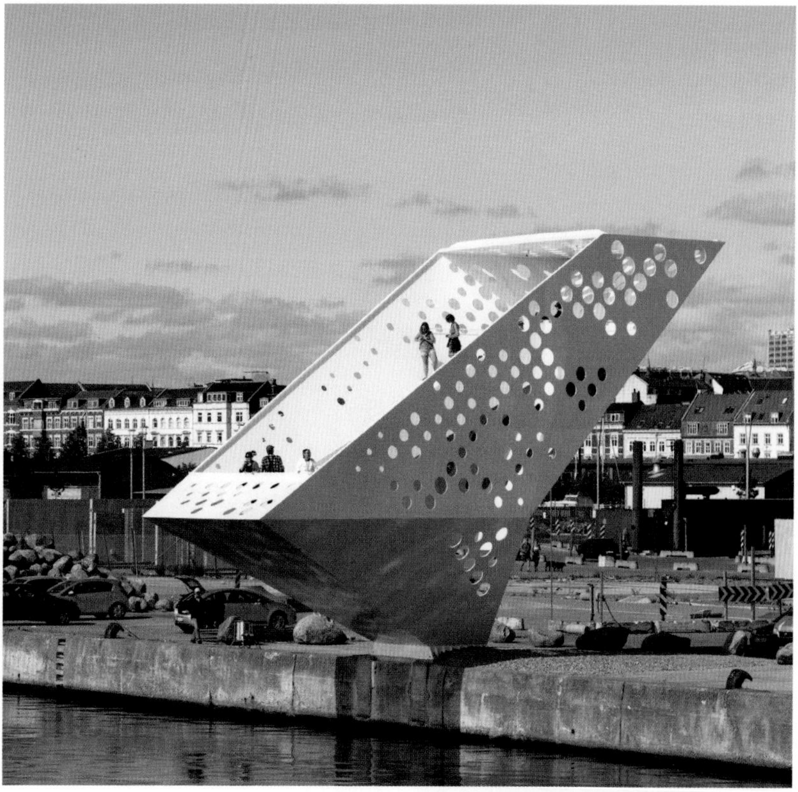

Torben Eskerod / Dorte Mandrup Arkitekter

Salling Tower

106 I

Bernhardt-Jensens-Boulevard
Dorte Mandrup Arkitekter
2015

The white Salling Tower is the new landmark and meeting place at the port of Aarhus – sponsored by the Salling Foundation and designed by Dorte Mandrup, who refers to the building as "sharply cut origami". According to the architect, the tower is an "urban sculpture with an architectural concept", the style of which contains nautical references, such as sails and portholes. Steel plates with a thickness of up to 30 mm have been used for the construction. Together, these weigh over 80 tonnes. The tower was originally due to be built in a dockyard, but following the tender process the contract was awarded to a company specialising in steel construction. The tower is thus completely prefabricated and was transported in one piece to the location at Bassin 7. The large surfaces are perforated with round holes of differing size – affording views in a wide array of orientations – in order to scale back the overall weight and wind loads. In the evening and at night, the tower is illuminated from within and emits light across a long distance – just as a ship's navigational lights do.

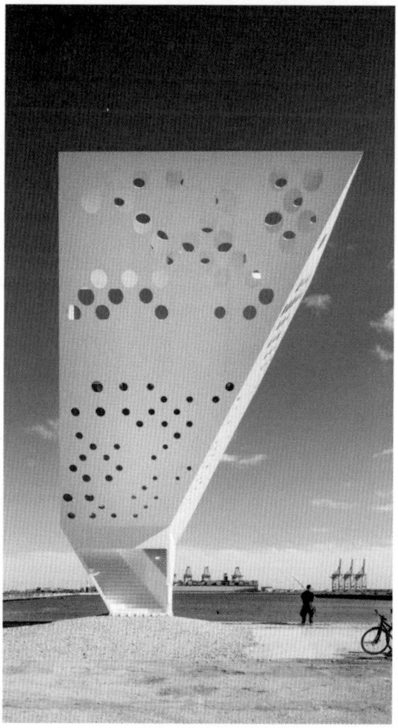

Torben Eskerod / Dorte Mandrup Arkitekter

Quintin Lake/dorte mandrup arkitekter

Harbour Pool

Bassin 7
BIG/Gehl Architects
2017

107 I

In common with the tower at the end of Bassin 7, the future harbour pool is also a gift courtesy of the Salling Foundation. The internationally acclaimed Danish architect Bjarke Ingels had already built up expertise in the construction of harbour pools. One of the first projects to be implemented by his former practice PLOT (together with Julien De Smedt between 2001 and 2006) was the harbourfront area Islands Brygge in Copenhagen which was a resounding success and a real eye-opener for citizens and politicians alike in terms of the significance of water as a recreational resource. Its success is to be repeated in Aarhus, where the harbour pool is part of the land development plan for the southwestern region of the new urban district of Aarhus Ø. The laying of the foundation stone in May 2016 also spelt the end of the temporary beach bar assigned to the undeveloped plot of land for years – to the great delight of the entire city. The new harbour is earmarked for construction in hardwood and is set to contain several swimming pools, an observation and diving tower, changing rooms and cafés and restaurants. It is scheduled to open in the summer of 2017 – roughly a year prior to construction itself at Bassin 7.

BIG

AARhus, Housing Development 108 I

Bassin 7

BIG

2018

AAR is the international airport code for Aarhus and lends its name to this proposed development. If we lend credence to the renderings of the architects and the marketing strategies of the brokers, "AARhus' magnificent architecture is intended to place the city of Aarhus on the world map." The new development at Bassin 7 will "convert fiction into fact". "People will be astonished, taken by surprise, draw inspiration from and fall in love in Aarhus." You will be "struck by restaurants, cafés, a small theatre, a series of bathing pavilions and much more" – "AARhus is thus the perfect setting for everyday life and recreation among people at large". According to the newspapers, the apartments are being "snapped up" at hitherto unheard of prices. The city of Aarhus is somewhat departing from the land development plan dated 2006 in order to pave the way for international consortiums with *starchitects* on board. The DNA of the design is to comprise "townhouses in the island-street quarter, and the residential blocks in Frederiksbjerg, combined with inspiration drawn from the towers of the city and the small, narrow streets, squares, cafés and restaurants within the Latin Quarter." The design is associated with the buildings by the BIG practice in Copenhagen, Shanghai or New York – a terraced landscape composed of stacked storeys with a recessed glazed façade, formally demarcated and defined by the contours and building alignments set out in the master plan, albeit with magnificent peaks of differing height at the corners which are in turn connected to the valleys of the common base. The large terraces of the private apartments on the uppermost storeys are staggered in height and define the coherent outline of the roof. All apartments have small balconies facing the inner courtyard which is to be designed as a large, communal kitchen garden. The garden is elevated two storeys above the site since garages are to be incorporated below. The elevated ground level is set to contain rental space for maritime activities, shops and communal areas which are to be accessible from the street. Small boathouses along the border of the basin are intended to inject life into the area surrounding the new building.

Julian Weyer/C.F. Møllers Architects

Havneholmen, Housing Estate ↑↓ 109 I

Bernhardt Jensens Blvd
C.F. Møllers tegnestue, 2016

Havneholmen is a new housing estate with 400 apartments on an attractive site in Aarhus Ø commanding views across the port, the city and the bay. The design is intended to evoke traditional canal houses with elevating mechanisms located outside. Accordingly, black steel girders, from which cantilevered balconies seem to be suspended, are placed on narrow white concrete slabs on the roof. The fully glazed façades boast an array of colours. The apartments placed within vary in size from two to five rooms with 73 m² to 145 m² of living space in order to foster a multifaceted composition of occupants. Roughly one third of apartments are configured for use by elderly occupants. The inner courtyards are relieved of traffic and planted with vegetation on a par with that in coastal regions.

Iceberg, Housing Estate ↓→ 110 I

Bernhardt Jensens Boulevard/ Jette Tikjøbs Plads
CEBRA (Aarhus)/Julien de Smedt, Louis Paillard (Paris)/ SeARCH (Amsterdam), 2013

The execution of this spectacular housing estate - the Iceberg (*Isbjerget*) – is the outcome of an international collaboration among three architectural practices. In 2007, the underlying design was awarded first prize in a competition, yet construction was postponed by several years owing to the financial crisis. The housing complex lies exposed on the peak of the new urban district of Aarhus Ø on the site of the former container port and draws its inspiration from the continuous movement of floating ice floes. Arguably in keeping with the architects' traditional approach to their work, the block perimeter development with a homogenous eaves height effortlessly dissolves into three L-shaped, parallel buildings and one tower block,

Julian Weyer/C.F. Møllers Architects

Jan Laursen / CEBRA

with the aim of furnishing as many apartments as possible with a view over the water. The complex contains 208 condominiums and rental housing across 25,000 m² of residential space. The variation in buildings inevitably gives rise to various types of dwelling – from small studio flats to maisonettes and penthouses. The façades consist of smoothly polished terrazzo with white aggregates, underpinning the idea of an iceberg. The entire complex features façades segmented into triangles. The partially cantilevered balconies have glazed balustrades in several hues of blue, intended to evoke the shimmering light commonly found within the interior of large expanses of ice.

Mikkel Frost / CEBRA

Mikkel Frost / CEBRA

Mikkel Frost / CEBRA

3XN

Lighthouse, High-rise

Helga Petersens Gade
3XN/Ultimo, 2018

111 I

The new urban district within the former container port is named Aarhus Ø, although it is also internationally known as *Aarhus Docklands*. Likewise, the flagship project at the peak of the jetty has been internationally baptised Lighthouse (see also 112). The original design dated 2012 contains a 130 m high high-rise with a façade similar to that of the lower buildings already established during the first phase of construction. The new high-rise is set to contain further luxury apartments, offices, a restaurant and a sky bar as well as a subterranean car park. Regrettably, it was established during the initial stage of construction, that the subsoil was unable to carry the load of a high-rise. This threw doubt on the feasibility of the project and it was suspended for an indefinite period. However, at the end of 2016 a new high-rise project was tendered which had been altered in keeping with circumstances. The execution of this is provisionally scheduled to take place by 2018. In the meantime, the vacant site has been used as a space for Urban Farming – likewise an international trend to reach Aarhus. The Island Garden (*Ø-haven*), as the area is known, is composed of more than 1,000 pallet gardens where intrigued urban dwellers, against payment of a symbolic rental sum, can cultivate vegetables and flowers and rear hens.

3XN

Adam Mørk / 3XN

Lighthouse,
Housing Estate

112 I

Helga Petersens Gade/
Jette Tikjøbs Plads
3XN/UN Studio/Gehl Architects
2013

The Lighthouse estate creates a new urban quarter within the former container port, where linear, angled terraced housing and a proposed high-rise are to establish a coherent environment in lieu of the block perimeter development. Curved balcony parapets in white fibre concrete, stainless steel, aluminium and glass connecting the individual storeys are used in the design for the circumferential façade. The unruly lines of the façade and the proportion of glass, amounting to 70 per cent, seek to evoke a maritime context. The development plan proposes a blend of private, semi-private and public spaces in interplay with a newly conceived promenade and a square offering recreational and leisure opportunities, thereby creating a safe and homogeneous community. In the planning phase wind and weather conditions were subjected to examination on site, in addition to urban aspects. The buildings are placed in relation to each other to prevent wind corridors as much as possible. All 400 apartments – of which 300 are condominiums and 100 for rental housing – have balconies, exposure to sunlight and a view across the water. The grounds are free of traffic. A subterranean car park for residents is located beneath the residential complex.

Adam Mørk / 3XN

AART architects

Pakhusene, Residential and Office Towers
Mariane Thomsens Gade
AART
2017

113 I

Pakhusene (Warehouses) denotes a complex composed of five towers with up to twelve storeys which – as one of the few new building projects in Aarhus Ø – teams apartments with commercial units to create a "quarter that never sleeps". Residents of the quarter have access to communal functions, such as sport and wellness resorts, conference rooms and a canteen as well as a roof terrace. Several of these functions are reserved for corporate users during the day, although private users may hire these in the evening or on weekends to host activities. The canteen is also to serve as a restaurant for the entire city in the evening or on weekends. The warehouses feature consistently dark brown brick façades. Three of the five towers with 15,000 m² of floor space were built prior to the end of 2016 (9,000 for offices and 6,000 for flats). Upon completion, the five towers will have 35,000 m² of floor space and a car park with 130 parking spaces.

AART architects

Heiko Weissbach

Z-Huset, Residential Block 114 I

Dagmar Petersens Gade
SAHL Arkitekter
(Today's Rambøll), 2017

The "Z-House" was given its name owing to its floor plan geometry: three large and two small terraced slab-like buildings with white façades enframe two triangular inner courtyards. Contrary to most of the residential buildings boasting a waterside location, the terraces and the balconies of Z-Huset facing the land are oriented to the west. The living rooms command views across the neighbouring marina and the Risskov forest. The northernmost slab-like building alone affords uninterrupted views over the bay in a northerly direction. Z-Huset is a (in Denmark) traditional building composed of concrete elements with load-bearing concrete interior walls and façades clad in white aluminium sheet which, together with the glazed parapets, lend the building a lightweight feel. The building complex solely contains exclusive condominiums with 87 m² to 204 m² of living space and was executed in several stages between 2011 and 2017.

SAHL Arkitekter

Havnehusene, Housing Estate 115 I

Dagmar Petersens Gade
ADEPT and Luplau & Poulsen/
Niels Boldt, 2015

Jesper Larsen / ADEPT

The Harbour Houses (*Havnehusene*) are a social housing block owned by the cooperative housing association, Brabrand Boligforening. The ten residential buildings with four to eleven storeys and one flat per storey were built on the construction site available as a classic block perimeter development around a leafy inner courtyard sheltered from the wind, thus enabling all apartments to benefit from a view across the bay on at least two sides. This approach complies with the requirements of the master plan for the new urban district of Aarhus Ø, according to which taller buildings must be oriented towards the new boulevard and decrease in height behind. The offer extends from two- to four-room apartments containing 80 m² to 115 m² of living space for both families and the generation aged fifty-five and older. In addition to these eighty-three "normal" apartments, there are a further 179 young people's and student flats within a compact building between the apartment blocks and communal facilities. Beyond the leafy courtyard complex, this includes, in particular, the roofs with viewing terraces and greenhouses which are accessible to all residences alike. To a certain extent the roofs are also landscaped in order to collect rainwater. Photovoltaic elements are located on the roofs and the greenhouses to produce self-sufficient electricity. Geothermal energy is used via geothermal heat pumps. All in all, by adopting these sustainable measures the building is seeking to achieve zero-energy status, a binding criterion specified by the Danish Building Code as of 2025. Therefore, clients and architects have more than met the general requirements.

Luplau & Poulsen

Martin Schubert/CUBO

Student Residences at the Port

116 I

Dagmar Petersens Gade/
Grethe Løchtes Gade/
Bernhardt Jensens Boulevard

Volcano ↓

Terroir/CUBO, 2013

The student residence named the Volcano (*Vulkanen*) has fifty flats and attempts to live up to its name with its façades which "burst open" in a number of places, similar to an eruption. The openings thus created are accentuated by hues of orange, yellow and red, marking the entrance to the building or the terraces lying outside which in turn forge a spatial coherence with an inner atrium. This interplay of colour is also continued within the atrium: the glazed parapets of the access balconies alternating in hues of orange, yellow and red, thus distinguishing themselves from the exterior and the interior walls in grey exposed concrete. The atrium has a basic temperature of 20 degrees, scaling back the heating requirements of the individual flats. The compact design of the somewhat cubic volume is to form part of the energy concept in order to meet the requirements posed by the Danish low-energy classification of 2015.

Grundfos ↘

CEBRA, 2013

The Grundfos student residence contains 159 student flats tailored to individuals, couples or flat-sharing communities. The façade design is based on the premises of the creation of a kind of *micro-Manhattan*. Each type of residence is arranged vertically atop of one another in vertical bands with individually selected materials and windows. Each of these high-rises is at an individual height to lend expression to the silhouette of the skyline. Similar to the Volcano, individual flats are rendered accessible via an atrium. Stairs and lifts lead to circumferential

Martin Schubert / Ringgaarden

Martin Schubert / Ringgaarden

access balconies, the parapets of which produce ceaseless reflections owing to their high-gloss surfaces, thus allowing daylight to penetrate deeply inside the building via the glazed roof of the atrium. The architects have integrated new technologies – including those by the sponsor of the building, the Danish company Grundfos – into the building in order to meet future requirements for energy conservation.

The Big Harbour House ↑

Arkitema Architects, 2013

The Big Harbour House (*Det Store Havnehus*) is a twelve-storey high-rise with ninety-nine student flats – predominantly two-room apartments. The entrance on the eastern side is marked by a corner of the façade which is recessed across six storeys and accentuated by gold shimmering aluminium panels. Communal facilities such as a laundry and a raised terrace are located on the ground floor level which is oriented towards the west. The apartments are arranged around a circulation core simply featuring a safety stairwell and a lift. Common recreational balconies and terraces have been integrated on every two storeys. The architects have achieved their ambitious objective of meeting the rules on energy efficiency (earmarked for 2025) already today by adopting a façade system comprising highly insulated compacted concrete, low-energy windows, decentralised ventilation systems and heat exchangers, among other things. Visible elements testifying to the production of self-energy are photovoltaic elements enframing the south-eastern windows as well as a photovoltaic array on the roof. The common feature binding together the four student residences on one plot is the attempt to forge identity in a place where – short of a development plan – there exists hardly any urban context that architects could draw on.

Mikkel Frost / CEBRA

Kjaer & Richter

Langelinieparken, Housing Development ↑ →

117 I

Langelinieparken
Kjaer & Richter, 2004

Since the relocation of industrial activities from the northern part of the port, the sea view is deemed once more to be a major quality attribute of residential housing. Accordingly, countless new buildings are being built anew in that location. The exclusive residential complex Langelinieparken consists of three units – two elongated, three- to four-storey slab-like buildings following the elevations stand on the common plinth of an underground car park embedded into the hill – without infringing upon the views from the listed residential development Klintegården (see 118) above, one of the most exclusive residential complexes from the 1930s. A third building has risen to seven storeys at the end of the path and marks the culmination of the north of the city facing the Risskov forest. The floor plan was designed with the idea of bestowing all apartments with a view across the marina in front, the new urban district of Ø and the bay situated behind – a postcard idyll commanding a high price. Accordingly, residential and recreational premises are oriented in a southeasterly direction, whereas bathrooms and bedrooms are placed on the side facing the land. The design of the façade which features a light natural stone cladding, balcony parapets made of steel and glass as well as decking and sun protection lamellae made of mahogany is intended to evoke maritime scenes. The elongated, aligned balconies are kept physically separate by

Kjaer & Richter

floor-to-ceiling storage space – also in mahogany – to lend a sense of privacy on the balconies. Shared functions have been adopted from the Klintegården residential development: in Langelinieparken there is also a dining hall and a foyer where art exhibitions are held.

Klintegården, Housing Development →

118 I

Skovvejen 44–46
Hans Ove Christensen, 1938

In the 1930s, Ove Christensen built four larger residential buildings in Aaarhus. The white residential block Klintegården, situated on a hill and placed atop the nearby marina like a crown, is the subsequent execution of the progressive engineer's social vision. Both new buildings with roughly 150 flats and guestrooms were conceived as a collective dwelling resort for families with working parents. Two villas on the property were integrated into the complex and used as common recreational spaces, guestrooms and childcare facilities. The two functionalist new buildings are oriented towards Skovvejen street and the bay. All residents and their children were to have the intervening grounds at their disposal as a safe and secure recreational environment. Flat roofs, white façades, large windows and balconies are also as much a part of the classically modern repertoire – in common with bathrooms and kitchens featuring hot running water, district heating and waste chutes, although these were considered to be a luxury in the period between the two world wars. The social vision in which all amenities were part and parcel of standard fittings financed by allocable shares in costs paid by the tenant amounted to a princely sum. In the end, it was only the upper echelons of civil servants and professors who could afford the technical achievements offered by the small three-and-a-half-room flats covering 50 m² to 60 m². The rental apartments were converted to private ownership as early as the 1970s. In 2013, the building ensemble was granted listed status.

Cort Adeler, Residential Building →

119 I

Cort Adelers Gade
3XN, 2010

This residential building lies within the former working-class neighbourhood of Trøjborg which emerged in the early twentieth century. Its streets are named after Danish naval heroes. The Wilhelminian quarter is dominated by four- to five-storey buildings composed of red exposed masonry with white Dannebrog windows. Since this project involved bridging the gap between the existing buildings, 3XN have designed the dwelling with a strip-structured façade – exerting a striking impact on the streetscape – to guide the eye of the observer from the pavement to the penthouse. The first floor is accentuated in the form of a bel étage. The ornamental vertical brick bonding varying in format illustrates the fact that the masonry in this concrete edifice is not part of the supporting framework. The floor-to-ceiling glazing between the brickwork is equally modern. The building contains ten apartments with 46 m² to 76 m² of usable space.

Adam Mørk / 3XN

Andreas Trier Mørch / KADK

Adam Mørk/ 3XN

119 I

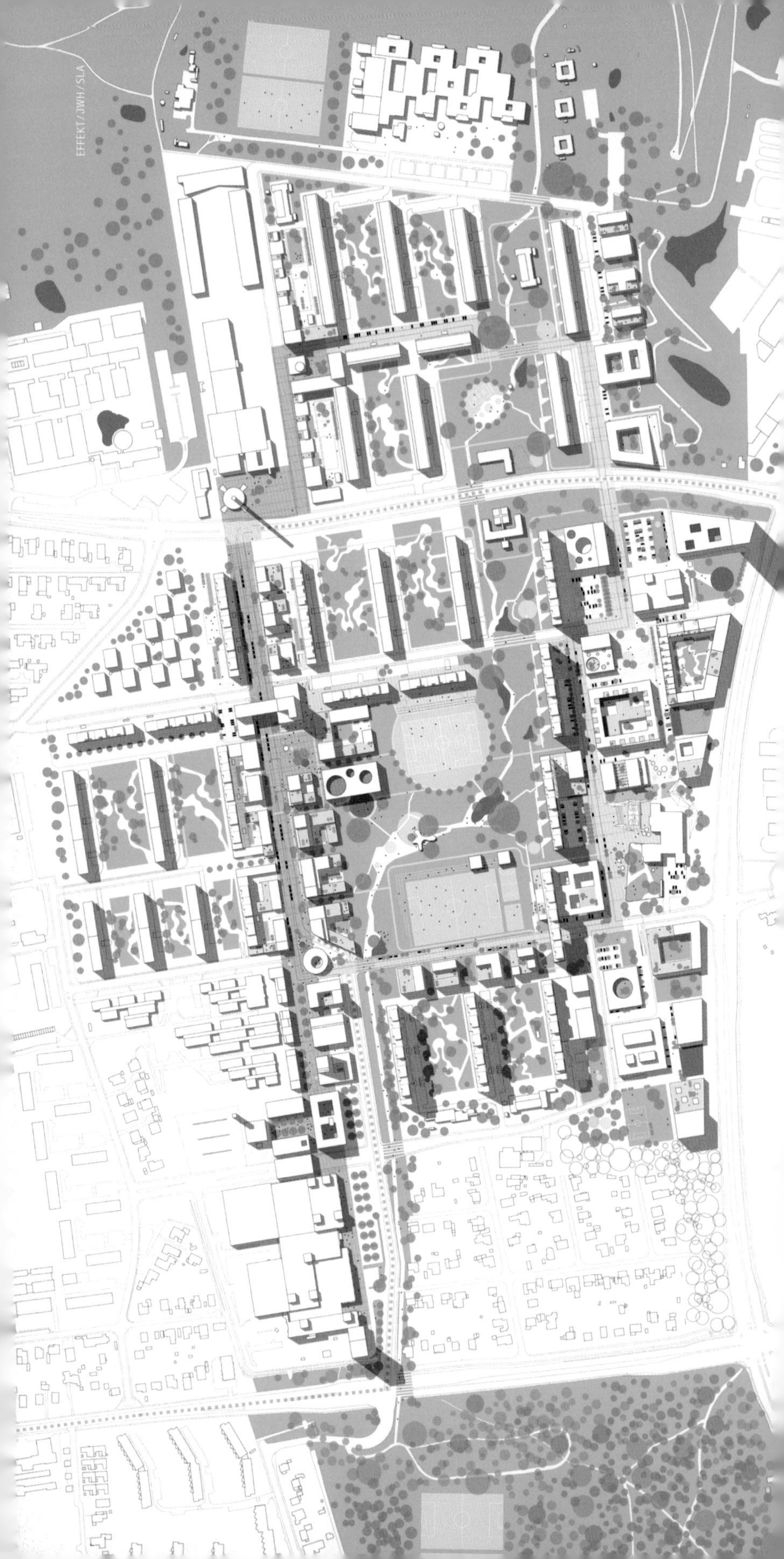
EFFEKT/JWH/SLA

Utopia in Aarhus

Stephen Willacy

Western Aarhus has seen some of the most ambitious housing projects in Denmark from the late 1960s into the 1970s:

- Holmstrup Park built in 1975 with 400 dwellings designed by Knud Blach Pedersen,
- Skjoldhøj Kollegiet student halls from 1973 designed by Knud Bach Pedersen & Knud Friis for 1,000 students,
- Bispehaven from 1973 with 972 dwellings designed by Architects Møller & Wichman and
- Gellerupparken and Toveshøj which were built between 1967 and 1972 by Knud Blach Pedersen.

These projects are the product of a period of hope where housing and planning policies and building technologies developed after World War Two.

There was an optimism in the wake of Le Corbusier's ideas which rejected the planning ideals of the likes of Camillo Sitte. Le Corbusier developed the open vision, *La Ville Radieuse*, providing air and light by designing tall buildings in green parks replacing historical Paris. He founded CIAM (*Congrès International d'Architecture Moderne*) where the committee advocated "cities without streets", where motorised traffic should be separated from pedestrians!

Modernist architects were fascinated by industrialisation where standardised prefabricated elements could be mass-produced and craned on to a site, reducing the need for skilled labour force, which was scarce. This efficiency could meet the massive demands for new homes in the post-war period, but it brought with it repetition, large areas of SLOAP (space left over after planning), segregated functions and separation of infrastructure. The new projects had not previously been seen on green field sites on the outskirts of traditional cities on a massive scale.

New tax rebates on the full amount on interest paid on mortgage loans made it advantageous to build single-family homes. Denmark's largest housing estate Skjoldhøjparken in western Aarhus consists of 1,014 dwellings. These *type-huse* were built as standard-houses adopting standardisation, industrial production in factory-like workshops, delivered and quickly assembled (not built) on site as a montage or kit-of-parts.

The largest public housing scheme in Denmark Gellerupparken and Toveshøj is a 110 ha district with 2,400 dwellings for 7,000 people established by Brabrand Boligforening (housing association).

This new town was built in the period of 1967 to 1974 and consisted of housing blocks from four to eight storeys, a student hostel, a crèche, a kindergarden, a combined primary-secondary school, a swimming pool, a sports hall, a culture centre with a library, a hotel, a local archives centre, a theatre, a church and a shopping centre. It could be seen as a completely independent and autonomous community.

← **Master plan for Gellerup**

Bazaar in the district of Gellerup

Today many residents are happy to live in Gellerup and Toveshøj, but a number of challenges lie ahead. The area is monofunctional, consisting primarily of housing, and could until this year appear closed off from the rest of Aarhus. Also, many inhabitants have little education and struggle in getting employment. The proportion of immigrants and descendants from non-Western countries is high, and the average gross income is very low compared with the same group in the region.

Transformation

In 2007 Aarhus City Council, together with Brabrand Boligforening, initiated a major process to prepare a new development plan for Gellerup and Toveshøj. This was approved by the City Council in March 2011. The vision is to transform and integrate Gellerup and Toveshøj into a new attractive multi-functional city district in Aarhus. Overall, the City Council has agreed to invest 1.9 billion DDK in the development plan.

With experience and documented research evidence from around the world it is proven possible to reverse developments in disadvantaged areas by changing the physical framework combined with social, cultural, environmental and economic initiatives to enable a new and vibrant sustainable community.

This combination will improve the liveability and well-being for the citizens in this city district as well as supporting a sustainable community with a strong sense of place. This is the first, largest and most ambitious urban transformation project of its kind in Denmark.

New Connectivity with the City

From being an isolated island, Gellerup and Toveshøj are being integrated with their neighbouring city districts by creating a network of roads. These streets create a new flow, as well as support better connectivity and accessibility between the new quarters. The new Karen Blixens Boulevard connects Bazar Vest and

Edwin Rahrsvej in the north with the shopping centre City Vest on Silkeborgvej to the south. Along the boulevard a series of new places and destinations have been initiated: a World Square with a Sports and Culture Campus including a public swimming pool, a community library as well as an activity centre. A string of shops and businesses connect with Instant City; a meeting/activity centre designed by Arkitema architects and sponsored by Enemærke & Petersen neighbours small clubs which will encourage engagement among local citizens of all ages, genders and ethnicities.
A new creative entrepreneur/start-up workshop with shops and offices will be up and running in early 2017. Adjacent in the central park the football pitches have already proven their popularity with local families as well as the daycare and healthcare centre designed by GPP Architects. The second stage of the light-rail line will increase accessibility to the city as a whole while reducing the dependency upon individual motorised vehicles.

New Central Park

Reduction in scale by dividing large open areas into smaller identifiable entities creates a greater sense of place, ownership and security. Landscaping with improved visibility over greater distances supports safer communities. Improved lighting, functional and atmospheric, whether in the streets or the landscaped areas, creates identities, higher degrees of ownership and safer environments. Renowned landscape architects SLA with EFFEKT architects are transforming this central park. At night, this safer park will also become the glue binding Gellerup and Toveshøj together and will become a destination in itself.
Following the demolition of four major housing blocks, space has been made available to develop the first major new quarter. Bazar Vest Plaza is located at the junction of Edwin Rahrsvej and Karen Blixens Boulevard. Here at the eastern corner, the new administration building for 1,000 staff from Aarhus City

Street in Gellerup

Council's Departments for Technical and Environmental Services and Employment and Social Services, together with the relocated police station, are currently being built. This project is the result of a Public-Private-Partnership competition where a team consisting of Arkitema Architects and Construction Company Enggaard won in partnership with the City Council. This building with seven staggered floor plates marks this corner at the highest point on Karen Blixens Boulevard and signifies its importance in the new quarter. The ground floor is designed as a porous and inviting place where the local population can intermingle with people asking the council departmental staff to run an errand. Wandering around it is possible to look up into five different "squares" with contemplative atmospheres, take in exhibitions, work in the Made in Gellerup start-up area, relax over a cup of coffee in the Risteri or use the auditorium which is transformed into a cinema. On the seventh floor the Liveable City Lab affords panoramic views across Aarhus. The multi-tiered floor plates create rooftop green oases where staff can hold meetings and eat lunch. Just across the boulevard on the corner is the new Brabrand Housing Association headquarters designed by CUBO architects. To the south, 400 new student residences designed by SAHL architects (together with NORD architects) are being planned, catering to students who have an interest in entrepreneurship. The ground floor is devoted to creating opportunities to meet like-minded people. The street façades along the boulevard will be active where people can look into and participate in the activities within. This new quarter kickstarts the regeneration of Gellerup. This move is already inspiring confidence and gaining interest from private investors.

Human Scale

A combination of transforming and renovating the existing housing stock and building privately owned homes is a high priority for the development

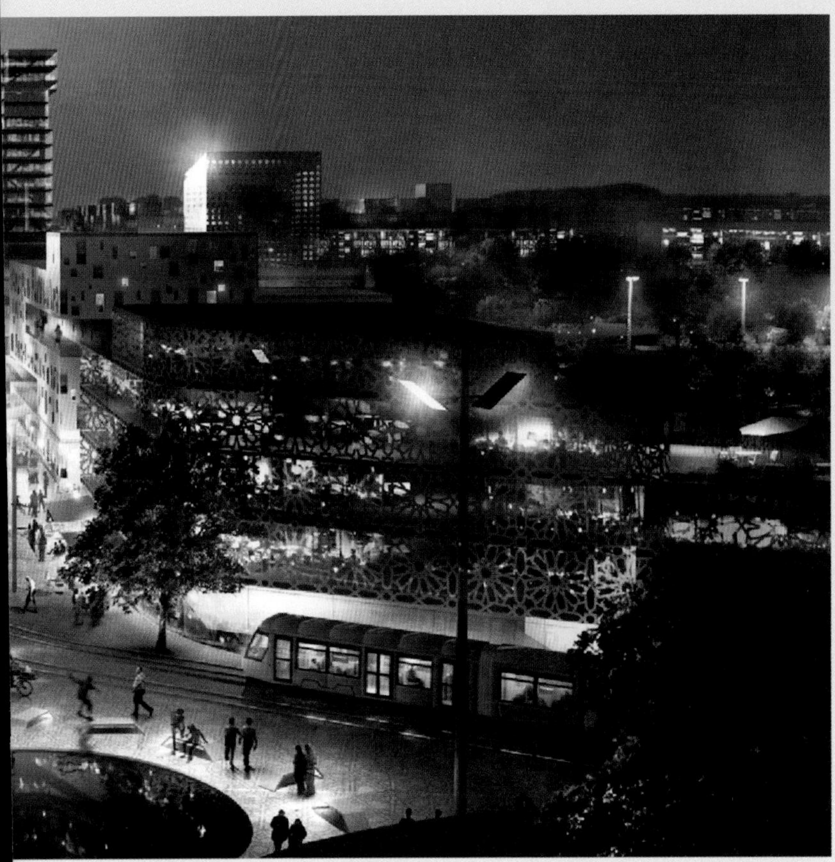

plan's success. Pilot projects have been initiated to transform two seven-storey and two four-storey apartment blocks. Human scale has been the mantra creating thresholds between the public, semi-private and private domains. The large anonymous car parking areas and impersonal access balconies will be transformed by introducing variation.

Townhouses will have their own entrance doors in the two lower storeys and small gardens will create intimacy and ownership. Shared entrances will have different characteristics and identities by using materials which have a tactility and age beautifully, such as brick and wood. Colour schemes facilitate personalised spaces and make it easier to find your way.

New privately owned and rented town houses combined with apartments arranged in urban blocks with façades with edge zones and front doors will create defined streets with green character which shall support the development of a friendly urban realm.

EUTOPIA

EUTOPIA is the name of a new culture base in an old disbanded theatre underneath the library and old hotel building adjacent to City Vest. EUTOPIA STAGE will be a one of the twelve full-moon events in the 2017 European Capital of Culture. During a week in July 2017 a large area of Gellerup will be transformed for the EUTOPIA festival.

The combination of these urban interventions will create a greater feeling of ownership and supports stronger neighbourhoods with their own identities fostering a new kind of community spirit. It would appear that we are re-thinking the visions of Camillo Sitte in favour of a more artistic, organic and people-friendly approach to urban living.

Westbound:
Tilst – Brabrand – Gellerup

Søbakke
Tilst Østervej
Grevested
Tilst
Langkær
Tilst Skolevej
Kileparken
Havkærvej
Blomstervej
Lundgård
121
Tilst
Viborgvej
Anelystvej
Råhøj
Eldalgård
Eldal
Viborgvej
Bredskiftevej
Holmstrupgårdvej
124
Jernaldervej
Skjoldhøjvej
Bremerholm
Voldbæk
Hjordhøjgård
123
122
Lundagergård
Grimhøjgård
Spobjergvej
Hasle
Bakker
Sintrupvej
Grimhøj
Dalgårdsvej
Holmstrupgårdvej
Grimhøjvej
Edwin Rahrs Vej
Mariendal
Langdal
126
Brabrand
Skovbakkevej
Hejredalsvej
Gudrunsvej
120
Dortesvej
125
Åby Ringvej
127
Højen
Stenbækvej
Lykkensdalsvej
Sigridsvej
Hans Broges Vej
Gundrunsvej
Truevej
J.P. Larsens Vej
Silkeborgvej
Brabrand
Skov
Gjellerup
Skov
Gjellerup
Egekrat
Louisevej
Aarhus Å
Gellerup
Sølyst
0
1 km
Brabrand Sø

Agro Food Park
Revelhøjvej
Herredsvej
Brendstrupgårdsvej
Dusager
Randersvej
Skejbyparken
Skejbygårdsvej
Brendstrupgårdsvej
Skelagervej
Nedergård
Brendstrupgård
Brendstrup
Olof Palmes Alle
Brendstrup Busvej
Nehrus Alle
Marienlystvej
Vester-
eng
Brendstrup Skov
Herredsvej
Bodøvej
Hasle Ringvej
Møllevangs Alle
Paludan-Müllers Vej
Staghøj
Katrinebjergvej
Hasle Ringvej
Viborgvej
Herredsvej
Åby Ringvej
le
Botanisk
Have
Vestre Ringgade
Fenrisvej
Vestre
Kirkegård
Den gamle
By
Viborgvej
Vestre Ringgade
Silkeborgvej
byhøj
Vibyvej
Åby
Anhøj
Viby Ringvej
Aarhus Å

J

127
125

122
120

Heiko Weissbach

Langkær Gymnasium
Kileparken 25, Tilst
Friis & Moltke
1975/2012

121 J

Against the backdrop of their designs for schools that had already been implemented (such as Risskov Gymnasium, see 089), the young architects Knud Friis and Ivar Moltke developed a flexible school building system in the 1970s which could be adjusted to meet changing needs. In all, six schools were built on the basis of this system in Denmark. The exterior walls consist of red masonry with horizontal bands of windows. Characteristic for these buildings are skylights oriented towards the north with steep roofs covered with Eternit, providing classrooms with exposure to daylight and natural ventilation. Langkær Gymnasium has three pupil streams. These are served by classrooms centred on natural science, a teachers' lounge and a sports hall. All rooms are rendered accessible via a coherent communal area, evoking an internal street network. Therefore, the building containing several hundred students remains as easy to survey as a village. The circular extension was planned a good forty-five years later by successors within the practice of the same name. Although the original buildings with their solid brick façades rest firmly on the ground, the bright new building at the end of a broad inviting stairway swells above the grounds, thus differing from the old orthogonal building in both form and materiality. The extension contains a multi-functional common room as well as recreational spaces to host activities. A connecting thread through the original circulation area containing meeting places is a spacious lounge featuring a library and a knowledge hub.

Friis & Moltke

Heiko Weissbach

Skjoldhøjkollegiet 122 J

Spobjergvej 6, Brabrand
Friis & Moltke/Knud Blach Petersen/Sven Hansen
1973

Situated amidst the green setting of Skjoldhøjkilen to the north of an industrial area is this student residence which has roughly 900 units across Jutland and is hence the largest settlement of its kind. The complex is dispersed across several village-like segments and is rendered accessible via an internal passageway unfettered by traffic, giving rise to diverging sequences with passages and squares – all the while offering a rapport with the green surroundings. The settlement has an asymmetric section – which is a commonplace feature of the Friis & Moltke practice – and apartments stacked on top of each other, opening up on to the grounds via extensive glazed areas. Inwardly, this is in marked contrast to the steep roofs sloping down to the narrow passages. Exposed concrete has been selected as the consistent building material, while the steep roofs are covered with asphalt. Knud Friis sought to create a "hierarchy of societies" in which residents are able to live together, as in an extended family, although there is also room for individualists. The residence has approximately 600 student rooms as well as one- and two-storey dwellings, of which roughly fifty are fully accessible or are tailored to families. There is a communal kitchen for every twelve rooms. This micro-society has its own laundries, workshops and other communal areas. The central building houses its own grocery store, a bar to host music events, a kindergarten and its own reception and administration. The artist Kasper Heiberg has built sculptures in the environs. The settlement was forced to undergo extensive concrete rehabilitation between 1987 and 1989.

Friis & Moltke

Friis & Moltke

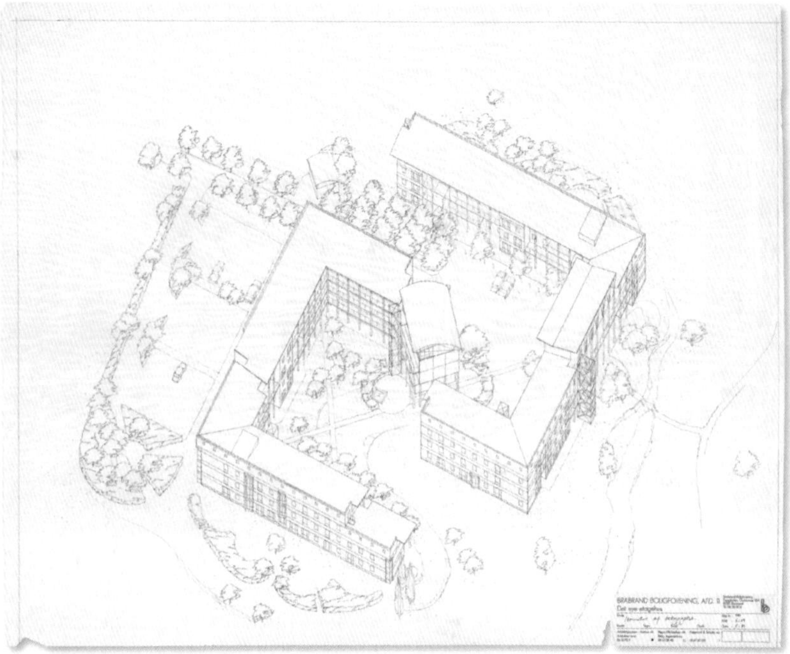

Tegningsarkiv Aarhus Kommune

Odinsgård 123 J

Stenaldervej 195–209, Brabrand
Arkitema Architects
1990

In 1983 the Danish Ministry of Housing held a competition entitled The New Apartment House for the development of multi-storey dwellings. The Arkitema practice won the competition with a design for a building system comprising prefabricated concrete elements (supports, ceilings, shafts, facades) and the flexibility in the design for the facades and the floor plans resulting therefrom as well as the reduction of construction time. Three prototypes of this construction system have been executed in Copenhagen, Rødovre and to the north of Aarhus. Odin's Court (Odinsgård) emerged in open countryside with two slightly offset, open, two- to five-storey residential blocks overlapping within a tower-like building standing in marked contrast to the low and dense neighbouring buildings prevalent at the time. Although one block containing the main entrance is given a more urban touch, the other with a leafy urban courtyard is more aligned with the landscape. The colour scheme obeys a simple logic: blue for the city, green for the land and contrasts with the striking colours of outdoor freestanding stairs and lifts. The settlement contains 103 two-, three- and four-room apartments as well as twenty student apartments and communal rooms within the central tower. The floor plans are organised around a quadratic sanitary core turned 45 degrees. Apartments are rendered accessible via access balconies featuring individual loggias which are designed as multifunctional transitional spaces mediating between the public and private realms.

Arkitektgruppen

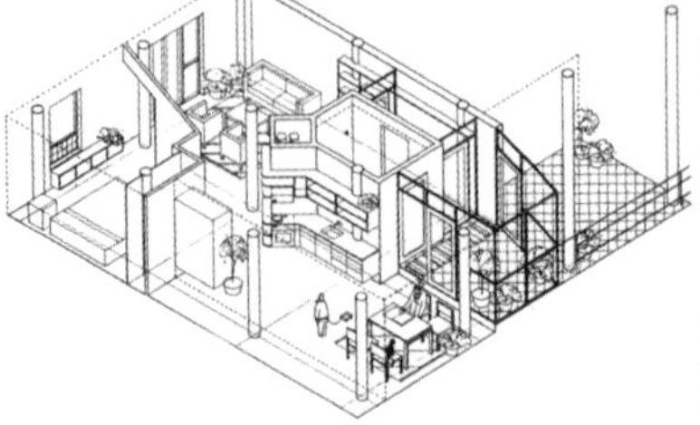

Arkitektgruppen i Aarhus/Arkitema

Friis & Moltke

Skjoldhøj Church

124 J

Jernaldervej 425, Brabrand
Friis & Moltke/Sven Hansen
1984

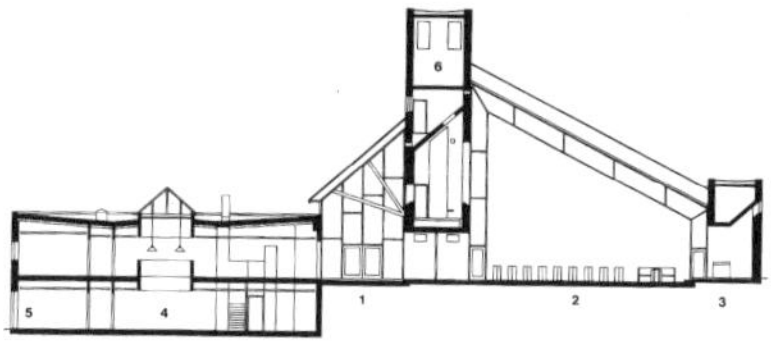

Friis & Moltke

Drawing influence from traditional village churches, this minimalist building – the individual sections and functions of which are discernible from the outside – is situated atop an exposed hill north of the city. Two steep copper roofs marking the fully glazed porch and the partially glazed church hall span three structures of varying heights and dimensions which are made of whitewashed masonry. The rooms may be connected to each other via mobile partition walls and jointly used to host larger events. In common with numerous other buildings, for the design of the interior fittings the architects also worked in partnership with the painter Emil Gregersen – who was accountable for the colour scheme of the partition walls, the altar and the baptismal font.

Friis & Moltke

Heiko Weissbach

Teknik & Miljø

Gellerupplan, Satellite Town

125 J

Dortesvej, Jettesvej, Lottesvej, Bentesvej, Gudrunsvej
Knud Blach Petersen & Knud Harbo, 1972
Arkitema Architects, 1996

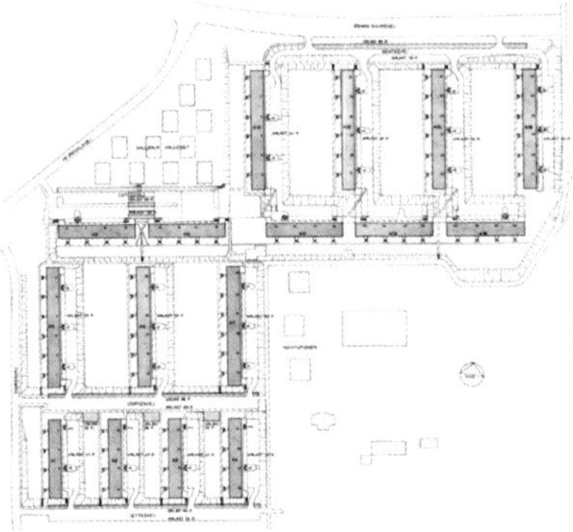

Danmarks Kunstbibliotek

One of the largest satellite towns across Denmark emerged – like so many of its type across the globe – during a period of economic growth and optimism. The architect Knud Blach Petersen designed a new town with 6,000 apartments for 20,000 people in line with the then housing policy and in accordance with the client, the social housing association Brabrand Boligforening. Merely half of that which was outlined was executed in three stages. The modular design, industrial production and assembly rendered possible comparatively large flats within four- and eight-storey buildings. Housing supply was enhanced by the location at Brabrandsø (the nearby lake) and infrastructure, such as shopping facilities, schools, a library, a theatre and a swimming pool. Passenger and car traffic were completely separated, in tune with the times. In the face of ever-mounting criticism levelled at the monotonous design for the new town with repetitive concrete elements, the necessity to let the apartments to vulnerable families soon became pressing. This spawned a ghettoisation of immigrants and a high rate of criminality. Damaged concrete emerged as early as the mid-1990s. The northern part of the settlement of Toveshøj underwent refurbishment – its design enhanced by newly marked entryways and coloured glassware in the form of balcony parapets. The beginning of the new millennium saw the launch of numerous social projects, although continuing unrest involving cars being set on fire and attacks on police and the fire brigade sowed the seeds of a large-scale process of urban change within the district (see Essay 6).

OPS Gellerup Nord

126 J

Edwin Rahrs Vej, Brabrand
Arkitema Architects
2018

The encumbered urban district of Gellerup is to be upgraded in terms of urban development and architecture (see Essay 6). Apart from overarching changes, a new building has been proposed that is born of a partnership between the public sector and private investors – hence the working title OPS. Apart from the administrative offices with 950 communal workplaces, the new building is set to accommodate a series of public functions, such as restaurants, open workshops and cafés, creating a dynamic ambience for young entrepreneurs. The ground floor is conceived as a covered urban space. Brick and wooden surfaces are intended to underscore the welcoming effect. The overarching architectural motif of stacked boxes offset in relation to each other turns into a tower in the middle, connecting public functions with individual storeys. The storeys of differing height are connected to each other via bridges. The uppermost box at the corner of the building juts out to a great extent and acts as an urban planning gesture as well as an observation tower, affording views across the new Gellerup and the bay of Aarhus.

Friis & Moltke

Detached House by Knud Friis 127 J

Højen 13, Brabrand
Knud Friis/Friis & Moltke
1958/1970

Knud Friis designed this "unpretentious and powerful" detached house with two storeys for himself and his family, occupying it prior to his death in 2010. It lies on vast wilderness lot bordering a beech forest to the east, affording a once unrivalled view to the south – particularly from the living room on the upper floor. Friis described his house thus: "This two-storey house aimed to capitalise on the four points of the compass so that each part assumes a special significance, distinguished by its rapport with the garden, the forest and the view. In particular, focus is to be placed on the relationship between the intimate garden and the vast landscape." In 1970 he extended it to the east in order to incorporate a wing in exposed concrete. The path through the house may be interpreted as a *promenade architecturale* in the vein of Le Corbusier. A large paved courtyard lies behind the garden wall. The façade on the ground floor has floor-to-ceiling glazing. Above it lies the upper storey which is fully enclosed facing the garden, like a concrete girder. A plain, single-flight wooden staircase connects both storeys. All structures are visible, the choice of materials simple and robust – concrete walls bearing visible traces of shuttering boards, brick partition walls painted white, stairs, door frames, wall panelling made from spruce wood, large Alta slate slabs with wide joints on the floor, cobalt blue door leaves and window frames as well as red banisters with coarse, black handrails made from solid wood. Pure Brutalism! A large proportion of the fittings were built-in, whereas loose furnishings comprised a range of classics

Friis & Moltke

Friis & Moltke

as well as those of Friis' own design. This was accompanied by a collection of artworks, artefacts and collectors' items which once filled the rooms – among them paintings, lithographs and reliefs by Danish architects, such as, for example, Emil Gregersen, Svend Engelund, Allan Schmidt, Aage Fredslund Andersen and Karin Nathorst Westfelt, as well as several landscapes by the architect. Several sculptures by the artist Erik Heide as well as unattributed stone masonry works have been installed outdoors.
Note: this house has been awarded listed status since 2008 and has been owned by Realdania By & Byg since 2011. In 2012 it underwent restoration and is today part of the collection of iconic buildings. It is not open to the public since it is rented out privately. A visit may be organised exclusively through Realdania By & Byg Klubben. For further information, please contact: info@realdaniabyogbyg.dk

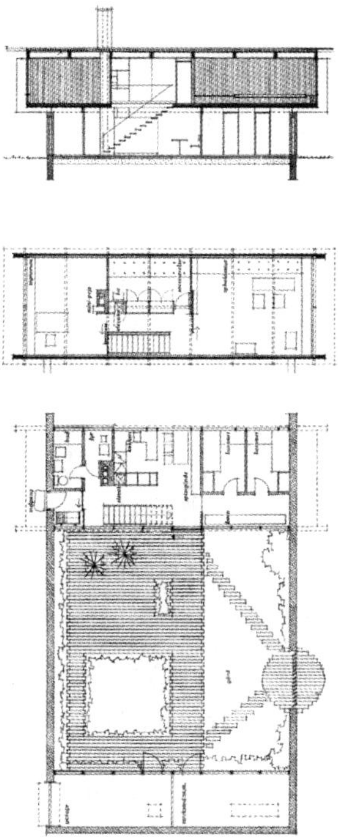
Friis & Moltke

Friis & Moltke

Southbound:
Viby – Højbjerg – Moesgaard

Edwin Rahrs Vej
Åby Ringvej
Åbyhøj
Silkeborgvej
Vibyvej
Gellerup
Aarhus Å
Brabrand Sø
Sølyst
Årslev Engsø
Viby Ringvej
Aarhus Å
Døde Å
Stavtrup
Viby
Ormslevvej
Ormslevvej
Århus Syd Motorvejen
132
Lemming
Skanderborgvej
Holmevej
Ringvej Syd
Kunnerup
Genvejen
Møllebakken
133
Christian X'S Vej
Hovedvejen
Jegstrupvej
Bjødstrupvej
Slet Møllevej
Slet
Kattrup
Hasselager
Ellemosevej
Grønløkke Alle
Jegstrup
Tranbjerg
Østerby Alle
Ellevej
Tingskov Alle
Overballe
Ingerslev
Landevejen
134
Østerby
Obstrupvej
Mårslet
Testrup
0
500 m
1 km

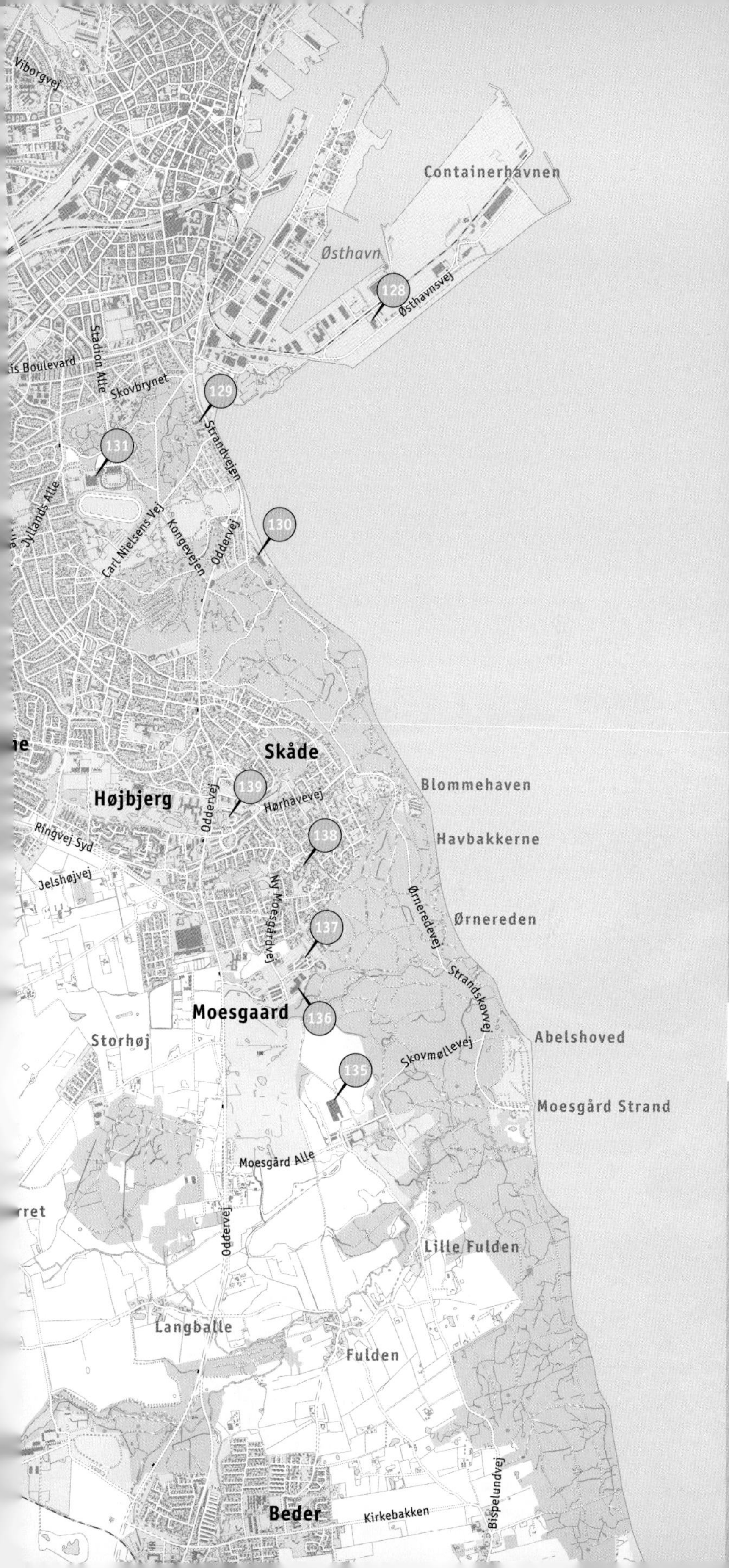
Viborgvej
Containerhavnen
Østhavn
128
Østhavnsvej
Stadion Alle
Skovbrynet
129
Strandvejen
131
Jyllands Alle
Carl Nielsens Vej
Kongevejen
Oddervej
130
Skåde
Højbjerg
139
Hørhavevej
Oddervej
Blommehaven
Ringvej Syd
138
Havbakkerne
Jelshøjvej
Ny Moesgårdvej
Ørneredevej
Ørnereden
137
Strandskovvej
Moesgaard
136
Storhøj
Abelshoved
Skovmøllevej
135
Moesgård Strand
Moesgård Alle
Oddervej
Lille Fulden
Langballe
Fulden
Bispelundvej
Beder
Kirkebakken

Tangkrogen

K

Julian Weyer / C. F. Møller Architects

Aarhus Havn, Port Centre
Vandvejen 7
C. F. Møller Architects
2015

128 K

The new administrative centre of the port occupies a central position at Pier 4. From here the administration has a sweeping view out over the port, the bay and the city. Office space is distributed across five storeys. Furthermore, there are workshops, storage space, a customer centre, security and a canteen. Spaces are available for rent by those firms in close vicinity to the port. According to the architects, the star-shaped floor plan of the building is intended to evoke an ice crystal, thus insinuating opportunities for further expansion without appearing unfinished. The first expansion stage involved a free-standing unit oriented around a triangular atrium to which further wings may be attached. The upper storeys are staggered in relation to each other and their surfaces decrease upwards. This gives rise to continuous spaces for the canteen on the ground floor and conference rooms on the upper floor. Each storey provides access to the circumferential balconies, the overhang of which lends the façades a horizontal structure and casts shade on the glazed façades below. The visible concrete shell comprising prefabricated elements has been augmented by materials such as oak parquet and orange steel staircases. The port centre meets the requirements posed by the Danish low-energy class 1.

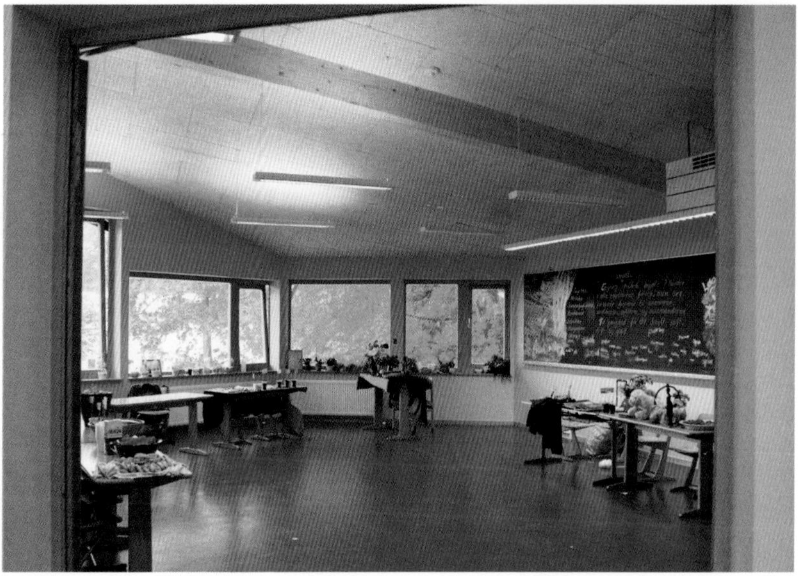

Schmidt/Hammer/Lassen

Rudolf Steiner School, Extension

129 K

Strandvejen 102
Morten Schmidt (SHL), 2009

Schmidt/Hammer/Lassen

Rudolf Steiner founded the first school in 1919 in Stuttgart. Today, there are sixteen Steiner schools in Denmark, of which that in Aarhus from 1955 was the second. The first classrooms were established in one of the large villas at Strandvej. The school has continued to grow, encompassing a further three historic villas and two extensions. The extension of 2009 was designed by Morten Schmidt, a former pupil, in structural timberwork and is used by children during pre-school years until fourth year. In keeping with the anthroposophic ideology, the building has no rectangular rooms, although each room has its own polygonal geometry. The sloping, cantilevered roofs and black façades are in marked contrast to the yellow window frames. The interior of the rooms is dominated by linoleum flooring in highly visible colours as well as raw, visible timber girders beneath the ceilings. With this design, an attempt is made to forge a relationship between methods of learning and architecture.

Schmidt/Hammer/Lassen

Friis & Moltke

Hotel Marselis ↑ 130 K
Strandvejen 25
Friis & Moltke/Thyge Klemann
1967

The greatest asset of this hotel is its rare and unique location in landscape terms – on the sloping ground above the beach, at the transition point leading to the forests in Marselisborg and affording views across the bay and the city. Facing the land, these three slab-like buildings aligned with one another and slightly offset seem almost enclosed owing to their façades composed of mocha brown exposed masonry. In contrast, the rooms with floor-to-ceiling glazing and narrow balconies open up on to the water. The building appears to contain two storeys on the entrance side, although a third storey containing a restaurant and a swimming pool has been slid under the bedroom wing on the side overlooking the water. Whereas initially the architects took account of the old villa and positioned the entrance here, the once elegant ensemble has been thrown off balance by subsequent extensions and a fourth wing containing bedrooms. In 2001, the hotel was sold to the Danish chain Helnan International. This spelt the end for the minimalist, robust interior with solid materials and the blunt detailing which had been the hallmarks of Friis & Moltke's local interpretation of Brutalism. Incidentally, the client himself was a mason and the hotel was his labour of love and life's work. He insisted that all bricks were handcrafted. These were further adorned with ceramic elements by the artist Jörgen Glud.

Stadium (Ceres Park & Arena) ↓ 131 K
Stadion Allé 70
Axel Høeg-Hansen, 1920
C. F. Møller Architects, 1954/1993
BBP Arkitekter, 2001

The stadium was originally built as a sports park and subsequently christened a stadium. Today, it bears the name of its current sponsor (a brewery) and is a multifunctional venue for sports, conferences and events. The original complex by Høeg-Hansen from the year 1920 sits as a demarcation line for the forest at the end of the then newly laid out axis Stadion Allé, with the tower of St. Luke's Church as a focal point and northern culmination of the axis. The architecture is classicist and the façades depicted in the national colours of red and white. The complex is tautly symmetrical and has a colonnaded courtyard with a glazed roof – from here one can reach two sports halls on the right and on the left. The large arched

structures are attributable to the central station by the architect Johan Daniel Herholdt in Copenhagen and, following its demolition in 1910, were reused in Aarhus. One hall became the target of an act of sabotage during the German occupation in 1943 and was burnt down. This hall wasn't rebuilt until just under ten years following the war and the capacity of the overall complex was expanded in the early 1990s. The sporting success of the premiere-league football club AGF triggered a growing demand for spectator seats, bringing forth the expansion of the southern grandstand in 2001 as well as the construction of a multi-functional hall catering for up to 5,000 spectators. A new football stadium is earmarked for construction prior to 2010, although no concrete plans are yet in place.

Torben Eskerod / C. F. Møller Architects

Torben Eskerod / C. F. Møller Architects

Ravnsbjerg Church ↓↗ 132 K

Grøfthøjparken 1, Viby
C. F. Møller Architects/
Jørgen Arevad-Jacobsen, 1976

The church lies in a traditional new development complex from the 1970s, although it sets itself apart in form and materiality. Situated on a small hill, it is visible from afar. The homogeneous mass of the red clinker – which is set apart from the belfry by two fine, concise incisions – gives it its distinctive appearance. A sole large circular window with a diameter of 5 m supplies the church with daylight. Next to the window is the organ located within the depths of the exterior wall. The steep mono-pitch roof slopes down to a small square where yet another separate part of the building is located, containing confirmation rooms and offices over two storeys. The entrance to the church is located on this square. The somewhat inclined walls guide visitors into the interior, the large volume of which has been brought vividly to life. At the rear there is a community hall which is separated from the church hall by a folding partition which can be retracted at the flick of a switch for major events. The altar and the pulpit are so located as to render them visible in either configuration of the space. The very special ambience of the church is inextricably linked to its dimensions and proportions, the overwhelming presence of the red clinker, the visible wooden beams of the supporting roof structure, the altar cross which was also designed in rough wood by the architect Erik Heide and, last but not least, the dramatic flooding in of daylight.

Heiko Weissbach

132 K

Torben Eskerod / C.F. Møller Architects

Torben Eskerod / Arkitema Architects

CCI Europe, Headquarters ↑↓ 133 K
Axel Kiers Vej 11, Højbjerg
Arkitema Architects
2001

The head office of the software developer CCI Europe lies on an industrial estate in Højbjerg, although it distances itself from its context with water basins and gardens. From the outside the building is a two-storey, rectangular volume clad in black granite which is located above a glazed basement floor and encircled by a water basin. Accordingly, the main entrance is rendered accessible via a bridge. The interior of the building is arranged around two atria: the stairway hall accessible to all and a somewhat secluded garden. The so-called monolith made of exposed concrete occupies a central position within the stairway hall and projects widely above the glazed roof. This contains an event space for 200 people on the lower level with conference rooms above. This free form is underscored by a glazed chasm in the roof, allowing daylight to enter the atrium. The ornamentation on the outer surface is attributable to the painter Jes Fomsgaard. In stark contrast to this is the traditional arrangement of the offices perpendicular to the atria, rendered accessible via galleries and bridges on three storeys. The roof garden on the second atrium has been planted with Scots pines and blueberry plants on a bed of blue gravel. Together with the floors fashioned from light-coloured wood, plenty of daylight and high-quality furnishings by renowned designers have given rise to a traditionally Nordic ambience.

Østerby Waterworks ↓ 134 K
Tingskov Alle 72, Tranbjerg
CUBO
2001

The waterworks were built to replace a former complex in the same place and comprise two buildings: a one-storey pump house and a two-storey building for the

Arkitema Architects

Ole Hein / CUBO

Moesgaard Museum/VisitAarhus

generation of hot water. The works are unmanned; functions are monitored electronically. Parts of the water treatment system must not be exposed to daylight and have been inserted into the earthworks of the hill facing the west. The façades are glazed on the side containing the entrance, while an office and a classroom on the upper floor open on to the landscape. All other façades are enclosed. The complex has been constructed from in-situ concrete, bearing visible traces of formwork. The roof and the façades are clad in zinc. The dark granite floor is in marked contrast to technical installations in stainless steel.

Moesgaard Museum ↑ 135 K

Moesgård Allé 15, Højbjerg
Henning Larsen/Kristine Jensens tegnestue
2014

This prehistoric museum has presided as an institution in Moesgaard Manor since 1970 and has rigorously expanded its permanent collections from the Old Stone Age up until the Viking era. The 2,000-year-old bog body of the Grauballe Man ranks among the most significant exhibits. The new museum's unique location on a slope amidst the hills of Skåde inspired the architects to create the design for a building that seems to grow out of the slope. The leafy and accessible roof of the new museum building is part of the landscaping entrusted to the practice of Kristine Jensen – the common thread underlying the surrounding landscape and the museum world. Visitors approach this extraordinary building from the car park from a westerly direction and may either reach the entrance domain via bridges from the side or flat sloped ramps on the roof. The path network creates recreational spaces and viewing posts to be enjoyed by the public, over and above its essential role of providing circulation. The central port of call is the spacious foyer housing the ticket shop, the museum shop and a café. This also provides access to the open spaces on the roof. From here, visitors can wander downwards across offset levels into the exhibition space – or back into antiquity. Inspired by archaeological excavations, an animated journey through the permanent collection and temporary exhibitions has been created where visitors gradually take a stroll through various stages of history. The central 12 m high exhibition space meets the highest technical standards and now also enables major international exhibitions to take place in Denmark, such as *The Terracotta Army and The Legacy of the Eternal Emperor* from the Chinese Mausoleum of the First Qin Emperor in 2015. This building denotes a rare marriage of nature, culture and architecture and has attracted wide international attention.

135 K

Hufton+Crow

Friis & Moltke

Scanticon, Conference Centre and Hotel (Today's Vocational School) 136 K

Skåde Skovvej 2, Højbjerg
Friis & Moltke/Sven Hansen, 1969

The positive economic trends of the 1960s led to the recognition that vocational training is a lifelong topic. Associations of architects and doctors were among the first to seek training centres which, in addition to the best education and technical equipment, provided overnight accommodation and the opportunity for informal exchange. The location on the southern outskirts of the city set amidst a green setting was ideal for the establishment of such a training centre. The architectural interpretation of the spatial programme denotes one of the finest examples of New Brutalism from the 1960s which the architects of Scanticon integrated into numerous oeuvres across Jutland. The exposed concrete building was and continues to be radical in its concurrent sobriety and the dramatic effect it imparts. It comes across as part of the peak elevation of the hill into which it is virtually carved. The terraced volume traces the soft topography with a simple geometry, underscored by the leafy roofs. All recreational spaces afford a view to the sky and across the landscape. The concrete walls cast in rough timber formwork and the over-dimensioned built-in furniture, handrails, window frames and luminaires set the mood of the spatial experience imparted within the interior. Custom-designed colour spectrums by the artist Emil Gregersen were conferred on textiles and construction components, bestowing life and warmth upon the cool rooms. Regrettably, the building's original dramatic effect has partially been lost owing to extensions and conversions, modifications to the interior and changes in usage.

Friis & Moltke

C. F. Møller Architects

Ny Moesgaard, Housing Development

137 K

Skåde Skovvej 5–83, Højbjerg
C. F. Møller Architects, 1998

C. F. Møller Architects

This two-storey settlement is aligned with the topography of the building plot. The houses in three rows incorporate the difference in altitude of 15 m. The ridges of their pitched roofs clad in zinc are punctuated by prominent skylights. The bright, whitewashed façades featuring meticulously laid out windows adorned with teakwood furnishings are in marked contrast to the green spaces between and behind the houses, hearkening back to Mediterranean influences. The settlement has eighty-four apartments featuring twenty-six different types and a floor space covering 70 m² to 126 m².

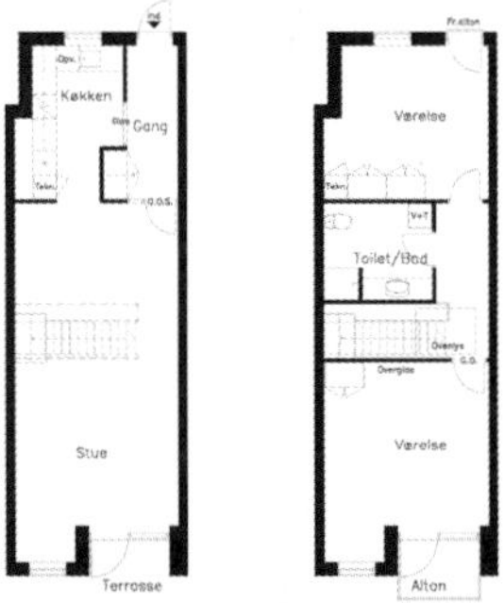

C. F. Møller Architects

Jan Kofoed Winther / C. F. Møller Architects

C. F. Møller Architects

Sandbakken, Housing Development

138 K

Sandbakken/Lerdalen, Højbjerg
C. F. Møller Architects/
Paul le Fevre Jacobsen, 1990

Sandbakken (Sandy Hills) is an exclusive residential housing development in southern Aarhus which arose within the vicinity of the forest and the beach on the hilly premises of a former brickyard with a quintessential fissured topography. The housing estate has two fundamentally different outdoor typologies: on the one hand urban courtyards which are accessible from each house and, on the other, the virtually unspoilt countryside encircling it. Several overlapping squares at 90 degrees to each other were laid out as the basis for the development plan. The two- to four-storey residential buildings trace the contours of the squares, forging coherent inner courtyards with recreational spaces unfettered by traffic. Communal facilities encompass underground car parks, washhouses and a pavilion on the lakeside. As with the university campus (see 030), the settlement with saddle roofs was constructed from yellow ochre brick, lending the complex a homogeneous appearance and making it appear to grow out of the former brickyard. The inference of exclusivity is underscored by the artistic interpretation of the courtyards by artists such as Merete Barker, Viera Colaro and Claus Jensen.

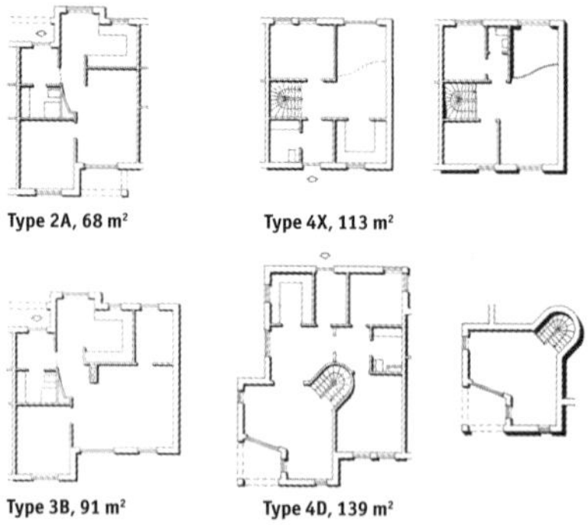

Type 2A, 68 m² Type 4X, 113 m²
Type 3B, 91 m² Type 4D, 139 m²

C. F. Møller Architects

C. F. Møller Architects

Adam Mørk/3XN

Emiliedalen, Housing Development

139 K

Emiliedalsvej, Højbjerg
Arkitema Architects/Kjær & Richter/SHL/3XN/Landskab & Rum, 1997

Schmidt/Hammer/Lassen

The Emiliedalen (Valley of Emilie) housing development executed with 157 apartments across several storeys was designed by four architectural offices and one landscape practice. The hilly topography of a former clay pit formed the point of departure for the development plan. Freestanding, two- to three storey apartment houses as well as two-storey terraced houses are arranged around a small village pond, upon which the communal building lies. The vaulted roof is a common feature among all buildings. The brightly whitewashed brick façades with a variety of windows are intended to evoke the qualities of modern architecture from the 1930s.

Heiko Weissbach

Schmidt/Hammer/Lassen

Epilogue: A New Airport in Eastern Jutland?

Those seeking to travel to Aarhus soon discover that the city does not have its own airport within its vicinity. The airport prefixed AAR lies roughly 35 km away in Tirstrup, the fourth largest airport in Denmark which was laid out by the German occupying forces in 1943. In addition, there are a further two airports serving civil aviation located in Jutland: one in Billund (approximately 100 km away) and one in Aalborg (approximately 120 km away). Holidaymakers from Jutland also enjoy travelling as far out as Hamburg-Fuhlsbüttel (approximately 330 km) from where they jet out on holiday. In spite of Intercity Express trains between the country's regions, it still takes three to seven hours to reach Jutland by train from the capital of Copenhagen. The airport in Aalborg recently underwent expansion in 2001 and 2013. The proprietor of today's global corporation LEGO commissioned the design for a first runway in Billund as early as the 1960s and this has evolved into the second-largest airport in Denmark over time. The growing self-confidence of the "uncrowned capital of Jutland" – Aarhus – has continued to yield studies and market analyses for a new Aarhus Jutlandia Airport since 1998, also called Green International Airport in Eastern Jutland. However, concrete implementation plans are not yet in place. In August 2016, the European Union had in fact thrown doubt on the need for a new airport on the grounds that the capacity of the existing ones is sufficient.

Møller & Grønborg

Annex

Buildings and Projects

Digits indicate the project number

Jan Kejser

Town Hall

Buildings and Projects

Digits indicate the project number

Architects

Digits indicate the project number

References

Books

Johan Bender: *Arkitekt Hack Kampmann*, Risskov 2014

Mogens Brandt Poulsen: *Den Gode Skole – og arkitekturmiljøet i Aarhus*, Aarhus 2015

Mogens Brandt Poulsen/Aage Lund Jensen: *Århus Arkitekturguide*, Aarhus 1999

Thomas Bo Jensen: *Inger og Johannes Exner*, Risskov, 2012

Kunstmuseet i Tønder: *Hans J. Wegner, A Nordic Design Icon from Tønder*, Tønder 2015

Olaf Lind: *Arkitektur Guide Jylland*, København 2002

Nils-Ole Lund: *Bygmesteren C. F. Møller*, Aarhus 1998

Poul Erik Skriver: *Friis & Moltke*, København 1997

Carsten Thau, Kjeld Vindum: *Arne Jacobsen*, København 1998

www

3XN.dk
aarhus.dk
aarhus2017.dk
aarhuswiki.dk
aarch.dk
aart.dk
adept.dk
architegn.dk
arkark.dk
arkitekturbilleder.dk
arkitema.com
asymptote.net
bbp.dk
big.dk
cebraarchitecture.dk
cfmoller.com
christiancarlsen.dk
claus-hermansen.dk
cubo.dk
dac.dk
danskebilleder.dk
dortemandrup.dk
effekt.dk
eplusn.dk
exnerarkitektur.dk
fladeland.dk
friismoltke.dk
gehlpeople.com
gpp.dk
henninglarsen.com
jdsa.eu
jwh.dk
kjaerrichter.dk
kristinejensen.dk
kunstbib.dk
luplau-poulsen.dk
mgarkitekter.dk
newaarch.dk
rubowarkitekter.dk
sahl.dk
schutze.dk
shl.dk
sleth.dk
thomasherzogarchitekten.de
transform.dk
unstudio.com
vandkunsten.com
visitaarhus.com

Acknowledgements

Authors
Johan Bender
Nils-Ole Lund & Anne Siri Bryhni
Mogens Brandt Poulsen
Gøsta Knudsen
Stephen Willacy

Additional Photography
Leif Wivelsted

Architects
Trine Berthold
Anna Mette Exner
Knud Fladeland
Mikkel Frost
Lena Kondrup Sørensen
Julian Weyer
Rie Øhlenschlager
Ole Østergaard

Aarhus Miljø & Teknik
Kirsten Lippert Olesen

Aarhus Stadsarkiv
Stadsarkivar Søren Bitsch Christensen

Danmarks Kunstbibliotek
Rune Rosenborg Rasmussen

Visit Aarhus
Mette Bygebjerg Petersen

Thanks too to all employees of those architectural practices who have contributed to this book with illustrative material and information, as well as to those photographers whose work was made available by the architectural practices.

Authors and Co-Authors

Heiko Weissbach (*1963), Architect
Resided in Denmark between 1983 and 2003. Studied Interior Design in Copenhagen between 1985 and 1988. Studied Architecture at the School of Architecture in Aarhus between 1989 and 1995. Guest studies under Prof. Enric Miralles at the Städelschule in Frankfurt in 1992. Worked at the CUBO practice between 1996 and 1999. Ran his own architectural practice in Aarhus between 1999 and 2002. Resided in Paris between 2003 and 2006. Has resided in Berlin anew since 2006. Worked at the Sauerbruch Hutton practice between 2006 and 2010. Member of the group of DGNB experts between 2009 and 2013. Project manager in property management for the German Federal Foreign Office since 2013. Author of *High-tech Architecture and Urban Ecology in Berlin* (1996).

Nils-Ole Lund (*1930), Architect
Diploma from the School of Architecture within the Academy of Fine Arts in Copenhagen in 1953. Resided in Norway between 1955 and 1973. Student under Arne Korsmo and Knut Knutsen in Oslo between 1955 and 1956. Ran his own architectural practice in Skedsmo between 1965 and 1973. Lecturer at the Norwegian Institute of Technology between 1963 and 1965. Professor at the School of Architecture in Aarhus as of 1965. Rector at the School between 1972 and 1985. Guest Professor at Washington University in 1976. President of the Association of European Schools of Architecture between 1987 and 1991. Architectural critic of the journals *Arkitekten, Arkitektur* and *Byggekunst.* Chairman of the Editorial Board of the *Arkitekten* and *Arkitektur* periodicals as of 1989 and many years forward. Author of *Teoridannelser i arkitekturen* (1970), *Bybygning* (1982), *Collage Architecture* (1990), *Nordisk Arkitektur* (1991, 3rd edition in English in 2008), *Arkitekt Henning Larsen* (1996), *Bygmesteren C. F. Møller* (1998) et al.

Johan Bender (*1931), Historian, Speaker
Senior teacher at Aarhus Cathedral School between 1958 and 2001. Author and publisher of numerous books and publications, most recently, *Hurra for Århus – Landsudstillingen 1909* (2008), *Arkitekt Hack Kampmann* (2014) and *Carl Nielsen – Komponistens liv i strejftog* (2015).

Mogens Brandt Poulsen (*1939), Architect
Diploma from the School of Architecture in Aarhus. Institute of Urban Development in 1971. Rector of the School between 1985 and 1991. Curator of numerous exhibitions, including on the architect Steen Eiler Rasmussen (1987) and Arne Jacobsen (1989). Author of *Arkitekturguide Aarhus* (1985, 1999), *Den Gode Skole – Historien om Arkitektskolen i Aarhus* (2015) et al.

Gøsta Thøger Knudsen (*1945), Architect
Diploma from the School of Architecture in Aarhus in 1973. Lecturer at the School as of 1986 and Rector between 1991 and 1997. Rector of the Danish Design School in Copenhagen between 1999 and 2007. City Architect of Aarhus between 2007 and 2012. Advisor to the Municipality of Aarhus since 2012. Ran his own architectural practice between 1972 and 1995. Chairman of the Danish Association of Architects between 1997 and 2006. Member of the Executive Board of the Housing Fund Kuben between 2004 and 2016 as well as of the real estate company of the research fund between 1996 and 2007. Awards in architectural competitions and author of numerous articles on Danish architecture. Participation in elaboration of atlases on monumental heritage. Served as Chairman of a committee of the Realdania fund which deals with the preservation of architectural heritage in rural areas.

Stephen Willacy (*1958), Architect
Studied Architecture in Oxford and London and has resided in Aarhus since 1984. Worked at the Kjær & Richter practice between 1984 and 1996. Self-employment for many years. Partner to the Schmidt/Hammer/Lassen practice between 2005 and 2011. Teaching and research at the School of Architecture in Aarhus for many years. Guest Professor at Arizona State University, Phoenix, USA, between 2001 and 2002. City Architect of Aarhus since 2012.

View across Aarhus Ø, the port and the city behind

Teknik & Miljø

The *Deutsche Nationalbibliothek* lists this publication in the *Deutsche Nationalbibliografie*; detailed bibliographic data are available at http://dnb.d-nb.de

ISBN 978-3-86922-560-9 (German)
ISBN 978-3-86922-561-6 (English)
ISBN 978-3-86922-562-3 (Danish)

Translation
Clarice Knowles

Translation of Essay 6
Stephen Willacy

Maps and Aerial Photographs
Aarhus Teknik & Miljø

Design
Masako Tomokiyo

Printing
UAB BALTO print, Vilnius
www.baltoprint.com

DOM
publishers